"*Maternal Desire* contains flashes of insight and expressions of deep sympathy, as when Ms. de Marneffe notes that our values inevitably determine what we consider to be our needs. She captures the exquisite conflicts that weigh on women, and . . . she writes movingly of the transfiguring effects of motherhood."

—Patricia Cohen, *The New York Times*

"De Marneffe's book isn't so much about the desire to have children as the desire to spend time caring for them once they're yours. . . . Her radical move is to urge women to think hard about what they *themselves* want or need from mothering, not just what their children want or need, and not what women's rights activists or psychological experts or right-wing politicians demand that they want or need. . . . *Maternal Desire* interweaves feminist history, psychoanalytic theory, subtle analyses of abortion and day care debates, and rich vignettes from de Marneffe's own mothering life."

—*Elle*

"One of the complexities of thinking about motherhood is that it's so hard to decide what—or, really, whose—criteria to apply. *Maternal Desire* . . . speaks to something real about the way that many mothers feel these days, which is that they are failing to measure up, personally or professionally."

—Elizabeth Kolbert, *The New Yorker*

"In joining motherhood with desire and pleasure rather than obligation, *Maternal Desire* is a subversive book. It undercuts the opposition of self-development and emotional connectedness, and affirms a woman's right to choose to spend time with her children. That this right is currently restricted to the economically advantaged is one of the scandals in our society. *Maternal Desire* demonstrates why women in our society will not really be free until all women have more power to shape their maternal lives."

—Carol Gilligan

"This is no sparkly-rainbow-and-dewdrop vision of mothering. De Marneffe, a mother of three, is clear-eyed about the demands of caring for small children. But as a clinical psychologist, she sees many women struggling to suppress a visceral ache to spend more time actively mothering. . . . *Maternal Desire* is an important addition to the literary canon on motherhood."

—Stephanie Wilkinson,
The Washington Post

"Daphne de Marneffe has tapped into something powerful and true about motherhood. Rigorously intellectual, passionately researched, and above all enormously generous and inclusive of all mothers—this is a book that deserves to be a classic."

—Dani Shapiro

"*Maternal Desire* places mothering just where it seems to a father to belong: neither as a woman's natural destiny nor as her inculcated duty, but as one of the chief desires of her life—a pleasure as real (and as problematic) as all her other pleasures."

—Adam Gopnik

"One of the most extraordinary books I have ever read . . . a brilliant, radical, and deeply poignant look at mothering and particularly *women's desire to care for their children* that should be required reading for all women. This beautifully nuanced, textured, and deeply accessible book helps put into words why it is sometimes so painful and difficult not to be at home, but never succumbs to any suggestion that this complexity can be remedied by a simple, functional solution."

—Arietta Slade, PhD, *Journal of
the American Academy of Child and
Adolescent Psychiatry*

"De Marneffe has a unique voice with an unusual capacity to hold the complexity of multiple perspectives. Recognizing the authenticity of different choices, she masterfully draws on current developmental theory to argue that women's subjectivity and sense of recognition can be found not only within the workplace but also within the mother-child experience. This remarkable, moving, and provocative book is about the passion of that experience."

—Susan Coates, PhD, Columbia
University Center of Psychoanalytic
Training and Research

ALSO BY DAPHNE DE MARNEFFE

The Rough Patch: Marriage and the Art of Living Together

MATERNAL DESIRE

On Children, Love, and the Inner Life

SECOND EDITION

Daphne de Marneffe, PhD

SCRIBNER

New York   London   Toronto   Sydney   New Delhi

Scribner
An Imprint of Simon & Schuster, Inc.
1230 Avenue of the Americas
New York, NY 10020

First Scribner trade paperback edition May 2019

SCRIBNER and design are registered trademarks of
The Gale Group, Inc., used under license by Simon & Schuster, Inc.,
the publisher of this work.

For information about special discounts for bulk purchases,
please contact Simon & Schuster Special Sales at 1-866-506-1949
or business@simonandschuster.com.

The Simon & Schuster Speakers Bureau can bring authors to
your live event. For more information or to book an event,
contact the Simon & Schuster Speakers Bureau at 1-866-248-3049
or visit our website at www.simonspeakers.com.

Interior design by Kyle Kabel

Manufactured in the United States of America

1   3   5   7   9   10   8   6   4   2

Library of Congress Cataloging-in-Publication Data is available.

ISBN 978-1-5011-9827-4
ISBN 978-1-5011-9828-1 (ebook)

For Sophie, Alex, Nicholas, and Terry
with love

Contents

Preface to the Second Edition

When preparing this updated edition of *Maternal Desire,* I asked my twenty-six-year-old daughter and her friends to read the book's first edition. Much had changed societally in the fifteen years since *Maternal Desire* had first been published, and I wanted to find out what parts of the book spoke to them and what parts seemed irrelevant or dated. I was particularly curious whether the fear that motherhood spells the end of identity and agency was as alive and well in their peer group as it had been in mine. I'd gathered from previous conversations that my daughter and her friends don't yet imagine having children, though most think that someday they will. They pass mothers with babies and little children on the street and undergo a mix of emotions common to ambitious young women in twenty-first-century America. They flinch from the notion of losing control over their bodies and emotions and time and feel a bit sorry for the harried moms ("stroller-tethered people," as one called them). Yet they also experience a flicker of fascination that feels indulgent to bask in and disorienting to explore. Would the idea of maternal desire strike them as a remote abstraction, immersed as they were in flesh-

1

ing out their adult identities in professional, creative, and sexual realms?

I was intrigued to discover that for this group of women in their midtwenties, *Maternal Desire* was gripping. They felt invited to engage and consider, rather than avoid or deflect, the complex questions for self and society that motherhood raises. It also spurred a subtle shift in their perspective on those stroller-tethered people. "When I see mothers with their little kids now," one said, "I am amazed at the nature of the labor. I feel more admiration and compassion for them and for my potential future self." Given that one of the book's overarching goals was to bring about this shift in perspective, I was gratified to learn that it could still serve that purpose for a new generation of readers.

The second edition of *Maternal Desire* draws upon the feedback of these young women, as well as my own personal, professional, and parental development. Since the first edition, I raised three children to adulthood, which I discuss at points throughout these pages. I have seen scores of patients in psychotherapy, both couples and individuals, and these experiences have honed my thinking on parenthood and intimate relationships. They have also provided material for the illustrative vignettes that I've added to this edition. (Where I offer clinical case examples, the persons described are composites.)

Since the book's 2004 publication, the culture-at-large has changed in many significant ways. The financial crisis of 2008, the omnipresent menace of climate change, the worldwide refugee and immigration crises (producing daily images of traumatized families), the opioid epidemic (producing images of same), and the upsurge of capricious and demagogic leadership across the globe all contribute to a collective sense of threat and insecurity. In such anxious times, many people respond by turning inward, looking to their family relationships for solace and safety. Yet, in the familial domain, mothers encounter, alongside professional, economic, and relationship stress, the contradictory pulls of technology-driven distraction on the one hand and the demanding edicts of "helicopter parenting" on the other. Perhaps more than ever, these conditions call for books, like *Maternal Desire*, that offer a thoughtful approach to negotiating the conflicting forces that animate mothers' inner lives.

There have been positive developments in society since the book's initial publication, too. Gay marriage has been legalized, gender fluidity has become a mainstream concept, and single motherhood is widely accepted. Alternative family forms have proliferated, and they have helped move our understanding of the desire to care for children even further from the essentialist views of "woman's nature" or "maternal instinct" that my book rejected. This new edition takes account of changes in gender norms and family arrangements, and it also puts to rest the tired trope of the "mommy wars," which pitted "working" and "stay-at-home" mothers against each other. In the 1990s and early 2000s, the conflict was on the tip of everyone's tongue, but even at the time it was recognized as a hyped-up distraction from the stubborn structural problems our society had—and continues to have—in integrating paid work with family life. Predictably—and depressingly—genuine issues of social, economic, and gender inequality were fobbed off as infighting among women.

Unfortunately, my book played a part in this polarized

debate. My goal was to discuss the mother's desire to "be there" for her child in terms of the desire's significance and value to *her*, the mother. I also aimed to help make the emotional experience of wanting to "be there" more accessible to more mothers. The book thus had two purposes: to describe maternal desire and to make a case for the emotional, relational, and social value of time with children. As a result, there was an occasional tension between description and prescription. Some readers felt I skated too close to arguing for stay-at-home motherhood, insufficiently emphasizing the many different ways in which universal needs for attachment and autonomy are constructively managed. Some felt I implied an optimal mothering context, which could be construed to ignore variations in economic necessity, paternal involvement, ethnicity and social class, couple dynamics, and a host of other factors affecting the lived reality of any given mother. I wrote the first edition of this book when I was deeply involved in raising young children, and that personal context led to both its bias and its conviction. It was my fervent belief that someone had to write from that state of immersion and make an intellectual argument that encompassed the importance of spending time caring for children *for the mother*. At the same time, there is no such thing as "the mother"; there are only individual mothers. In this new edition I take special care to differentiate the subjective experience of maternal desire from mothers' choices and to recognize and describe the variable and complex ways they interact.

Although the ideas I explore in *Maternal Desire* were originally sparked by personal experience, my larger aim was to bring scholarly rigor and seriousness to a category of experience that had often been deemed, even in feminist circles, retrograde, self-sacrificial, and trivial. At the time of its publication, the book's argument that mothers seek *self*-realization through caring for children was a radical proposition to many readers. In fact, part of its purpose was to try to understand why naming this widely felt reality was such a destabilizing and challenging act. Encouragingly, over the intervening fifteen years, *Maternal Desire*'s core concerns have been discussed with greater visibility and urgency. In academic research and psychological theory, as well as in literature and cultural commentary, the subjective experience of motherhood in the twenty-first century—its meaning, value, and variability across different social locations—has become one of our society's most avidly explored topics.

Researchers in fields as diverse as sociology, anthropology, history, film studies, career development, and public health have turned to the concept of *maternal desire* as a framework for rethinking issues about women, motherhood, and identity. Feminist scholars have identified maternal desire as a new theoretical direction in the study of motherhood, "one that begins from women's desires and pleasures, and from their own sense of the value and meaning of what they do." In writing *Maternal Desire*, I drew inspiration from Adrienne Rich's conviction "that only the willingness to share private and sometimes painful experience can enable women to create a collective description of the world which will truly be ours." That project continues to claim more cultural terrain, in the form of novels, memoirs, essays, short stories, and movies. In the context of this canon, the arguments for women's "responsibility" not to center their lives on children have come to seem increasingly simplistic, if not tone-deaf, to the chorus of creative voices that are giving our understanding of mothers' experience greater specificity, texture, and depth.

Finally, contrary to the subtle misogynistic tendency to dismiss maternal desire as the preoccupation of a privileged few, research and clinical practice are teaching us about its role in psychological health across different populations. In interviews with Rwandan genocide rape survivors, anthropologists found that the women's emotional experience of maternal desire influenced and enhanced their modes of resilience in the face of trauma. Therapy groups offered to stressed mothers at a London counseling center helped participants bear their ambivalence and self-judgment, which in turn enabled them to feel more effective as parents and take more pleasure in mothering. Current psychoanalytic writers have turned attention to mothers' "unique desires and developmental sequence, her own voice and subjectivity." They also investigate the relevance of maternal desire to the optimal stance of the therapist. Like a mother in a responsive relationship with her child, a therapist must meet the patient with "a willingness to wonder, an expectation to engage" and "manage forces as best she can without attempting, in a desperate way, to control them."

Passionate engagement as the basis of self-actualization, resilience, and growth—for *both* mother and child—was, and is, the key human insight at the heart of the book. Audre Lorde wrote, "The sharing of joy, whether physical, emotional, psychic, or intellectual, forms a bridge between sharers which can be the basis for understanding much of what is not shared between them, and lessens the threat of the difference." Between any two people, including mother and

6

child, the sharing of feelings is the essential understanding and respect for difference. My goal was to use pleasure and joy as the starting point for exploring mothering's potential for fulfillment, empowerment, and freedom.

Maternal Desire offers an argument, but also a sensibility—an attention to nuance, complexity, and diversity, as well as a tolerance of ambiguity. This sensibility is always in danger of breakdown when it comes to highly emotional issues at the core of identity, such as sex and parenthood, perhaps particularly when quick fixes, catchphrases, and war cries are the order of the day. I want the book to serve its readers by providing room to reflect and permission to turn their experience over in their minds without any pressure to act or react, but with a receptivity to feelings (including difficult ones), an acceptance of uncertainty, and an excitement at exploration. Just as a child needs first to be seen before he can see himself, so too does a mother. I hope this book gives its readers the experience of being seen.

1

The "Problem" of Maternal Desire

It would seem that everything it is possible to say about motherhood in America has already been said. Beckoning us from every online platform, beaming out from every news satellite is a solution or a revelation or a confession about mothering. Yet in the midst of all the media chatter about staying on track, staying in shape, time crunches, time-savers, and time-outs, there's something that remains unexamined about the experience of motherhood itself. It sways our choices and haunt our dreams, yet we shy away from giving it our full attention. Treated both as an illusion and as a foregone conclusion, it is at once obvious and invisible: the desire to mother.

The desire to mother is not only the desire to have children, but also the desire to care for them. It is not the duty to mother, or the compulsion to mother, or the concession to mothering when other options are not available. It is not the acquiescence to prescribed roles or the result of brainwashing. It is the longing felt by a mother to nurture her children; the wish to participate in their mutual relationship; and the choice, insofar as it is possible, to put that desire into practice.

Maternal desire is at once obvious and invisible partly because it is so easily confused with other things. Those fighting for women's progress have too often misconstrued it as a throwback or excuse, a self-curtailment of potential. Those who champion women's maternal role have too often defined it narrowly as service to one's child, husband, or God. Each view eclipses the authentic desire to mother felt by a woman herself—a desire not derived from a child's need, though responsive to it; a desire not created by a social role, though potentially supported by it; rather, a desire anchored in her experience of herself as an agent, an autonomous individual, a person.

I juxtapose *maternal* and *desire* to emphasize what we still feel uncomfortable focusing on: that wanting to care for children, even with its difficulties, is an important source of meaning and identity for many women. We resist reflecting on its implications because we fear becoming mired in clichés about women's nature, which will then be used to justify gender inequality. But when we avoid thinking about maternal desire or treat it as a marginal detail, we lose an opportunity to understand ourselves and the broader situation of women. Clearly, not every woman wants a child and not every mother finds meaning in caring for children. But for those who do, or wonder if they do, it's time to have a deeper conversation.

LIKE SOME WOMEN and unlike others, I had always imagined being a mother. When we were young, my sister and I whiled away our afternoons in an ongoing saga of siblings with four kids apiece, each with a set of twins. In our imaginings, we withstood car crashes, camping disasters, hurricanes—this was Motherhood as Adventure. Despite our awareness of the upheaval in contemporary thought about women's roles in the sixties and seventies when we grew up, we enjoyed this game, in part because our own mother made it clear that she loved raising children, and we happily modeled ourselves on her example.

If my childhood fantasies bore out later in my life, they didn't predetermine my path toward motherhood. I don't believe that early maternal feeling is a prerequisite for becoming a mother or being a good one. Rather, I now see these early feelings as a kind of seed of potential, one that gradually developed into a physically involving, emotionally complex, and psychologically transformative desire to care for children. The realization of that desire began with the birth of our first child, when I was several months shy of completing my PhD. Overnight, motherhood became thrillingly and dauntingly real, filled with our newborn daughter's suckling, her startle, her drunken contentment after nursing, her nocturnal waking, her nerve-jangling cries.

As I moved from the abstractions of expecting a baby to the absorbed bodiliness of infant care, I still loved my work as a psychologist. While pregnant I'd been committed to building a psychotherapy practice for children and adults,, and I looked forward to continuing my research projects on childhood trauma and gender development. Yet, something about taking care of my child changed me. As a new mother, devoting long hours in the library or at my therapy office didn't feel good, and I held my work in abeyance. I was fortunate to have a profession in which I could make my own schedule, but the more hours I spent with my baby, the better I felt, in myself and with her. Whenever I was out of the house for more than a few of hours, I felt an invisible tether drawing me home, and then, when I was with our baby, I couldn't imagine a worthwhile reason for leaving her.

Yet, when I took account of my values and my enduring sense of social responsibility to continue my work, I experienced an inner conflict, questioning whether these new feelings were something that I could fully endorse and embrace. During feedings at 4:00 a.m., an hour ripe for morbid rumination, I would wonder if my reluctance to leave my daughter revealed some sort of weakness that I couldn't quite acknowledge or pin down. I'd probe the nature of my seeming lack of willpower, but despite my background in thinking through psychological issues, I couldn't find clarity or even a satisfactory vocabulary for describing how I felt. This led to some vaguely disorienting conversations with friends, each of us struggling to explain our different choices and different constraints, each of us finding ourselves both defensive and exposed. Yet what was the nature of this defensive posture? Where did it come from, and why couldn't we talk about how motherhood had changed us, or hadn't, without getting bogged down in the kind of stock generalities ("work's so much easier than home," "kids need their moms") that so often stymied such conversations?

As my desire to spend time mothering gathered force within me, I kept noticing how hard it was to talk about. Usually comfortable expressing myself in words, I found myself strangely inarticulate on this topic. The only time distress ever drove me to shop was after a respected mentor bemoaned over lunch my post-motherhood lack of professional productivity. Rather than find a way to explain to her

my shifting priorities, I responded, as if in a trance, by pur-
chasing a hideous mauve suit as a sop to my vanished profes-
sionalism. I never wore it. A few weeks later, my obstetrician
genially asked what I was up to, and I muttered something
about having turned into a fifties housewife. It was as if the
moment words began to form in my mouth, they instanta-
neously tumbled into the well-worn groove of cliché.

I was aware that my conflicts and fear of judgment bore
the stamp of my own idiosyncratic psychology, and eventually
I stopped expecting this complex of feelings to dissipate; I
simply learned to live around it. Over the next five years, it
sat in the background of my thoughts, familiar enough to be
regarded as an uneasy companion, flaring up when I faced a
difficult choice about how to allocate my time. Things took a
turn, though, when I became pregnant with our third child
five years later. I remember taking a walk in the first few weeks
of pregnancy along a bike path near our house and feeling
a surprising sense of lightness. It surprised me because I'd
imagined that, though the child was very much wanted and
planned, my spirit of welcome would be weighed down by an
array of practical worries and the old familiar psychological
concerns. Instead, though mindful of the challenges that lay
ahead, I felt an almost giddy sense of freedom.

Poised as I was in that sliver of time between becoming
pregnant and the descent into nausea and bone-tiredness,
I knew that soon even thinking would exhaust me, so I was
impatient to figure out what was making me feel so light.
Suddenly, a childhood sense-memory of learning to ride a
bike came to mind—in particular, the feeling of being at
the final stage of not knowing how to do something and
tipping overnight and without conscious effort into the

most elementary stage of knowing. It captured a transition I sensed within myself, from a model in which children were fitted into the mold of my previous life to a new sense in which mothering was the center from which my other priorities flowed.

My feeling of freedom didn't diminish the real economic, emotional, and practical demands of having another child. Still, I found it compelling, in part because its source—my shift of emphasis toward mothering—felt so transgressive. How was it that at the dawn of the twenty-first century, the ancient imperative that women mother their children felt somehow liberating and new? Those thoughts led me to reflect on the complexities of women's experiences of mothering young children in America today. They stimulated me to reconsider questions I had long pondered about the place of motherhood in the psychology of women. Eventually, they drove me to use my training as a psychologist, my practice as a psychotherapist, my sympathies as a feminist, and my ongoing experience as a mother to try to understand how we evaluate and live out, socially and individually, the desire to care for children. And ultimately, that exploration became this book.

NO MATTER WHAT our differences may be, every mother I've ever known has grappled with her own version of similar questions: Where should caring for children fit into one's life? How should one understand, think about, or talk about the feelings involved? What are we to make of our desires, our ambivalence, our guilt? No one expects to have easy answers. But it seems that so often our culture's response is framed as a matter of figuring out the minimum amount of time one can spend with one's children without doing them any real damage. Rarely does public discussion take account of the embodied, aching desire to be with their children that many mothers feel. What's more, the vocabulary for this desire seems so limited, the language available for exploring it so constricted, that it is hard to grasp what part the desire should play in one's decisions and in one's assessment of oneself.

There is a complicated blend of emotions at the heart of these issues, as well as a complicated overlay of social messages. On this minefield we step gingerly around our own feelings and those of others, balancing self-revelation and self-concealment in an effort to respect others' choices, maintain friendships, avoid giving offense. Women's desire to *have* children is now fully respectable and in public view. Remote are the days when the radical feminist Shulamith Firestone identified childbearing as the root of women's oppression, and the ubiquity of fertility treatments attests to the lengths people are willing to go to have children when they want to. But the territory that remains occluded, dogged by contention and strangely unspeakable, is the subject of caring for children—of spending one's hours and days with them, of "quantity time," and of its meaning and value to children and mothers alike.

The historical reasons for this silence are abundantly clear. For most of human history and in many parts of the world today, women have had little choice in being mothers. "A woman can hardly ever choose," wrote the novelist George Eliot (born Mary Ann Evans) in 1866. "She must take the meaner things because only meaner things are within her reach." Motherhood has always meant sacrifice—of economic power, of personal freedom, and sometimes of life itself. In the fight for gender equality, women have correctly understood that a chosen and desired motherhood is essential to our rights and freedoms. We have recognized the strategic risk of emphasizing women's maternal role, the very role that for millennia defined our existence. It has therefore been crucial to put front and center women's equal access to social roles and rewards *other* than motherhood, such as professional opportunity, economic justice, and sexual autonomy.

Today, women are mindful of how precarious our rights and freedoms continue to be. Yet during the socially transformative decades that saw motherhood conceptualized as disempowering, important aspects of what makes maternal desire so compelling to many women were misinterpreted or lost. Mothers continue to recognize the impediments to earning power and professional accomplishment that caring for children presents, but the problem remains that caring for their children *matters* deeply to them. What if we take this mattering seriously, put it at the core of our exploration? Even to pose the question is to invite almost instant misconstrual. It's as if this would recommend to women to live through others, forsake equality, or relax into the joys of subsidized homemaking. But that reflexive misinterpretation is itself evidence of how difficult it is to think about maternal desire as a positive aspect of selfhood.

Consider, for example, the view that caring for one's children amounts to self-sacrifice. When it comes to their economic well-being, it is all too true that women sacrifice themselves when they become mothers. But in terms of emotional well-being, a mother often sees her desire to nurture her children as an intrinsically valuable impulse. This tension presents contemporary women with one of the key paradoxes of their lives as mothers: that some of what they find meaningful about mothering can also be construed, from some vantage points, as self-sacrificing. At moments in the day-to-day life of every mother, the deferral of her own gratifications or aims is experienced as oppressive. Managing one's rage, quelling one's desire to walk out the door on squalling children and dirty dishes, and feeling one is going to faint of boredom at the sheer repetitiveness of it all are some of the real emotional and moral challenges that caring for children routinely presents.

Yet when a mother relinquishes control over her time, forgoes the satisfaction of an impulse, or surrenders to playful engagement with her child, the surface quality of capitulation in these decisions can also obscure their role in satisfying deeper motives and goals. These deeper goals have to do, ultimately, with the creation of meaning. In the seemingly mundane give-and-take of parenting—playing, sharing, connecting, relaxing, enduring boredom, getting mad, cajoling, compromising, and sacrificing—a mother communicates with her child about the possibilities and limits of intimate relationships.

This process can be extraordinarily pleasurable. It can also be filled with difficulty. In motherhood, we consent to make space for a child, in our emotions and our body. We accept responsibility for a completely dependent being, and at times the responsibility feels like an encroachment, an imposition, even an invasion. It takes great strength to find the necessary resources within ourselves. We accept and desire a relationship defined by *responding, being affected, being needed,* and *enabling the other to come into him- or herself.* We relinquish control, we are touched, we change. This desired relationship benefits children, mothers, and humanity itself, but seen through the wrong lens or experienced in frustration, it can be swallowed up by the hotly contested political waters surrounding the idea of mothering activity as "disempowerment" or "submission." When this occurs, we risk losing sight of the deeply-held personal and social values about responsiveness and responsibility that this relationship expresses.

FUNDAMENTALLY, OUR RELATIONSHIPS with our children and our desire to care for them have to do with time: time is an essential ingredient of every satisfying emotional relationship, and the tough choices we make between our children and our other commitments are a product of our limits as temporal beings. Yet spending time with children is culturally devalued and personally conflicted. Mothers today worry that their power, their prestige, and their very identities are at stake. They've absorbed views that hang in the cultural air: mothering is a sacrifice for the sake of the child; mothering is of lesser value by not being paid work; careers enhance personal growth, while caring for children produces stagnation. Those who are partnered sometimes seek to circumvent the problem by carefully monitoring their division of labor. They fear a scenario in which their duties diverge and conceive of pre-parenting life as the norm and the ideal. As one prospective mother said of her husband, "I'll resent it if he can still do everything we used to do, and I can't."

In the shrinking American middle class, time with children is also a "luxury" many parents feel they can't afford. If current statistics are correct, American women are having fewer children than they would like. Like so many basic necessities of life—health care, good schools, fresh air— motherhood has turned into something of a privilege. Mothers at all socioeconomic levels face difficult decisions regarding spending time with children, and the devaluation of maternal desire operates at various levels of social and economic reality and in many intersecting ways. If we opened our eyes to the commonalities in mothers' experiences, it could generate some political consciousness, even solidarity, about the larger-scale problems that the social devaluation of caring for children inflicts upon everyone.

This social devaluation brings with it missed opportunities that can never be recaptured or regained. In the popular American mind-set, there's always a second chance. So it comes as a shock to realize how fast children grow up and how quickly they no longer crave your company or respond to your influence in the ways they once did. The time-limited nature of mothering small children, the uniqueness of it, seems almost like an affront to women's opportunity, demanding that mothers respond at distinct, unrepeatable moments with decisions about how to spend their time. Unfair as it may seem, the fleetingness is real. That should point us toward prizing, personally and socially, this brief period of our lives.

With respect to the well-being of children, psychological research unambiguously demonstrates that responsive, sensitive, and secure relationships with caregivers are at the heart of every aspect of healthy development—from brain maturation, to stress response and resilience, to the capacity for emotional intimacy. With respect to the well-being of parents, adult development researchers advise that we spread our professional and personal obligations evenly over the course of our lives, providing ourselves more flexibility throughout and reducing the emotional stress of parenthood in particular. These findings are linked: providing children sensitive and responsive care *depends on* and *amplifies* parents' pleasurable, desired engagement. As a society, we need policies concerning work and family that recognize the value of shared time together—for the sake of children and parents alike.

MOTHERHOOD CALLS FOR a transformed individuality, an integration of a new relationship and a new role into one's sense of self. This is a practical and a psychological transformation. It is clear that as a society we are grudging and cramped about the practical adjustments required by motherhood, continually treating them as incidental and inconvenient. Like an irritated bus passenger who is asked to move over and make room, we appear affronted by the sheer existence of mothers' needs. But the practical difficulties have far-reaching psychological effects. They shape how we appraise and experience the whole issue of inner maternal transformation, the "space" we allow motherhood to occupy in our psyches.

We are at a promising cultural moment for expressing and describing female desire. Yet to inhabit our desires and bodily experience fully and without apology, we need new narratives about both sexuality and motherhood. Historically,

20

mother and *desire* do not belong in the same phrase. Desire is about sex, and motherhood is about practically everything but sex. In Victorian times, blooming young women contracted odd symptoms—paralyzed arms, lost voices—because social mores inhibited women's awareness or expression of their sexual desires. By contrast, their roles as mothers were sanitized and idealized. Today, young women's free expression of their sexual desire is central to identity and empowerment. It's maternal desire that gives rise to more troubling questions of self. For a certain class of contemporary woman, it's almost as if the desire for sex and the desire to mother have switched places in terms of taboo.

My goal for this book is to provide a framework for thinking about women's desire to care for their children in a way that is consistent with feminist ideals and free from sentimentality and cliché. This task necessarily means evaluating the most significant ideological approaches, scientific research, political issues, cultural norms, and social practices that relate to mothering today. Specifically, it involves the following, as the book's chapters will respectively elaborate: a critical appraisal of twentieth-century feminism in an effort to formulate how maternal desire can offer opportunity, rather than simply oppression; an exploration of the resources that psychology and psychoanalysis can provide women who need help thinking through their perspectives on (potential) motherhood and childcare; a frank, nuanced account of what it means to encounter both the pleasurable highs and ambivalent lows of maternal experience; a dispassionate survey of contemporary policies and the ethical standards that our society applies to the hot-button issues of childcare, fertility technologies, and abortion; a comparative look at how our society prepares (and doesn't prepare) young women and men for the prospect of parenthood; and an honest discussion of what our culture truly values and how we strive to spend our time.

The sense we make of motherhood has a powerful impact on women living their day-to-day lives, so my goal is ultimately therapeutic. The creation and nurture of children transforms men and women alike. These activities also provide a unique opportunity for reconsidering the premises of one's life. We live in a culture that enshrines acquisition but profanes care. When a person, still most likely a mother, feels the desire to care for her children, our tired cultural scripts shed little light on the profundity of her situation. This book offers a new view of maternal desire, including its qualities, its effects, and its pervasive devaluation and misinterpretation in our individualistic culture. I hope it proves useful to women reflecting upon their lives. More than that, I hope it frees them to tap into their own sources of human happiness.

2

Feminism

Every woman's feminism is a love letter to her mother. "For my mother" is the most usual dedication of a feminist book. The author offers her own reading of her mother's life, and if the book is about motherhood, she grapples with her mother's choices and constraints in light of her own. This effort takes as many forms as there are feminists. For some, it's about taking the measure of her mother's thwarting at the hands of male power. For others, the impulse is to repair and redeem the limits of her mother's life through achievement in her own. Even when a book grieves maternal absence or betrayal, it is often a cry of pain about what could have been were it not for the mother's suffering in a sexist world.

Whatever else feminist discussions about motherhood may be, they are passionate. The disagreements about children and work, the appropriate role of day care, and the needs of mothers, children, and families are not just glib debates or about superficial differences. They cut to the core of the values and goals we cherish. Because our beliefs arise from the wordless observations and lessons we take from own families, we often experience our convictions as gut reactions ("I don't know how I know it, I just do"); they can feel as close as our breath.

Historically, second-wave feminism focused on loosening the grip of women's conventionally defined roles, working to secure the right not to have children (birth control, abortion) and the choice not to stay home caring for them (employment opportunity, universal day care). Third- and fourth-wave feminism have focused more extensively on the body and sexual expression, while also attending more closely to the intersectionality of gender (and its fluidity) with race, class, culture, and sexuality. Regardless of era, though, feminism's consistent goal has been to address problems that affect women as a class, to free them from unjust incursions into their bodies and psyches, and to lift restrictions on their opportunities. Obviously, mothers' desire to care for their children belongs on this agenda.

Too often, though, this topic has elicited feminist suspicion as a retrograde deferral to patriarchally defined gender roles or has been presented as a self-annihilating contrast to self-actualizing desires like the pursuit of sexual freedom. We need a fresh feminist look at maternal desire, both in light of the practical conditions of women's current lives and the powerful cultural ideas that contribute to women's perceptions of themselves. We need to develop a more satisfying, more complex understanding of what women get from mothering—not only the rewards of being responsive to children, but also the ways in which mothering is responsive to self.

A Feminist History of Middle-Class Mothers

I once talked to a graduate student who described to me her thesis on women's sexuality, a sophisticated analysis of the subtle interplay of psychological and social forces in women's perceptions of their own agency and desire. But when we began to talk about motherhood, she promptly recited a series of platitudes condemning it as a mind-numbing, self-sacrificing trap. Despite the ever-increasing diversity of writings on motherhood, belief in the inherent contradiction between motherhood and self-actualization remains alive and well. Even for this woman, who prized careful thinking, it was acceptable to hold an extraordinarily simplistic opinion of motherhood. Stubborn assumptions about the profound incompatibility of motherhood and selfhood continue to resurface, even when social conditions have vastly changed.

This odd opposition also shows up in the divergence between historical research on the roles of American women and the uses to which this scholarship has been put by popular feminism. The past few decades have seen an emergence of feminist historical scholarship devoted to understanding the lives of middle-class American women in the eighteenth and nineteenth centuries and to tracing the ideas of "domesticity" from that period that continue to influence us today. The Industrial Revolution in the early 1800s—about which the feminist writers Barbara Ehrenreich and Deirdre English remark, "'Revolution' is too pallid a word"—transformed the social conditions and dominant ideas that governed ordinary people's lives. Rapid economic growth, urbanization, a shift from subsistence to commercial farming, the replacement of home-based with factory production, not to mention developments in politics, education, and religion, all wrought profound changes in family life and the lives of women.

For married women and mothers, daily life came to

revolve less around the production of goods such as food, cloth, and soap and began to focus more on the care of children and the upkeep of the home. Married men increasingly assumed the role of provider by making their way in the "cold world" of the capitalist economy. Out of these changes arose a new ideology of domesticity, which idealized the caregiving and homemaking roles of women and lent a naturalistic and ethical air to the separation of male and female spheres, as if this rapidly evolving, socially constructed phenomenon had a basis in nature and the moral good.

The ideology of domesticity, though powerful, was also contradicted by some of the actual material conditions of the era. For one, single women were gaining unprecedented access to employment (albeit at wages far scanter than men's). Married women threw themselves into civic and religious causes such as temperance and abolitionism, which gave them a public voice and confirmed their Christian (and domestic) values of love, nurturance, and good works. Wherever women devoted their energy, though, the general perception of motherhood was one of special esteem, as the civic and spiritual importance of this practice was continually acknowledged and amplified. The development of women's "separate spheres," especially for middle-class whites, at once emphasized the paramount importance of the roles women played in the household and created a community of activist mothers committed to advocating for social betterment. This community was the precursor to the first-wave feminist movement for suffrage and women's rights; ironically, then, the foremothers of modern feminism also helped build precisely the domestic structures that their intellectual and political heirs later critiqued. Grasping this mixed historical picture can help us better understand the complex dynamics of the present.

Though historians underscore women's gains *and* losses during this period, the interpretation of their scholarship in works of popular feminism tells a more one-sided tale. The Industrial Revolution, it is asserted, removed remunerative and *meaningful* work from the home. Thus bereft, women were left with what remained, namely childcare and housework—thin gruel indeed. Such writings also assume that the work of caring for children or tending a home was relatively thankless, devoid of any of the creativity that purportedly adhered to candlemaking, weaving, or any of the other "productive" activities from which women were now excluded. And viewing the past through a present-day lens, these popular writings tend to focus on what it meant for women to have to forgo employment in order to care for their children, neglecting what it meant for women to have to forgo caring for children in order to work.

The idea that nineteenth-century mothers caring for children were left at home with "nothing" to do has been argued on the basis of the debatable claim that childhood itself is something of a modern invention. This interpretation dwells on how brutal parent-child relations used to be and the historical absence of an ideal of tender affection in the family. We are told, for instance, that before the sixteenth century in Europe, "parent-child relationships appear to have been much less emotional. What is seen today as a deep biological bond between parent and child, particularly mother and child, is very much a social construction." Nurturing child-rearing practices spread during the eighteenth century, but by the nineteenth century, the account goes, this norm of nurturance had become something of a shackle for women. "The idealization of mother love, vigilant attention to the needs of children, and recognition of the unique potential of each individual came to dominate child-rearing ideology," writes the economist Juliet Schor. We are left with the impression that whatever good resided in this ideology, it oppressed women by idealizing motherhood and pressuring mothers to devote their energy to their children. Although it is hard to believe that the earlier, less tender model of child-rearing would induce nostalgia, it is held up in many ways as preferable to what came after: the installation of middle-class women as "angels in the house" and the fashioning of child-rearing into an activity that demanded the investment of time, thought, and emotion. Discussion remains muted on how or whether those investments could pay dividends worthwhile in themselves.

When the high valuation of the mother-child bond is cast as an unjust limitation, it is difficult to ponder the positive meanings that being able to focus more on the care of their children might have had for mothers themselves. In reality, when seen in the context of what came before, the ability of middle-class women to oversee children's development was conceived as progress. Furthermore, middle-class mothers were in no sense left idle when they stopped weaving their own cloth and tilling their own soil; rather, their activity was directed toward different social and familial ends, including the increasingly solicitous care of infants and children. That care included, then as now, pleasure and satisfaction. "That most interesting of all occupations is begun—the care of my child," writes Abigail Alcott in 1831, "and delightful it is—I would not delegate it to angel—I am at times most impatient to dismiss my nurse that not even she should participate with me in this pleasure." Yet, then as now, mothers also struggled. "My time is abundantly occupied with my babies," Alcott writes in 1833, soon after the birth of her second child (Louisa May). "It seems to me at times as if the weight of responsibility connected with these little immortal beings would prove too much for me—Am I doing what is right? Am I doing enough?" Alcott's reflections indicate that self-doubts and struggles were not rooted solely in women's position as mothers in patriarchal society; they were the struggles anyone assumes in trying to do meaningful work.

Perhaps the main source of irritation for today's feminist critics of nineteenth-century domesticity is the latter's unapologetic belief in the indispensability of mothers to children, for this belief, above all others, reverberates in our current conflicts and debates. In the nineteenth century, middle-class mothers began to take their work as parents extraordinarily seriously, and for better or worse, we are inheritors of that tradition. Whereas then the focus was religious character, now it is psychological health; but in Alcott's concern about her children's souls, we can detect a spirit similar to our own. Critics may charge that children's need for continual maternal attention is little more than a "social fiction." But if we're honest, we can't leave it at that. Much as we may fear that an intensive model of mothering constrains women, or much as we may rail against today's overinvolved and overanxious parenting ethos, we cannot dismiss the value to children of parental attention or the sincerity with which many desire to give it.

It's All Drudgery: The Problematic Collapse of
Housework with Caring for Children

In her classic work, *The Second Sex*, Simone de Beauvoir contends that "the child is the foe of waxed floors." Betty Friedan, in *The Feminine Mystique*, likewise laments the predicament of the mother who focuses her considerable energies on getting spots out of her carpet rather than on larger social goals. Though the familiar feminist target of compulsive housekeeping has evaporated—largely because most mothers work and long ago gave up hope of a spotless house—a tendency persists to view childcare and housework as dull, repetitive maintenance activities and to lump them together as one demeaned, poorly remunerated, tedious task.

A parent caring for children and keeping house is obviously not paid for the work, and we can respond to this in various ways. When the measure of gross domestic product (GDP) was first created in the 1940s, debate was spirited on whether "home production" (housework and caregiving) should be included. Unpaid home-based work lost out, and as a result women's work in the home was effectively "disappeared," redefined as economically worthless. Some believe that since home-based work is unpaid, it *is* of low worth, and that anyone acting in rational self-interest would refuse to be stuck at home. Others reject the idea that pay constitutes the only legitimate measurement of intrinsically valuable home-based activities. Still, those who tend home and children may still justifiably feel disempowered or constrained by their financial sacrifice.

It is easy enough to concede the drudgery of housework; yet, because caring for children also takes place in the home, childcare is then tacked on, with hardly a thought to the fundamentally different characters of the two endeavors. This tends to obscure, rather than clarify, the character of mothers' work lives. The desire to care for her children can, and often does, motivate a mother to make choices she wouldn't otherwise make, such as sacrificing income or taking on a larger proportion of household responsibilities. Even if we grant that housework can be dull, doing it is redeemed by its being accomplished with more or less success while tending to children. In fact, housework may be especially suited to the hovering background attention that children often need from their caregivers.

The author and activist Charlotte Perkins Gilman was neither the first nor the last to compare the work of mothers to that of domestic servants. Every mother has days when she feels her children treat her as a domestic. But an equally relevant comparison might be between mothers and artists or between mothers and professors. Mothering is one of many kinds of work perceived as meaningful by its practitioners even when society doesn't reward the vocation handsomely. Artists are rarely well paid, but people continue to make art because it has intrinsic value. Professors might view their work as socially devalued because they are often remunerated poorly, but they count the expansion of human knowledge as a worthy goal. No one lives on love alone, and love shouldn't be the only reward of motherhood. As Ann Crittenden observes, we don't insist that a professional ballplayer forgo pay because he enjoys his job. But neither should motherhood's less quantifiable rewards be viewed as worthless. The desire to care for her children can, and often does, motivate a mother to recalibrate her sense of "value" or "compensation," leading her to forgo income and to take on a larger portion of the household work necessary for family life.

To understand this motivation, it's important to understand that goal-directed activity in parenting differs from goal-directed activity in most vocational situations. To feel effective as a parent, and to engage in parenting pleasurably, a person needs to be in tune, at least some of the time, with the pace and rhythm of her children. The effort to tightly control the rhythm of young children's lives usually results in frustration, conflict, and a sense of inadequacy for both parent and child. Parents will often intentionally try to create an environment that fosters spontaneity, play, the injection of emotion, and a continually shifting balance of structure and flexibility. If creating this environment is a goal for parents, they may be motivated to take on less gratifying chores of household management in order to cultivate conditions conducive to parent-child harmony.

Critics have noted that in Betty Friedan's world, credit goes to those mothers who get out of the house, pursue careers, and brave such problems as "finding nurses and housekeepers." The problems of the "nurses and housekeepers" themselves don't rate, nor does the possibility that mothers whose work is domestic service for others might regard their own domestic life as source of relative freedom and agency. A different slant on domestic work surfaces in the critique of mainstream (white) feminism by those who consider the ways that class, race, and ethnicity affect a woman's experience of motherhood. This critique examines, among other things, the reality that the family lives of women of color have historically been regarded as secondary to their usefulness as cheap labor. Immigrant women, particularly from the Global South, today leave their homes and children with relatives to care for those of more privileged families. Clearly this cadre of underpaid and socially dislocated workers don't have freedom of choice as to whether to invest time and attention in their own domestic spheres. Strains of feminism that devalue domestic work not only risk demeaning the emotional labor that takes place in the home, but also reflects an insensitivity to the range of circumstances in which mothers of different class, race, and power positions find themselves.

It's All Trivial: The Problematic Collapse of Mothering into "Femininity"

In her 1991 exposé, *Backlash*, Susan Faludi cataloged feminists who retrenched in the 1980s. She criticized Sylvia Ann Hewlett for concluding that most women didn't even want feminism; Betty Friedan for backsliding into a sentimentalization of domesticity; and Carol Gilligan for developing a psychological theory that appeared to legitimize the notion of women's "difference." These writers were all interested in how motherhood figures into the way we conceptualize equal rights, women's liberation, and feminism's goals. But Faludi and other similarly inclined thinkers reject versions of feminism that give any special consideration to women in their capacity as mothers. Eager to refute the perennial and perennially wrongheaded tendency "to conflate 'mothers' with 'women,'" they counter with a troubling conflation of their own, treating motherhood as just one more optional feature of "femininity."

In this view, adjusting our laws or economic incentives to recognize and protect the value of a mother's emotional and economic investment in her family amounts to a flight from equality and a reification of feminine "difference." The critic Wendy Kaminer, for one, appears to see no meaningful distinction between the two in her account of feminist history:

> Retreating from equality and questioning the efficacy of rights, feminists in the 1980s began demanding special protections for women. . . . Only women get pregnant . . . opponents of equality intone; so they demand laws that treat the sexes differently, in respect of their reproductive roles, as if the mere possibility of becoming pregnant makes women uniformly more compassionate, nurturing, cooperative, more sexually submissive, and more interested in family life than men.

Kaminer thus dismisses the particular requirements of mothering as just one more manifestation of "difference feminism," a school of thought that foregrounds women's purported psychological tendencies toward empathy, nurturance, and relatedness. In so doing, Kaminer glosses over a crucial issue: it is not a woman's abstract proclivity to nurturance and compassion that might legitimately serve as the basis for maternity leaves, preferences in custody disputes, and the like; rather, it is her *actual participation* in family relationships. In real life, any woman who risks losing her job because of a difficult pregnancy does not want extra time off or sanctioned leave in order to gain unfair female advantage or be treated as "special." Rather, she wants it in order to protect her status as an adult in the workforce, as well as her own health and safety and that of her unborn child.

The way out of this confusion is to think more carefully about the word *special*. *Special* in the sense of "exceptional, primary, or esteemed" is expressed in the idea that women have unique propensities for caring, nurturing, and peacemaking, which emanate from their femaleness, their capacity for motherhood, or their experience as mothers. But *special* in the sense of "particular or distinct" is the relevant meaning when considering pregnancy, lactation, and parenting small children (the first two biologically limited to mothers, the latter empirically associated with mothers). These specific, practical, necessary activities are carried out by mothers for the continuation and flourishing of human life. On that basis, they deserve legal and economic consideration. That these maternal activities are sometimes viewed as *special* in the first sense does not delegitimize their *special* status in the second.

Ironically, the most vociferous defenders of women's reproductive rights with regard to contraception and abortion are sometimes the least forceful voices when it comes to defending women's reproductive rights as pregnant workers or new mothers. When Kaminer writes of her own "youthful desire for both equality and the pedestal," she sees it as a microcosm of the larger "historic conflict between protectionist feminism, which emphasizes traditional notions of gender difference (the moral strengths and practical weaknesses of motherhood) and equality feminism, which challenges gender stereotypes and roles." Placing the pedestal and motherhood on one side of the ledger and equality on the other, she associates protecting women's rights as mothers with being worshipped for one's femininity.

As a further example, witness an exchange between lawyer Anita Blair and editor Barbara Jones in a *Harper's* magazine forum on women in business:

> BLAIR: As a lawyer, what I find often happens is that some-body is pregnant, and she's having a terrible time of it and missing a lot of work. That person may be fired for missing work. That's not the same as getting fired for being pregnant.
>
> JONES: But if we want a next generation, and if women are working, working women are going to have to have babies, right?
>
> BLAIR: You've still got a job that needs to be done. The deal between the employer and the employee was not "I'm going to pay you regardless of how many hours you come to work." The deal is "You work, you get paid."

In this particular version of equality, unequal burdens will fall on women who become mothers as a matter of course. But that particular inequality doesn't seem to bother Blair much.

What is striking is that both "equality" feminists and "difference" feminists overlook how motherhood is often the first time women feel grounded in an identity freed from stereotypical feminine concerns. Though it is elementally connected to body and to sex, in its most vital, useful, and responsive moments, mothering is not about gender. The novelist Toni Morrison eloquently describes her experience as a mother:

There was something so valuable about what happened when one became a mother. For me it was the most liberating thing that ever happened . . . liberating because the demands that children make are not the demands of the normal "other." The children's demands on me are things that nobody else had ever asked me to do. To be a good manager. To have a sense of humor. To deliver something that somebody else could use. And they were not interested in all the things that other people were interested in, like what I was wearing or if I were sensual. Somehow all of the baggage that I had accumulated as a person about what was valuable just fell away. I could not only be me—whatever that was—but somebody actually needed me to be that.

This "falling away" that Morrison describes is one of the reasons why attempts to "feminize" women's experience of motherhood so often miss the mark. Like soft-focus videos about labor and childbirth, they try to render tame and frilly the raw power of female sex and motherhood. "Most of the instruction given to pregnant women is as chirpy and condescending as the usual run of maternity clothes," writes the novelist Louise Erdrich. "We are too often treated like babies having babies when we should be in training, like acolytes, novices to high priesthood, like serious applicants for the space program." When femininity and motherhood are falsely linked, what gets lost is the character of motherhood as vividly self-expressive and goal directed. Equality feminists may treat motherhood as another feminine option, and difference feminists may imply that it expresses feminine qualities of self. But neither captures the ways that motherhood transcends the trappings of gender, putting us in touch with the deepest meaning of being human.

Queer Mothering

The simplistic alignment of motherhood with "femininity" in mainstream culture and feminism has permeated some queer discourses as well. "Real lesbians don't have kids," remarks one woman to a researcher studying lesbian mothers' paths to pregnancy. Another sees a "seamless connection between being a 'normal' girl and becoming a mother." However, our consideration of the way motherhood transcends gender should make us consider how it transcends norms of sexuality as well.

The poet and critic Maggie Nelson questions the "presumed opposition of queerness and procreation." She asks whether, instead, there is "something inherently queer about pregnancy itself" in that it "radically alters one's 'normal' state, and occasions a radical intimacy with—and radical alienation from—one's body." In this framing of the question, she highlights a way in which patriarchal bias echoes in queer culture; in patriarchy, the privileged position is maleness, and in queer culture, the privileged position is the "nonbreeding" nonconformist. Nelson asks how pregnancy, "an experience so profoundly strange and wild and transformative," can "also symbolize or enact the ultimate conformity?" She sees in both biases a common theme, namely, "the disqualification of anything tied too closely to the female animal."

In *Of Woman Born*, the poet Adrienne Rich also critiques the tethering of "feminine" gender characteristics with heteronormative models of parenthood by distinguishing between motherhood as an experience—an embodied field of relating between persons—and as an institution, which forces mothering practices into a strict mold designed to serve the interests of men. Although Rich did not discuss this distinction with respect to her own perspective as a lesbian until her book's second edition, by dividing the experience of mothering into the patriarchal overlay of oppressive ideas and the potential for authentic relationship, she creates a place for maternal desire that is distinctly defined in contrast to the patriarchal order.

Rich therefore lays the groundwork of a theory of how the very practice of motherhood can be politically revolutionary and subvert pernicious social conditions and norms. For one, Rich emphasizes the mother's role as a model of resistance, aligning some of a mother's most important qualities (trustworthiness, courage, ethics) with an activist political stance toward society's injustices. This emphasis allows Rich to demonstrate, for instance, that a poor and oppressed mother's fight for the sheer survival of her family through long hours of paid work away from her children is a positive expression of motherly love, not simply an absence.

Second, while Rich laments that women's "active energies have been trained and absorbed into caring for others," she affirms that the energies "trained and absorbed into caring for others" are *also* the sources of the "trust and tenderness" that people need most "deeply and primally" from their mothers. Rich notes that the developing child's need for a mother's trust and tenderness does not necessarily cooperate with tidy political categories. For example, when a daughter needs her mother to honor what she cares about in order to feel understood—and what she cares about is her Barbies and her princess costume—a mother may struggle with the conflict between exercising political resistance to problematic cultural norms while at the same time being responsive to her child. This paradox raises complex questions for our society, including for feminist and queer discourses and for mothering practices more generally. In transmitting values to children, parents continually confront their own politics with respect to both the need for social change and the provision of stability. Rich illuminates how it is often the parents most persecuted by systemic prejudice who explicitly and radically conceptualize their parental roles as necessarily involving active political critique and opposition.

The mounting research on queer motherhood—as well as on the many other families where gender identifications, sexual orientation, number of parents, or genetic relatedness differ from traditional norms—demonstrates that, contrary to prejudice and stereotypes, alternative family forms are not a risk factor for children's mental health. According to Susan Golombok, a pioneering researcher on family relationships, "family structure—including the number, gender, sexual orientation and genetic relatedness of parents, as well as their method of conception—does not play a fundamental role in children's psychological adjustment or gender development." What *does* matter is the quality of the relationships—the parents' relationship with the child, the parents' relationships with each other, and the family's relationship to their larger social environs. By taking us out of old oppositions and dichotomies, this research helps us finally regard what the writer Annie Leclerc calls "the profound taste we have for children" through a less gendered lens.

The increasingly widely lived experience of new family forms confirms the genuine variability in people's desires with respect to love relationships and children. Simultaneously, as a culture we have shifted toward the belief that whom we desire and love is an essential component of our identities and as such deserves to be freely exercised and legally protected. As part of these considerations, we must also recognize that many kinds of people—male, female, intersex, genderqueer—view caring for children as central to their basic identity.

"One of the gifts of genderqueer family making," Nelson writes, "is the revelation of caretaking as detachable from—and attachable to—any gender, any sentient being." Anyone can take the position of a loving, desiring, engaged parent. But *someone must take it*. The role calls us into extraordinarily challenging, deeply felt states: "caring for others" is no easy thing. In opening ourselves to the other's dependency on us, we consent to being "tossed about," "loved too much," "detested," and to "serving as a buoy, as a lifeline," as the psychoanalyst Viviane Chetrit-Vatine puts it. As I've written elsewhere, parenthood "inevitably and necessarily involves the stubborn reality of the flesh," and that's one reason it is so hard. Amid fatigue and stress and personal struggles, every parent must find a way to connect to their parental desire so that the child can be vitally connected to his own desires and passions, to his own creativity.

One of the stresses that nontraditional families face is pervasive prejudice against their legitimacy as parents and familial units. In my therapy sessions with one lesbian couple, we explored how much pressure they felt to be seen as model parents and how difficult that was in light of their daughter's special needs. They both felt a subtle skepticism from those around them and realized how hard they worked to "measure up." This couple had quietly suffered for quite a while, reluctant to seek help, because they felt so vulnerable to being judged. Most "traditional" families are spared from this kind of parenting stress.

Still, one of the revolutionary promises of queer thought on the formation of nontraditional family structures is that all of society will stop seeing relationships of dependency, help, and care as inherently "feminized"; with stereotypical associations such as "passive," "submissive," or "weak." Likewise, the evolution of family forms should also encourage us all to think more deeply about the place we want children and childcare to have in our lives. Instead of connecting the desire to parent with the position of a demeaned "female animal," perhaps we will learn to recognize caregiving as central to the larger project of human growth and flourishing.

Connecting Motherhood and Desire

A friend of mine once asked, genuinely curious, "Why would you want another baby after you've already had one?" She couldn't understand my wanting a second child, and her wondering about it was equally incomprehensible to me. People really are different; they want different things. There are as many forms of feminism as there are feminists because what each of us believes in and desires bears the stamp of our unique history.

Yet, whatever our individual vantage points, mothers share a common predicament: we all deal in one way or another with the splits and conflicts in our lives. From time to time we try to fortify ourselves in our choices by disowning our competing motivations, perhaps by elaborately insisting on our contentment at home with children or by espousing our belief in the importance that mothers also pursue their own careers. But the reality for most of us is that we are torn, and we live with a sense of conflict, sometimes flickering, sometimes flaring, hour by hour, day by day.

The sources of our conflict are various, but Adrienne Rich puts her finger on an important one: our ability to strive in the outer world usually entails our absence from our children and diminishes our in-person participation in the "trust and tenderness" that they need "deeply and primally." Historically, this predicament has been an unremitting reality for poor mothers; today, however, many middle-class mothers also experience a version of this plight. The very structure of work, whether performed by necessity or choice, dictates ongoing dilemmas between providing material subsistence and tending to our children's emotional and psychological needs. Anyone who works to keep her health insurance or make the rent and leaves her child at day care encounters a conflict between meeting the material and emotional needs of her child that can be truly agonizing. When work is chosen or deeply satisfying, some things are easier, but it does not banish conflict or dispel the pain.

What is painful is not only our awareness that we might not be providing what our child wants and needs. It is also the experience of what might be described as a thwarting of self. Having a child creates not only a new living, physical being, but also a relationship between two people. The desire to mother is in part the desire to participate in that relationship and in the creation of another human personality through our unique capacities, through our own personality. When that desire is insufficiently fulfilled, we often experience this lack as pain. Like the artist or the poet, a mother can feel she is not truly living her life or being herself if she feels deprived of the time and emotional space to relate to her child. She can still nurture and support her children, still feed them and put a roof over their heads, but her sense of creative contribution can be diminished. To feel fully engaged in this creative process does not necessitate round-the-clock togetherness or perfect attunement. But it involves a physically felt need for time together in which both mother and child come to discover and progressively know each other.

Ironically, buried within the founding text of feminism's second wave, Simone de Beauvoir's *Second Sex*, is a powerful philosophical understanding of this desire. You won't find it in de Beauvoir's discussion of pregnancy and motherhood, though. Rather, it's in her analysis of erotic love and the relation of the sexes, where woman has historically been seen as "object" to man's "subject." (In a similar way, according to one type of feminist analysis, a mother becomes the "object" to her child's "subject," and thereby loses her own subjectivity, agency, and freedom.)

De Beauvoir argues that love relationships are unique because in them we accept and even embrace the struggle to see ourselves *and* the other as both subject *and* object. This effort is a struggle because it's never easy to remain flexible in our picture of others and ourselves. It is difficult, de Beauvoir argues, to take pleasure in being the object of another person's desire *and* to maintain a stable sense of being a fully desiring subject in one's own right. I contend that this difficulty also characterizes how hard it is for a mother to stay connected with her identity as someone in the world while also fulfilling the essential, if temporary, need to constitute the "whole world" for her baby. To maintain our sense of autonomy and freedom within relationships of dependency is a lifelong psychological struggle for each of us. As the philosopher Nancy Bauer writes, "The essential struggle is with myself: I struggle to let go of a fixed picture of myself, to risk letting the other teach me who I am." Letting the relationship with the other *teach me who I am* is the risk and reward of sexual love. It is also the risk and reward of a desired motherhood.

No one in his right mind would suggest that a sense of power and effectiveness in the world is attained at the cost of lopping off one's sexual impulse; however, women are often asked to take for granted that we have to compartmentalize maternal desire if we want to achieve power and effectiveness in the world at large. For contemporary women in developed Western countries who have access to birth control and a broad range of potential life paths, motherhood is more than at any other time in history a self-chosen project. However, working women with small children tell me in therapy all the time, "Maybe I'm just spoiled." They wonder what's wrong with *them* that they can't adjust to their sense of dividedness, and their inability to banish guilt becomes just one more thing about which to feel guilty. "Success," it appears, is synonymous with getting rid of your yearning to be with your children or your belief that they need you. Rather than understanding their predicament in a social and historical context, these women feel that they should just be able to deal with their internal conflicts through savvy or strength of character or denial of their feelings. They see their distress and conflict as a personal failure, as a problem of *self.*

The feminism I espouse takes as its focus the issue of what exactly contributes to an authentically fulfilling experience of motherhood and what detracts from it. It's not useful to side with one aspect of women's lives while devaluing another; characterizing motherhood as perpetually oppressive is just as wrongheaded as claiming it is exclusively a path to joy. The question my feminism asks is not how to free mothers to go to work or how to free them to care for their children; it is how mothers can grapple with the demand for self-dividedness, an issue inherent in our structures of work and embedded in our neoliberal "ideals" about the autonomous self in capitalist society. Insofar as feminist traditions have valued the lives of women by framing individual achievement at the expense of achievements in relationships of dependency, feminist discourse has played a part in creating the sense of dividedness women feel today. This dividedness cannot be addressed by endlessly reversing the hierarchy of value. Instead, we need a feminism that articulates truer, more complex stories about how a woman's maternal desire relates to her search for meaning and her desired place in the world.

3

Psychoanalysis

Caroline, a thirty-year-old consultant, contemplated with some excitement her promising new relationship. In therapy sessions with me, I noticed her occasionally interrupting her complaints about work with smiling, hopeful outbursts. "I can almost imagine getting married and having babies with him," she said one day, but then blushed and quickly followed up with, "Here I go, trying to escape from the real world." She *did* have a lot of professional challenges, and her relationship *was* still young. But as I watched her, my strongest feeling was that she was actually embarrassed about admitting to me, or perhaps even to herself, her intense desire for marriage and children. As we explored this together, she said, "I feel so weak and dependent to be pinning so much hope on something that's so out of my control. It's almost babyish." She switched gears, turning her thoughts from the "babyish" part of herself to the problems presented by an actual baby. "If I'm serious about my career, there's no way I'll be able to deal with a kid needing me all the time. People who make it at my company all have wives at home."

Over several months, as her romantic relationship

deepened, Caroline continued to characterize marriage and motherhood as a kind of shrinking from challenge. But these pronouncements began to feel increasingly rote to me, offered to placate me somehow, or to remind herself of who she was supposed to be, even if her heart wasn't in it. When I asked more about it, we discovered she saw me as a "powerful feminist" who would look askance at her "girlie" aspirations. This view of me linked up with her view of her mother, who'd always praised her for her independence and warned her never to depend on a man financially. One day, after she ran into me at a clothing store with two of my children in tow, her picture of me shifted, and she wept "with relief" that maybe I was a bit like her.

One reason it was hard for Caroline to think about her maternal desires was that the life changes implied by those desires, and the identity she'd assume, felt at odds with the kind of goal-oriented activity for which she'd always been rewarded. Caroline did not feel she was considering the differences between two paths to meaning or two avenues to satisfaction; she felt that her dilemma involved mature, goal-directed activity—work—on the one hand and an amorphous mass of feelings—motherhood—on the other. Somewhere buried under her sense of inadequacy, Caroline felt that fostering another person's happiness by devoting her energies to parenthood was a direct way to do good in the world and to feel happy herself. But that seemingly "soft" belief was almost impossible to square with a self-image as "achievement oriented" or "adult."

Motherhood is, in the first instance, a relationship. To explore maternal desire at a level deeper than social commentary, we need a psychology, such as psychoanalysis, that takes relationships as its focus. Within the broader field of psychology, which studies the brain, mind, and behavior, psychoanalysis is a subdiscipline that focuses on people's *subjective experience* and on improving that experience through psychotherapy. Most people today do not encounter psychoanalytic theories of human psychology on the psychoanalyst's fabled couch, but rather in the broader culture and in their own assumptions. In daily life, we tend to take for granted that we have desires and conflicts we keep out of awareness that have an ongoing impact on our feelings and choices. We accept, for instance, that some things about our current interactions reflect aspects of our formative past: we might subconsciously expect our boss to act like our perfectionistic mother and therefore find ourselves feeling a strangely familiar resentment toward her, or we might notice that we treat our child when he's badly behaved the way our disciplinarian father treated us.

Psychoanalysis's unique contribution is that it explores the human psyche through the relationship of therapist and patient. In so doing, it powerfully illuminates the nature of intimate relationships more generally. But psychoanalytic theories also underlie a body of scientific research that has conceptualized and tested models for how the mind is formed in our earliest parent-child relationships. Aided by suggestive findings from mother-infant research, psychoanalytic approaches help us think more clearly about children's development, but also the mothers' development—specifically, how responsiveness to children relates to the development of the self.

Early Women Psychoanalysts on
Motherhood and Ambition

Despite the historically male bias of psychoanalysis, women were among the field's key players from its beginnings in the early twentieth century. They asked many of the same questions about motherhood that Caroline was asking herself: What is the relationship between individual aspirations and maternal feeling? How are we to think about and manage the conflicts between them? These women also sought a satisfying synthesis of theories of female development that would be consistent with their own subjective experiences as mothers and ambitious women.

In the preface to her book *Motherhood and Sexuality*, written almost seventy years ago, the Argentine psychoanalyst Marie Langer asks, "Does a woman engaged in a professional career experience obstacles to her realization of motherhood, and if so, to what extent? . . . During my adolescence it was a frequent topic of conversation. . . . Later I had to abandon the question at the theoretical level so that I might resolve it in practice. Only when I recently read a book with the alarmist title *Modern Woman: The Lost Sex* did I begin to think again about the possible incompatibility between motherhood and career." Langer's question is remarkably fresh, and her consideration of the "possible incompatibility" between maternal and professional aspirations remains a contested social and theoretical ground in the present. Even the scaremongering 1947 *Modern Woman*—which contended that post–World War II women who left the domestic sphere were psychologically disordered—echoes in certain strains of today's pop-psychological commentary and reactionary cultural criticism (Yikes, women are "losing their femininity"!).

Helene Deutsch, Freud's colleague and one of the first psychoanalysts to take up the complexity of maternal desire, experienced a profound personal struggle with motherhood whose scars can be traced in her writing. She believed, for instance, that breastfeeding was an ultimate maternal achievement, yet she herself felt drained by it. She deeply desired more children but had an avowed hatred of her mother, which she felt hampered her own ability to care for her child. As an adult, her son spoke resentfully of her absence and her tendency to fire caregivers to whom he had become attached. Deutsch felt keenly that mothering took her away from her work, yet she also felt that the child's inevitable developmental separation from his mother was "the tragedy of motherhood."

These painful personal experiences and contradictions form the focus of her analysis of motherhood. She takes individual differences seriously and understands all human activity, including mothering, as inevitably characterized by conflict. Clear-eyed about how being a mother involves conflicts between real and different desires, she also tries to articulate something about the mother's desires regarding her child:

In order to thrive, the baby needs his mother and the mother needs her baby. . . . Whenever [some women] are away from their children, they are seized by a peculiar and irrational feeling of restlessness and worry; sometimes they describe it as "longing." . . . It is the natural pull at the psychic umbilical cord. The younger the child, the shorter the cord, and the more the pull is burdened by neurotic additions and excessive dutifulness, the more painful it is.

Deutsch continues, "This kind of longing is not comparable to any other emotion; it is neither pure dutifulness nor love."

Then as now, the difficulty for women is that the feelings involved in what Deutsch terms "motherliness"—"the mother's deep longing for a more intimate relationship with her child, her justified concern for his emotional development, and her feeling of guilt for neglecting him"—can be experienced as opposed to "the interests of her own individuality." Deutsch's therapeutic approach is to be gentle toward the conflict and realistic about the trade-offs. "Very often the situation can be mastered only by means of a compromise," she writes. "The task of the psychologic adviser is to give these women permission to compromise. . . . They themselves must accept as a necessary result of the compromise the fact that by reason of it they are missing something important."

Karen Horney, another early woman psychoanalyst, was the first to introduce an affirmative personal perspective on mothering into psychoanalytic theory. Horney's mother, whom Karen called "my great childhood love," died at around the same time Horney gave birth to the first of her three daughters, perhaps strengthening the intensity of Horney's own experience in mothering her infant. According to her biographer Susan Quinn, Horney "felt trapped, in the beginning, by the undeniably feminine position in which pregnancy placed her," but her experience of childbirth and mothering an infant compelled her, "for the first time in her professional life, to take an independent position." Specifically, it led her to frame a psychoanalytic viewpoint in which motherhood stands on its own as a rewarding physical and emotional experience. In 1926, Horney wrote:

> At this point I, as a woman, ask in amazement, and what about motherhood? And the blissful consciousness of bearing a new life within oneself? And the ineffable happiness of the increasing expectation of the appearance of this new being? And the joy when it finally makes its appearance and one holds it for the first time in one's arms? And the deep pleasurable feeling of satisfaction in suckling it and the happiness of the whole period when the infant needs her care?

Horney's incredulousness is aimed at the distorted and woefully incomplete theory of penis envy, which in her view attempted to hide and compensate for the envy that *both* males and females naturally have for the sexual capacities they don't possess. She is the first to unequivocally state the pleasures and power of female sexuality and the maternal.

Marie Langer's answer to her own question about how to reconcile mothering and professional life lay in the direction of recommending society "educat[e] women so that as adults they are capable of sublimating a part of their maternal instincts." Her language is antique, and the notion of "maternal instinct" is vague, biologistic, and universalizing. Yet, as in Horney's views, there's something refreshingly matter-of-fact in her acknowledgment that for some women the experience of self includes an embodied wellspring of maternal desire that can help a mother be a nurturing, living presence through the ordeals of bearing and raising children and, crucially, can offer a powerful source of energy for other pursuits as well. Drawing on their psychoanalytic training, their personal experiences, and their clinical practices, these three thinkers—Langer, Deutsch, and Horney—each theorize how the pleasures that women seek in motherhood, physical and emotional, are neither in any way suspect nor subordinate on the hierarchy of value. They also remind us that an eternal problem for any individual mother is that navigating competing desires always means some degree of compromise and loss. Their theories offer a powerful means for exploring both the desires and compromises of motherhood, even as the nuances of their messages are always at risk of disappearance—including within psychoanalysis itself.

The Feminist Turn in Psychoanalysis

For those of my generation who read feminism and psychoanalysis, Nancy Chodorow's *The Reproduction of Mothering* and Jessica Benjamin's *The Bonds of Love* were the consummate feminist texts that took the inner life of women seriously. I probably read each book half a dozen times, each time with a deeper understanding of the arguments and a renewed appreciation for their elegance.

Yet, when I returned to the books after I became a mother and experienced the relationship with my children myself, I found my respect for them was undiminished but my emotional reaction had changed. Both authors acknowledge that women may find gratification in mothering, but this gratification is not treated as a motivator or first cause. Their arguments appear to operate from the premise that something is inherently disempowering in being a mother caring for one's children, that patriarchal society has instigated and enforced this disadvantageous position for women, and that it is a goal of theory to unearth the unconscious tributaries feeding this oppression. Chodorow and Benjamin foregrounded the mother's psychology as well as the baby's, but the authentic pleasure and meaning that a mother derives from caring for her child is not fully articulated. The result is that key features of a mother's subjectivity, including her sense of agency and self-expression in mothering, drop from view.

Chodorow's goal in *The Reproduction of Mothering* is to explain why generation after generation of women assume the role of primary caretakers for their young. By posing the question "Why do women mother?" she demonstrates that mothering is not simply biologically determined, but also socially and psychologically created. Her main thesis was that mothers experience more intense and enduring feelings of oneness with their daughters than they do with their sons, resulting in the creation of stronger propensities for empathy in daughters and for independence in sons. Her psychological theory joined with her politics in the solution she proposed to this gender asymmetry: fathers and mothers should equally share parenthood, and mothers and fathers should assume similar roles in social and economic life. In terms of personality development, this would result in richer capacities for empathy among men and less conflict-laden individuality for women.

Chodorow's account begins from the premise, grounded in the theory and research available at the time, that the earliest relationship of an infant to his or her caretaker—almost always a mother—is characterized by a sense of "merger" or oneness. The concept of merger captures the infant's utter dependence on the caretaker and his basic need for human contact. But it also connotes that the infant is incapable of experiencing his mother as a separate being or of distinguishing fantasy from reality.

This premise—the idea that a mother and baby begin their life together in a state of complete identification or oneness—has come in for a thorough rethinking and revision since her classic work was published. The mother-infant research shows that human development does not follow a linear progression from fusion to autonomy; rather, feelings of oneness and separateness oscillate throughout life. A baby can first conceptualize and yearn for an experience of merger only in the course of developing an increasingly distinct sense of self. A mother with a mature sense of autonomy will at times experience with her baby a mingling of self and other. At every stage of life, our separateness creates the potential for intersubjective sharing, while our experiences of oneness replenish and enrich our individuality.

The research findings do not contradict how utterly dependent the baby is on the caregiver. Nor do they undercut the reality of the transient states of melting into each other that mothers and likely babies experience. Nor, obviously, do they undo the fact that an average mother is likely to feel at times as if her life has been taken over by her infant and that she no longer has the same clear-cut experience of self. But they do help us make sense of our intuition that images of oneness or fusion do not adequately capture the interpersonal dynamics of mother and infant. And they help us create a narrative more true to our experience that in the interaction between a mother and baby, both parties express a great deal more individuality than the somewhat swampy metaphor of merger evokes.

This subtle point is crucial because it changes our picture not just of the baby, but also of the mother. Once we take account of the genuine relating that takes place between mother and baby, we begin to notice how the idea of mother-baby merger, when subjected to a certain feminist sensibility, tends to characterize mothers' experience of caring for babies as at odds with their individuality. To give one example, Chodorow argues that since the baby is completely dependent, he or she will "employ techniques which attempt to prevent or deny its mother's departure or separateness." Chodorow neglects to differentiate between a baby's desire to maintain proximity, which is due to attachment, and his desire to deny that the mother is a separate person, which is a highly speculative psychoanalytic assumption. Conflating the two distorts how we see the mother's relationship to her child. If we imagine that the baby's wish to deny separateness is identical to his wish to maintain proximity, we're likely to view it as healthy for the mother to have a dose of suspicion toward the child's bids for proximity and protests against separation. Indeed, we will see it as the mother's duty to frustrate the child to help her child develop a sense of "reality." Mothers who "give in" to their babies' putative denial of separateness are in danger of prolonging their children's refusal to accept their independence.

This view misunderstands and pathologizes a mother's own motives for minimizing separation from her child. Like her baby, who is bonded to her by a powerful attachment, the mother is bonded by a powerful motive to give care. It's problematic to characterize what a mother wants for herself as wholly distinct from what she wants to experience with her babies or to provide for them. In fact, one of her most powerful desires for *herself* is often to relate to and care for her baby. When that desire is subsumed into a notion of merger of distinct identities, it gives rise to an image of mothering as passive, infantile, and depleted of agency and desire.

In *The Bonds of Love,* Jessica Benjamin gives a highly original account of how, in every close relationship—whether between mother and baby, intimate partners, or even therapist and patient—our ability to see the other as a full person with different desires and needs from our own is in a continual state of breakdown and repair. In Benjamin's telling, mutual recognition—the child's and the mother's acknowledgment of each other as persons—is particularly vulnerable to breakdown during a developmental phase that Margaret Mahler terms rapprochement, which begins around fifteen months. Benjamin argues that this period brings forth the child's most vehement struggle against recognizing his mother's separate identity and goals. Whereas Mahler portrays the rapprochement struggle as involving primarily issues of separation, Benjamin emphasizes the child's wish to *control* his mother's comings and goings. In her view, when the toddler becomes aware of his frustrating limitations, he tries harder to assert his will. He gains some temporary sense of mastery in forcing his mother to participate in his plans, but this endeavor also constitutes a refusal to recognize her as a person with her own goals.

If the toddler's agenda is to control his mother, it is not surprising that the mother should be understood to be maintaining her selfhood if she asserts herself and refuses to kowtow to his will. Benjamin repeatedly illustrates maternal limit-setting with examples of the mother's leaving the child, which puts in bold relief the reality of the mother's independent agendas and her child's objection. In this scenario, if a mother capitulates to a child's bids for her to stay, she risks depriving him of the opportunity to accept the subjectivity of others. From that angle, the mother who wishes to minimize separation, either because that is what the child wants or because that is what she wants (or what they both want), begins to look like a clingy saboteur of her child's healthy disillusionment.

Benjamin's drama of a maternal assertion of autonomy in response to a child's demand for control expresses a dominant image behind one strand of contemporary feminist thinking about mothering. According to this view, a good mother must hold fast to the ballast of her independent aims, not capitulating to the domineering child's insistence that she be "just his mother" and nothing else. But the problem is that a mother's "renunciation of her own will" is not the same as a mother's having "sacrificed her own independence." According to Benjamin, when a mother doesn't insist on her independence, this situation "trap[s] mother and child in an emotional hothouse and make[s] it difficult for either one of them to accomplish separation." Again, it seems that the only way for psychological separation to be accomplished is for the mother to insist on her independent selfhood, repeatedly operationalized as the ability to leave. In reality, the kind of independence Benjamin is getting at is an internal autonomy, a connectedness to one's own desire, and a sense of authorship in one's life. These capacities bear no necessary or inevitable relationship with the mother's ability to pursue independent goals away from her child.

Benjamin and Chodorow are exceptionally nuanced thinkers, and their perspectives on the issues they took up have changed and deepened over time. Chodorow, reflecting later on her earlier views, writes about the pressures she felt "to choose between one position that seemed biologically determinist and entrapping of women and another that claimed women's feelings about mothering and their potentially reproductive bodies were the product of social structure and cultural mandate. . . . On a more personal level," she continues, "I, along with many feminists of my generation, did not in our twenties and early thirties adequately understand how mothering is actually experienced . . . and many of us were ourselves not prepared for the powerful, transformative claims that motherhood would make upon our identities and senses of self." Benjamin's subsequent work uses her earlier analysis of the inevitable tensions between mothers' and babies' needs to consider the broader question of "how there can be two subjects in one relationship." Specifically, she has explored the ways that a therapy relationship helps people achieve mutuality by "negotiating the sticky compromises and paradoxes of a dyad in which there is mutuality but asymmetry, identity of needs but conflict of needs, deep attunement but also difference." Her 2004 article "Beyond Doer and Done to," where she fully conceptualizes these issues, is one of the most widely read in psychoanalysis.

Unfortunately, however, their nuanced ideas have been translated in popular books about motherhood more simplistically as a mother's right and duty to avoid the perils of putting a child's needs before her own. Even in professional journals where Benjamin's theory is subtly debated, her feminist assertions go uncritiqued. "At this point in cultural history," write three sophisticated clinicians, "the family context mediating the child's conflict [in toddlerhood] still tends to be organized by the traditional, culturally determined scenario in which women mother, such that mothering requires a repudiation of true agency and desire." Concepts like Chodorow's "merger" can feel pretty close to the mark for some women, since becoming a mother can involve a profound destabilization and transformation of one's former self. But when the necessary changes toward a more porous identity and more fluid boundaries are characterized as inflicted on women by sexist society and women internalize a sense of inferiority for not feeling more solid and unitary, it vastly oversimplifies a complex and meaningful internal process.

Such self-critical ideas still hold sway over some women, who express anxiety about losing their taut bodies, clear goals, and social approval if they descend into the engulfing world of mothering. A thirty-three-year-old marketing director in therapy with me was planning her first maternity leave and decided to take a minimal amount of time off and go back to work at full capacity, even though her job allowed for more flexibility. She was understandably concerned about maintaining her professional standing and expertise. But her realistic concerns were intensified by fears of how her identity would be changed by having a baby. As a therapist, my work was not only to help her navigate the external pressures and biases she would face in her workplace. It was also to explore the power of her feeling that she was moving from "form" to "formlessness" and to help her consider not only her fears about loss of control, but also her hopes about the pleasures of relating and the possibilities for growth.

Mutual Responsiveness between Mother and Child

There is an odd disconnect between the portrayal of motherhood as requiring the "repudiation of true agency and desire" and the explosion of research pointing toward how centrally a baby's and a mother's intentions and desires figure into their creation of mutual satisfaction and pleasure. Many extol the contribution mother-infant research has made in replacing the image of mothers as "extensions of babies" with a more accurate picture of mothers as full persons. But comparatively little has been said about the light this same research might shed on mothers' desire to care for children, let alone the meaning of that desire with respect to mothers' identities and goals.

Yet, in minutely describing the processes by which mothers and babies together create a satisfying pattern of interaction, the research brings into focus some of the capacities that mothers bring to these interactions. These capacities conform, in all relevant particulars, to the characteristics we commonly associate with a sense of self: the ability to reflect, to interpret, to enact goals, to respond to others flexibly and creatively, and to share pleasure.

The mutual responsiveness of baby and caregiver begins in the earliest weeks of a baby's life, when baby and parent already relate to each other via exquisitely tuned interactions that are, in the words of the late researcher Lou Sander, "little miracle[s] of specificity." At three or four months, babies and parents engage in face-to-face play of extraordinary coordination and nuance that lays the groundwork for patterns of pleasurable relating and intimacy throughout life. The caregiver and her baby are increasingly active partners, continually and subtly shaping each other's actions to achieve a gratifying rapport. By nine months, babies deliberately seek to share feelings and intentions with others, for they now begin to grasp that other people have minds like their own. Parents commonly talk about this as a "great age," for the parents and the baby both find a special delight in the baby's first awareness of sharing subjective states with others.

By being responsive to her child over time, a mother communicates that she values her child's inner life. That leads him to value hers. In contrast to Benjamin's account, a child's attempts to feel all-powerful and cancel out his mother's needs are not an inevitable by-product of toddlerhood. According to the psychologist Karlen Lyons-Ruth, such behaviors, when they occur, "appear to be rooted in the mother's much longer-term difficulties in providing a responsive relationship, which includes genuine affective engagement and effective comforting and soothing of the infant at times of stress." Toddlers with responsive caregivers also vigorously assert their needs and oppose their parents, but they are able to integrate their "initiatives into the social give and take while maintaining warm relatedness." In other words, they assert their needs while staying in touch with and recognizing the caregiver as a person.

Parents encounter this truth throughout development, particularly in those moments when we feel our relationships with our children are going right. We comfort our little girl when she has hurt herself, wash her cut, kiss it, and put on a Band-Aid. When she sees we are sad, even at age one or two, she hugs us or sings us "Happy Birthday." She feels secure and close when we accept and respond to her feelings, and when we respond, we confirm her view that "when I need or want something, Mommy understands and responds." This model of relationships in turn guides her interactions with us. Or, an older son uses his imagination to figure out the "exact right present" for us; he aspires to know us for who we really are, having so often experienced that same recognition from us. Such moments could be described as peak experiences of parenthood. They are fully saturated moments, bringing us satisfaction of two kinds: pleasure in our child's eagerness to know us and make us happy, and a sense of success in having nourished our child's own empathic capacities through our responsiveness to him. This loop of empathy, I think, is what is most likely to get parents and children through difficult times, be they the storms of toddlerhood or the rebellions of adolescence.

Circling back eighty years, we can see that Helene Deutsch recognized features of maternal responsiveness that today's mother-infant researchers have empirically identified. "The mother's task," she wrote, in slightly archaic terms, is "to enter into her child's feelings" so that she can "achieve the inner certainty that enables her to grasp the volatile expressions of childish life and to intervene now in a reflex manner, now with critical deliberation. . . . The great 'wisdom' of mothers results from the blending of two functions, the affective-intuitive and the intellectual."

The research confirms that a mother's responsiveness combines both her willingness to enter into the emotional state of her child—what we commonly call empathy—and her ability to reflect and offer a different perspective. She both *feels with* and *thinks about* her child. When a baby is distressed after an injection, for example, mothers who are most effective at soothing typically do two things: they mirror the baby's emotion, sometimes with a sad face or by saying "Ouch," then they shift affective states, sometimes using humor or irony. The mother joins the baby's feeling (mirrors emotion), then takes a perspective on it, saying, in effect, "Join me and let's shift to another emotional state." In this way she helps her baby gain perspective on his own experience and learn to manage his emotions.

Throughout life, sensitive responsiveness is what makes relationships comforting, satisfying, and a source of mutual understanding. As adults, and as mothers, we also need and deserve to receive, and give to ourselves, the same kind of curious and compassionate attention that we give our children. Psychotherapy is one place where people can seek to cultivate and express these capacities, while friendships and partnerships are more common ones. Mom blogs have also emerged in the past two decades as a responsive community for sharing experiences, being heard, and for feeling helped. "Women online find they 'let go,'" writes the sociologist Kara Van Cleaf, "and find an expanded sense of pleasure and self. Digital media is particularly conducive to experiencing the pleasure of letting go, in part because it is done with others. The risks of subverting dominant narratives or the status quo are minimized when there's a virtual group nodding their heads in agreement, via the hearts, likes, etc., of social media platforms." As of 2016, there were an estimated 4 million self-identified mom bloggers, making online mother communities a readily accessible source of support that enhances—and even supersedes—on-the-ground relationships. As one twenty-five-year-old woman said to me, "I've learned way more from *PBFingers* and other mom blogs about pregnancy and motherhood than I have from the actual women in my life."

Empathy Is Never Perfect

As a therapist, and as a mother, my ability to perfectly attune to another person is fleeting at best. That is not a personal failure; it's being human. The mother-infant research I've discussed supports the premise that our relationships with our children are not about the need to be perfect, to know exactly what we are doing, or to anticipate all our baby's needs. The normal back-and-forth between two people who care for each other—the miscommunications, the repairs, the repeated attempts to connect and to elicit each other's interest or pleasure—are the "stuff" of parental care, empathy, and secure attachment.

The earliest roots of these processes have been studied during a period in babies' development when, as the researchers Beatrice Beebe and Frank Lachmann write, the only goals of the "infant's repertoire of interactive capacities . . . are mutual attention and delight." Studying the timing of vocalizations between mothers and their four-month-old babies, they found that an optimal degree of coordination in their rhythm—neither too much nor too little vocal overlap—contributes to their feeling in tune with each other. In some fascinating experiments, Joseph Jaffe and colleagues found that a middle range of adult-infant coordination of vocal communication at four months is related to secure attachment at one year, suggesting that the healthiest patterns of interaction are neither too tightly matched nor too mismatched. Whereas disordered attachment relationships at one year were found to be preceded at four months with a pattern of overly tight vocal tracking, indicative of vigilance, wariness, and anxious monitoring, secure pairs are able to allow each other "more 'space,' more room for uncertainty." Throughout life, in good relationships, each partner feels trusting enough and free enough to apprehend and respond to her own and the other's feelings and thoughts.

Though babies and mothers are partners who cocreate their interaction, a mother's internal model of intimate relationships is extraordinarily powerful in shaping the baby's own. The study of attachment shows that the crucial link between a mother's own childhood attachment experiences and her child's attachment security is the mother's capacity to reflect and think coherently about her own past. In other words, *regardless of how insecure her own childhood attachment was*, the mother's ability to take perspective on her own past relationships predicts her own child's security. How exactly might this work? If a mother can reflect deeply and incisively, she can more accurately perceive and understand her own and others' thoughts and feelings. This makes her more likely to be able to respond sensitively to her child. The researchers Peter Fonagy and Mary Target define a secure bond as "one where the infant's signals are accurately interpreted by the caregiver." A baby develops a secure attachment by virtue of the caregiver's reliable recognition of his needs and desires and the provision of an appropriate response.

Even in good relationships, empathy is never complete. Miscommunications happen all the time. It should come as a relief to mothers to know that there is no such thing as the perfectly attuned caregiver; in fact, the inevitable moments of being out of tune give each person an opportunity to reach to understand the other's mind. Researchers have found that a baby's development into a happy, confident, curious child is likely associated not with a caregiver's perfect responsiveness, but with her ongoing attempts to course-correct after misinterpreting her child's signals and to find ways to restore positive feelings after negative interactions.

In clarifying the specifics of early mother-child interactions, the research begins to illuminate a deeply felt but inadequately theorized aspect of a mother's experience: that her ability and desire to respond to her child contribute not only to her recognition of her child but also to her own sense of pleasure, effectiveness, and self-expression. The research also suggests that a mother's separateness and individuality are amply recognized by her child in normal interacting. The child's recognition of the mother does not hinge on the mother's dramatic demonstration of independence or assertion of autonomy. Instead, a mother's assertion of selfhood can be as powerfully effected through the more subtle communications of difference. These also have the potential to express and convey the mother's sense of self; these also have the potential to provide her recognition as a person in her own right. It is precisely this potential of seemingly "small" interactions to fully engage the personality of both baby and mother that has gotten lost in the broad-brush appraisal of caring for children as an abdication of self.

Compromise and Flexibility, Love and Loss

Among the most pressing emotional and practical questions mothers struggle with is how to walk the line of providing for the various needs of others and themselves. Each mother, whatever her roles, must find a way to balance togetherness and separateness, as well as the feelings of love and loss that go with them, in her own life and with her children. She must respond to her children in ways that are appropriate to their stage of life and her stage of motherhood, and she must find a way both to mourn the losses and embrace the opportunities that accompany her children's growth into more independent people.

Maggie was a stay-at-home, married mother with a two-and-a-half-year-old son, and she had gotten a great deal of satisfaction from her role. She felt that she had never been so much "herself" or so happy with her life until she became a mother. However, she came to see me for therapy because she had gotten into conflict with her husband over his complaint, "You never want to go out." Friends were finding it exasperating that everything revolved around her son's schedule. By insisting that her son's well-being should always be their top priority, she was losing connection to her husband and friends.

After meeting for a while, I felt that Maggie was having a hard time facing the inevitable losses that motherhood, and life, presented her. For one, she couldn't quite accept her little boy's development from a babe in arms into a more independent child. The reality that he needed something different from her as he grew—something equally essential—was difficult for her to adjust to. Historically, she'd had troubles with her own mother around autonomy and separation, her mother having transmitted the message that Maggie was "abandoning" her when Maggie asserted her own interests or wishes. Maggie's feelings of guilt, fear, and loss of control in moments of separation hindered her ability to foster the degree of autonomy that would best nurture her child and aid in her own development.

One day, I shared with her the research findings about mothers and babies' overly tight vocal tracking as an indication of vigilance and anxious monitoring. It helped her think about the ways that her inflexible control resulted from a sense that relationships are only safe when people proceed in lockstep; in her world, difference meant separation, and separation meant anxiety. After that, we used this mother-baby image to gradually help her create more space to discover and reflect on what her son needed. She realized that she tried to keep her fears of separation at bay by doing everything "right," but it meant controlling those around her and distancing them as a result. I said to Maggie, "What's important to your son is not that you *know* what he needs and feels or instantly anticipate it with no gap, but that you *try to understand* what he needs and feels. That takes time, and effort, and even failure. The gap isn't an unbridgeable abyss. When you struggle to understand him—that *is* bridging the gap. Then you can feel close again."

As we worked together, Maggie began to be able to bear her uncertainty and take more time to decipher her own feelings and her son's. She got better at what she called "sitting with the swirl." Feeling accompanied and understood by me and relaxing into the safety of our relationship helped her gain confidence that the effort to understand her son was more important than anticipating his every need or adhering to rigid rules. As her emotional flexibility grew, she also understood the pressures she had been putting on her husband, friends, and extended family. She began to make more room for the needs and desires of all the important people in her life.

Mothers who feel a keen sense of loss as children grow up may deal with their feelings through outward action: "I'll have another baby" or "I'll breastfeed longer." They may avoid letting go or inwardly feel confused about what they are doing for their child and what they are doing for themselves. One mother, describing another's decision to continue nursing a three-year-old, concluded that the child was "not yet emotionally ready to wean. The comfort and closeness of nursing were still vital to the child's well-being." Framing the issue solely in terms of the child's needs, she didn't reflect on why the mother might feel that continuing to nurse was the best way to comfort her now preschooler.

Psychological conflict and the need for compromise are inevitable. The challenge is to meet them with awareness, emotional flexibility, and a reflective perspective. Often the answer is not an outward change in role balance as much as an inward, psychological one. That said, a key social issue is the *actual* lack of flexibility in mothers' lives. The emotional flexibility on which mothers draw in relating sensitively to their children and themselves is marred by the inflexibility of their work situations. Greater flexibility in the workplace and more humane family-leave policies lessen mothers' sense of conflict, thereby creating conditions for their optimal responsiveness.

Regrettably, recognition of the crucial centrality of emotional responsiveness to the remediation of almost every social ill is virtually absent from public health debates. It's also muffled in the mainstream conversation about motherhood in late capitalistic society. If market research is any indication, many sources of solidarity for mothers, such as influential mommy bloggers, have migrated from "raw and authentic" blogs, where the goal was responding to the feeling that "I want to feel less alone," to the Instagram feeds of "influencers" and "pitchwomen" who post "pretty objects like cooling pies and evergreen sprigs tucked into apothecary vases, with hardly any chaos in sight." Unsurprisingly, the corporatization and commodification of maternal concerns don't offer the best support to mothers. As the author Bunmi Laditan writes, "Companies don't want to align themselves with the difficulties of motherhood. They want to align themselves with people who are winning."

WHERE DOES ALL THIS leave women such as Caroline, the patient I described at the beginning of the chapter?

The insights from psychoanalytic theory and research do not put an end to the perennial argument about why or whether a mother *should* be spending her time caring for her children. Instead, they help us think about the question of why she might *want* to do so. They demonstrate the extraordinarily nuanced, though rarely articulated, awareness of self and other on which her caring activities are based. They illuminate the mother's improvisational responsiveness and the moment-to-moment appraisal of the child's and her own needs, desires, and frustrations, both within her relationship with her child and beyond. They clarify some of the genuine mental and emotional challenges with which mothers struggle in everyday interactions with their children, and they help us conceptualize and practice the skills that are called upon and developed. Taken together, the findings give us more explicit knowledge about something that usually remains implicit: the activities of mothering can, and often do, enrich and deepen the complexity of personalities of both child and mother, and in those activities mothers can, and often do, find enormous meaning and satisfaction. In these ways, the research helps us to describe more accurately what women who want to mother aspire to experience.

This perspective might help women such as Caroline look differently at the tension between her maternal and professional ambitions. In particular, it might help her disentangle her desire to mother from a set of ideas she has about that desire. For reasons partly motivated by her own wishes and fears, she has espoused ideas, readily available in the culture, that wanting to care for children is regressive—politically, personally, economically. If she is ambitious or mature or truly autonomous, this story goes, she "should" want something different. It might be a relief to her to consider that there is another way to look at her desires, one that does not eye them suspiciously as a retreat but rather permits her to imagine what, for her, would be the most satisfying way to express them.

4

Pleasure

I *am in the supermarket, the one with natural foods and mag-*
azines about mysticism and yoga at the checkout stand. There
is an issue of a magazine called Mothering. *On the cover is a*
chubby, delicious baby who has just raised his head from nursing.
Next to his cheek is the answering curve of his mother's breast. I am
transported to a time of life when my baby is about six months old;
when, his tongue-lips-gums quivering, sometimes still latched on,
sometimes taking a break, he looks up at me with sparkling, happy
eyes. Something impish is in his breezy latitude, in his growing
expertise at doing two things at once. In the picture, the camera is
exactly where my eyes would be if I were the nursing mother, so look-
ing at the baby's face tugs me into a physical moment of pleasure. I
feel it in my throat, in my belly, in my involuntary smile, and in a
startling, ridiculous welling up of tears. The delight I feel at being
at the receiving end of those eyes is almost overwhelming, like a gush
of uncontrollable laughter.

Nursing is one instance when we might feel this rush of connection, but there are many. An adoptive mother may feel
it when she first lays eyes on her baby. We may feel it when

we hold our baby or engage her gaze or when she graces us with her first social smile. This delight surely encodes our mammalian heritage, the powerful evolutionary mechanisms that ensure that we will reproduce the next generation. But our distinctively human awareness of this delight, as well as the way complex emotions and memories interweave with it, relates our experience of intense maternal pleasure to our larger sense of meaning and purpose. Maternal pleasure is a portal into peak experiences of communion with others, and many people privately feel that parenthood is set apart, even sacred, among their ways of seeking higher meaning in life.

Yet, our relationship with motherhood's potential for pleasure is far from straightforward. For one, the experiences are by nature fleeting: the pleasures we share with a child so easily evaporate in the moment. They are often swamped by external conditions such as poverty and job stress, health crises and marital strife. For any given mother on any given day, the sheer challenge of multitasking, shifting gears, and not having time for oneself, combined with the usual chronic lack of sleep, can turn moments of potential pleasure ("Mommy, will you play a game with me?") into a tangle of inner conflict. Emotional challenges such as depression, anxiety, or baggage from childhood can feel as debilitating as any external impediment.

Beyond these issues, there's something about the all-encompassing sense of responsibility aroused by motherhood that insidiously pulls us toward anxiety and even negativity. For example, I've been struck by the stories of women I've known who have anticipated a second child with a feeling bordering on dread. Mothers have many legitimate anxieties about pregnancy and the responsibility of additional children. Ambivalence, plus hormones, makes weepers of us all. But in each case, these women, all of whom took immense delight in the childhoods of their first kids, portrayed their pregnancies as a misfortune that befell them. Their justified reasons for wariness aside, it still struck me how much more fluent they were in articulating their dread than their desire. Similarly, a scholarly book argues in prose assiduously pruned of emotion that the ideology of intensive mothering is a social construction that undermines women's well-being. In the author's acknowledgments, however, she erupts with mother-child pleasure: "I smother with kisses, shower with flowers, and promise an endless supply of frozen yogurt desserts to my beloved mother." It's as if adult seriousness and academic rigor cannot occupy the same universe as mother-child pleasure.

The difficulty in taking pleasure in having or caring for children does not begin and end with the social pressures on mothers; it also involves the complex relationships we have with our own potential for delight. Any full investigation of motherhood must include a focus on this issue. First, when we ask ourselves what place maternal pleasure should have in our lives and what conditions facilitate our access to it, it's important to recognize that we're not sentimentally gushing over the "little pleasures"; we're talking about genuine ethical and social goals that relate to being responsive parents and engaged, compassionate members of society. Second, when we're frustrated in our ability to take pleasure in mothering, and we wonder what we should do or feel about that frustration, useful ideas exist for how to cope, persevere, and recapture the psychological states that we seek.

The seeking after maternal pleasure also prompts deeper

questions about the larger human project of making and finding meaning in the world. How is meaning created, and what does the time we spend with our children have to do with that endeavor? What does mothering have in common with other human meaning-making activities? And, perhaps most important, how can we cultivate practices that deepen and extend the meaningfulness and pleasure of mothering in a way that also promotes the same values in our wider communities? Three frameworks from psychology help to chart this terrain: studies of mother-child communication and attachment, the experience of time in parenthood, and the concept of mental "flow." Using these ideas, we can consider maternal pleasure from a variety of perspectives, looking at what's involved, what we seek through it, and what makes it harder or easier to sustain.

The Pleasures of Connectedness through Voice and Language

Describing her feeling after her first child's birth, one woman said, "When the nurse placed him in my arms, I felt that I had knowledge of something very powerful that made life completely comprehensible. I remember feeling very light, as if every burden was lifted from me. It made me understand why some people search for ecstatic experiences of revelation in religion." Many women don't feel anything like this at the moment of birth (I was so spent from the pain of my first birth, I asked not even to be shown my baby for several minutes). But others do, and still others experience it when they are holding their baby, biological or adopted, in the first few days, weeks, or months of life.

If we listen to what women say about this experience, we

hear them use expressions such as "getting it," "waking up," or "being in touch with the meaning of life." They describe moments when everyday perception is shot through with a deeper sense of meaning and reality. Some women physically and emotionally experience this sense of a deeper reality in childbirth, where the physical changes produced are second only to those produced by death. In our unfolding relationship with our children, we sense an integration among the various registers of our experience: the yearning for closeness, felt as a physical need; the emotional desire to tend and nurture and satisfy; and a spiritual aspiration to penetrate beneath the surface of things, to be, as Robert Frost writes, "tripped into the boundless." This quality of wholeness—of integrating our physicality, our conscious intentions, and our unconscious wellsprings of desire and need—characterizes the most engaged, satisfying moments of caring for children.

In the weeks, months, and years after childbirth, one of the most powerful and pleasurable ways we continue to forge these connections with our children occurs through the voice—human speech, its rhythms and cadences. When we talk to a newborn, we have no illusion that she understands what we are saying. But our effortless patter feels "right"; we know intuitively that there is much more to speaking to our child than just verbal meaning. Research confirms that intuition. Newborns are extraordinarily sensitive to the nuances of maternal speech. They recognize and prefer their mother's voice to all others, and the basis of that preference is laid in utero. They recognize their mother's voice with such sensitivity that they can recognize extremely subtle variations in her speech patterns. Researchers asked pregnant women to read a Dr. Seuss story to their fetuses in the third trimester. Once born, the babies paid more attention to a tape recording of their mother reading the Seuss story they knew than they did to one that they didn't know.

The way mothers tend to talk to their babies has certain widely observed features, leading scientists to name it motherese. What's distinctive about motherese is that particular rhythmic and musical patterns of mother-infant vocalization convey specific meanings. According to the linguist Steven Pinker, motherese "has interpretable melodies: a rise-and-fall contour for approving, a set of sharp, staccato bursts for prohibiting, a rise pattern for directing attention, and smooth, low legato murmurs for comforting." Motherese demarcates and differentiates through its emotional-vocal quality, and the relation of certain meanings to certain vocalization patterns is so widespread across cultures that it appears to be universal. This apparent universality suggests that mothers intuitively know that utterances paired with emotional tone will communicate best to very young children. The mother's purpose in motherese is therefore not to "teach" her child language; rather, she recognizes that meaning is communicated through vocal-emotional quality, and she combines words and intonation to communicate emotional messages, such as those that are comforting or admonishing. In this way, the mother and the child develop a feeling-laden, relational experience of language from early on in their bond, forging a connection that optimally enables the child to remain in vital contact throughout life with the earliest feelings of wholeness and with the vivid, emotive tone of his first experiences with language.

Affect attunement is another example of a mother's

feeling-laden use of language and another conduit for intense experiences of mother-child pleasure. Until their babies are around nine months old, mothers tend to imitate their baby's behavior or vocalizations, modifying them slightly ("improvising") to add interest. Around nine months, mothers tend to add something new to these exchanges, what Daniel Stern calls affect attunement, which probably emerges in response to the babies' growing ability to share subjective states. Rather than closely imitating her child, a mother begins to match more loosely the affective state her child is expressing in one mode (for instance through a physical gesture) with an action in a different mode (for instance, a vocalization). As an example: "A ten-month-old girl finally gets a piece in a jigsaw puzzle. She looks toward her mother, throws her head up in the air, and with a forceful arm flap raises herself partly off the ground in a flurry of exuberance. The mother says 'YES, thatta girl.' The 'YES' is intoned with much stress. It has an explosive rise that echoes the girl's fling of gesture and posture." The impulse to affectively attune also continues in our relationships with older children. When my five-year-old sat with me at Fourth of July fireworks long ago, we reflexively squeezed each other at the bursts of most spectacular brilliance, and these physical expressions relayed and intensified our shared delight.

In Stern's research, the most frequent reason mothers give for attuning to their baby is not to communicate an imperative (to calm down, energize, or change behavior); rather, it is to attain interpersonal communion. "Communion," he writes, "means to share in another's experience with no attempt to change what that person is doing or believing. This idea captures . . . mother's behavior as seen by experimenters and by the mothers themselves." Mothers commune with their babies for the act itself, for the sheer mutual enjoyment of sharing a moment. It is an intrinsic satisfaction, an embracing of what unfolds between two people.

The psychological literature on the way mothers and children use their voices, sounds, emotions, and verbal utterances to build a close interpersonal connection—rather than convey meaning for purely utilitarian ends—captures something important about parental pleasure in relating to children. As children's verbal capacities expand, their close connection to their emotional life endows their use of language with rich metaphorical possibilities. One three-year-old boy asked if "yesbody" would be there, meaning the opposite of "nobody." Another greeted his too-hot oatmeal with the exclamation "Very fiyaplace!" Children's creative, evocative use of language is delightful to us in part because it surprises us and breaks open our usual habits of thinking.

More generally, though, our interchanges put us in touch with our own embodied emotional life in a new way, weaving in memory and empathy. Helping our children give verbal form to feeling and enter into the shared social world is not some sort of didactic exercise. It involves our whole selves, integrating multiple levels of our conscious and unconscious experience—physical, verbal, and emotional. This continues throughout childhood into adolescence and beyond, whether through shared humor, childhood neologisms, family jokes, texting and its array of emojis, or joint enthusiasms for music or nature. My now-twenty-six-year-old daughter and I still call each other by nicknames we coined decades ago, and we have a whole shared language of references to vacation misadventures, odd elementary-school teachers, pets' personality quirks, sibling games, and children's movies. When these are called up in the present, enjoyment from multiple eras converge. One of the great pleasures of parenting adult children is that our entire trove of shared experience hums in the background, enhancing and deepening our current conversations.

Psychologists describe this sense of integration with reference to emotion and language, but it has also been explored over the centuries by mystics and religious faiths. Transcendent moments, or glimpses of "the center," occur when the unconscious awareness of oneness is apprehended by the conscious mind. This feeding of the conscious mind by unconscious sources, this enriching, deepening, and rendering more resonant the acts and moments of lived experience, is what religious ritual, myth, and poetry are designed to do. At its best, talking to our children partakes of this quality; together, we participate in a way of being in the world where body, emotion, imagination, and memory fluidly communicate.

Such encounters are by their nature both immersive and transitory, which is one reason why they are hard to call to mind after the fact or to imagine in the abstract. The pleasures of interacting with a child are found in the singular moment, the individual event; in that sense, they may be less akin to the pleasures of a "job well done" and more akin to how we experience beauty. "Beauty always takes place in the particular," writes Elaine Scarry, "and if there are no particulars, the chances of seeing it go down." Staying in touch with the pleasure that these moments afford is challenging, not only because of the genuine difficulties of raising children, but also because the tendency to generalize the entire child-rearing enterprise according to available (and often disparaging) narratives effaces the particularities that make it rewarding. When we substitute well-worn tropes for more nuanced reality, we make it harder to experience what moves us most deeply.

Attachment, Security, and Joy

Here's a vignette about a little boy and his mother, taken from the writing of the psychologist Susan Coates:

> A young toddler, barely two, is playing in the backyard; he excitedly pulls at and sniffs some flowers while making excited but unintelligible utterances. His mother can see his pleasure, a pleasure that differs from her own, and smiles in recognition saying "You really love those colors, don't you? You are a guy who loves flowers." . . . The child looks at the mother, sees himself, and smiles; there is a recognition and a discovery of a part of the self held by the other. By virtue of being sensitively met, the child comes to experience loving colors and flowers as part of his notion of himself, and this notion has emerged in the transitional space created by the mother's attuned response. He has been met by his mother in an unobtrusive way such that her needs have not been imposed upon him; thus he has the experience of his own creativity.

Coates's vignette captures the essential element of a secure parent-child bond: sensitive responsiveness. A sensitively responsive parent is warm, affectionate, and attuned to distress signals. She interprets them accurately and responds to them appropriately and promptly. More broadly, she conveys an attitude of curiosity and respect for her child's inner life and takes the view that *understanding feelings* is fundamental to rewarding relationships. In being loving and dependable, the mother helps her child to see himself as lovable and worthy of care. By having his mother appreciating and reflecting on what he feels, the child learns to appreciate and reflect on his own feelings and hers. These behaviors and inner attitudes on the part of the mother create a safe haven and secure base for her child.

If, as the attachment researchers Jeremy Holmes and Arietta Slade put it, "a safe child is a happy child and a happy child is a safe child," something similar holds for mothers. A mother's sense of security allows for a more pleasurable interaction with her child. A research study examined the relationship between a mother's behavior with her toddler, her perspective on her relationship with her toddler, and her memories of the attachment quality she shared with her own caregivers of her youth. It found that a mother who displayed "the capacity to flexibly access and integrate a range of thoughts and feelings relative to her relationship with her own parents" most often experienced joy in relating to her child. It is a bit of a shock to see the word *joy* anywhere in an academic study, but there it is: "joy, coherence, and richness of perception" in the mother's relation to her toddler were correlated with her own "autonomous-secure" status, as measured by the Adult Attachment Interview (AAI), which asks parents about their memories of their own early attachment relationships. Joy and pleasure are more easily shared when people feel secure.

A mother's insecure attachment experiences with her own former caregivers are understandably a barrier to creating mutually joyful experiences with her children. Some mothers grew up with parents who were not responsive to their distress, and they bear a special burden: it's not easy to give your own children an experience of comfort and calm you didn't receive yourself. But as parents we aren't doomed to repeat the past. As I discussed in the last chapter, researchers have found that a mother's rating as "secure-autonomous" on the AAI is not based on her actual attachment experiences with her own parents, good or bad, but rather on the way in which she *reflects on and communicates about* her own early attachment with the interviewer in the present. Parents who speak coherently and with self-awareness about their own pasts are most likely to have securely attached children. Parents rated "insecure-dismissing" of attachment produce narratives of their childhoods that are constricted in emotional expression and low on introspection. Parents rated "insecure-preoccupied" tend toward incoherence and intense, chaotic emotion. These two insecure groups try to deny or easily become flooded by their early emotional pain, and their children's attachments to them are judged "insecure" when assessed at one year. By contrast, the "secure-autonomous" parents can see themselves and their children more clearly; the parents are more responsive to self and others as a result, and their children's attachments to them are rated "secure" at one year.

This research suggests, in effect, that one of the most powerful means for healing from our past is mindfulness. When we are mindful, we are attentive to *and* accepting of our experience. Attending to and accepting the reality of our emotional pain means that we adopt a nonjudgmental, curious attitude toward it, letting it "be"; we neither become fixed on it nor push it away, but let it pass through us. As the therapist Jon Allen observes, avoiding distressing thoughts and emotions amounts to "trying to avoid one's own mind—a futile endeavor." Often as not, the attempt to avoid pain leads to numbing behaviors such as eating, drinking, or devoting all one's attention to screens.

How can we mitigate or accept our own mental stumbling blocks and painful memories in the service of facilitating fuller lives with our kids? For one, we can consider that compassionate acceptance is at the heart of mindfulness, and that the attentiveness and acceptance of mindfulness is at the heart of sensitive responsiveness. Sensitive responsiveness is in turn what creates a sense of security. To cultivate these qualities toward our children, we need to also cultivate them toward ourselves. Supportive adult relationships help enormously, and we should give ourselves the time and space to nurture them. Satisfying marriages and intimate relationships can help us revise our dysfunctional scripts, no matter how challenging our childhood was. Talking to trusted friends— whether to unburden ourselves, review our actions, give and receive solace, or share humor—is an utter necessity. Even reading fiction or watching great TV can remind us that others don't have it all together either. Psychotherapy and mindfulness meditation can help us become gentler on ourselves. Ultimately, gentleness toward ourselves can help us become more open to pleasure in relationships.

Mothers also find valuable support in community online, sharing, as the blogger Alice Bradley describes, "our lopsided, slightly hysterical, often exaggerated but more or less authentic experiences. If one blogger writes about, say, her bad behavior at the doctor's office, then maybe at some point, some freaked-out new mother is going to read that and feel a little better—less stupid, less ridiculous—about her own breakdown at the pediatrician's." The flip side is giving yourself permission to avoid the endless drumbeat of social media comparison, and to honor your need to turn away from feeds and friends that are not truly responsive or fulfilling.

A Deepened Experience of Time

When we are pregnant, the utterly novel condition of having another within us, a being that we slowly invest with subjectivity, changes our relationship with our own unconscious and our sense of time. In this transitional space, we undertake mentally something akin to what our bodies do physically. We knit together a being, out of illusion, reverie, fantasy. Pregnancy impels at least momentary glimpses of a different way of being ourselves, of being *in* ourselves. A vast and rich psychological literature brims over with clinical vignettes about the bizarre dreams and intense fantasies that accompany the body's toil at building a baby. I page through the journals I kept during pregnancies and postpartum and am struck by their efflorescent imaginings, their depiction of mental states that are closed to me now. When happy being pregnant, we feel that good things come from those parts of ourselves we don't control and that we can't directly see. That may be what the writer Faye Weldon means when she remarks that having children gives a woman confidence in her creativity.

Pregnancy also heightens a feeling of living in multiple time frames simultaneously. The psychoanalyst Julia Kristeva contrasts "cyclical" time (of gestation and biology), "monumental" time (eternity), and "linear" time (history). In pregnancy, all three ways of experiencing time are accessible in a heightened way. When we conceive a child, history is in the making. Rarely do we feel so "up close" to a process that changes the course of things forever. One day we are not pregnant, the next we are; somewhere, sometime, as we browse online, buy the groceries, meet a deadline, sleep and dream, a vital connection is made, a journey is traveled, a zygote is implanted. All the while we busy ourselves, doing the things we always do. Yet, dimly, we know that biology is launching, in its implacably repetitive and cyclical way, a unique human destiny. We are part of both the cycle of life and the march of history. A pregnant woman commonly feels, for the first time in her life, that she is participating in an "eternal" female activity, joined with other women across time and place. And she's also shocked to realize how little thought she's given to the fact that every single human she encounters issued from another woman's pregnancy.

As the relationships with our children unfold, we enter into a more poignant and complex sense of time. On one level, they make us aware we are participating in an ancient practice, endlessly variable but repeated across the generations. Parents often feel the urge to extend the sense of connection to their children to a broader connectedness to the world. Parents sometimes return to the religious practices of their youth or forge new ones once they have children, but religious practices in no way exhaust the forms taken by this parental impulse toward ritual. My husband liked to spend Sunday morning with our children looking at crabs at the beach; the writer Louise Erdrich compares her children's baths to church. Whatever form we give them, our sacred practices express the sense of connectedness we feel with our children and extend the bond to our broader relationships with other people and the natural world.

On another level, our relationships with children, along with their milestones, birthdays, and physical growth, make us acutely aware of the passage of time and of loss. On parenting websites, I read mothers' heartrending posts about their children's going off to kindergarten, and as a mother who has sent three off to college, these reflections remind me of how many of these bittersweet transitions parents live through. When our children were in early childhood, my husband and I set about hanging family pictures. We couldn't believe they'd lain in boxes for four years, that we had not had one spare afternoon in all that time to hang them. When we unwrapped them and leaned them against a wall, one was of our daughter and son taken when she was three and he was six months old. We were startled to realize that the picture had been recent when we wrapped it for our move. But just in the time it had taken us to set up house—a blink of an eye, it seemed—the picture was from the distant past, another era of our life entirely. I remembered the day the picture was taken, but I didn't remember what my daughter's voice sounded like then or the precise heft of my little son in my arms. In the absence of memory, what comforted me was time. I knew I had been there and that I had done with them and for them, day in and day out. That helped me bear all I had forgotten.

Still, as in so many parenting moments, alongside loss there is renewal. When my youngest child turned three, I started remembering how it felt to be me before I had children. I began listening to music again. I read novels and felt the characters' lives more acutely. I became reacquainted with the shape and feel of solitude. It wasn't that I was alone much more often. But I was alone in my head more. I had more psychic room. I was wistful about the loss of a certain naive belief that having my children had constituted a final destination. They were changing, I was changing. My daughter's legs were growing gangly, she had precise ideas. The two boys were old enough now to share a perfectly self-sufficient imaginative world. I loved them as deeply and cared for them as much, but sometimes I noticed a new voice inside saying, "It's their life." At an earlier point, this feeling of distance would have felt a bit heartless. Now, in some way I couldn't quite define, it seemed right, both for me and for them.

The wedge of distance that grows as one's children grow mingles excitement and sadness, freedom and guilt. When children are little, we often feel that everything we do is of supreme importance. This state of mind is fully adaptive for the task at hand. But as a seasoned parent who has been through the babyhoods, childhoods, and adolescences of my children, I see over and over the ways that they were never really under my control, were never anyone other than who they were going to be. Now, as a mother of children in their twenties, the pleasures are different, but just as deep. Development doesn't end, and I can see in the faces of my children, in the tilt of their heads and their singular streaks of humor, the babies and children they were as well as the people they are continuing to become. We relate as complex individuals who are at varying stages of life, but each with perspectives to offer the other. As hard as childhood struggles can be, adult struggles are more high stakes, and my ability to protect my grown children is limited. But being a resource of comfort, support, and understanding for them connects me, as it always has, to my deepest wellsprings of pleasure in being their parent.

The Experience of "Flow"

In addition to experiencing special temporal registers, mothers of babies and small children often perceive themselves to be in different mental states from those to which they were accustomed. Some say, "I've lost my mind," while others talk about knowing what to do vis-à-vis their child but not knowing *how* they know. Mothers of babies can be uncharacteristically inarticulate about their day-to-day tending and interacting with children. I think this reflects having one foot in unconscious process and the other in conscious process. As the writer Anne Enright observes, "Motherhood happens in the body, as much as the mind." It's not that mothers of infants are bereft of their sense of self, their cognitive faculties, or their boundaries. Rather, they are tuning in with their babies in a way that is specific and nuanced but hard to describe. They are acting on what psychologists have called implicit knowledge, a nondeclarative, nonverbal sensitivity to their interactions.

As I suggested in my discussion of vocal connectedness and secure attachment, this level of "implicit knowledge" contributes to the pleasurable affective dimension of parent-child interaction, which grows richer and more complex once children become verbal. Analyzing what went on when I conversed with my very young children, I was seeking a feeling of "rightness" or "fit" between how I expressed myself and how they would take in what I communicated. For example, my three-year-old might ask a question or comment ("Mom, Mom, there are gray clouds! It's going to rain!"), and in my response, I would use intonation and quality of voice, in combination with words, to try to open up a new area of curiosity for him. Maybe I would say, "Well, you know what?"—getting him positioned mentally to receive new information—"That's actually fog. And sometimes fog or clouds means it's going to rain, but sometimes it doesn't. Have you ever noticed that sometimes in the morning it's kind of cloudy, but then it gets sunny?" He might say, "Yeah . . ." "Well, where we live, we sometimes have fog in the morning, and then the sun comes out." I was trying to communicate information; but I was also trying, not quite consciously, to create an experience, one that embedded the specific information in an emotional exchange where he felt his interest was shared and where I adapted my response to his capacity to digest information.

Seeking this "rightness" was not always automatic or effortless. Particularly when I was tired, the feeling in these interactions was of pushing against a slightly resistant medium. That quality of effort suggests one of the striking features of parenting interactions, whether talking to a preschooler or comforting a baby: they require effort toward a goal, however dimly perceived and unelaborated, and satisfaction and pleasure result when the goal is met.

This goal is so different from what we commonly think of as a goal that it is almost unrecognizable. Yet, we can understand it better with reference to the psychological notion of flow. *Flow* is an evocative term for "enjoyment" or "optimal experience," studied by the psychologist Mihaly Csikszentmihalyi, among others. Flow experiences, whether they arise from a tennis match, meditation, or work, tend to have a number of things in common. Action and awareness are fused in a state of total concentration and involvement. People lose self-consciousness and have a sense of heightened responsiveness to the task at hand. In relationships, an interaction is truly enjoyable when it entails a stretch toward something new, meaningful, or challenging. The effort to stretch one's awareness or skills, the intention to share and discover something new, intrinsically involves seeking greater complexity, which contributes to psychological growth.

Parents commune with children for the sheer mutual enjoyment of sharing the moment, but absorption in the moment also serves certain goals. They are not goals that a mother would name as such; somehow, to say that one is attuning to one's child "to enhance interpersonal growth" sounds woefully incomplete. Still, on an unverbalized level, what goes on serves goals of connection, growth, and happiness. When I am in a state of flow, I am graced with self-forgetfulness. I am not preoccupied with myself, but rather I'm keenly responsive to the interaction at hand. After the experience of absorption and challenge is over and I am returned to self-awareness, the self I reflect upon is changed, "now enriched by new skills and fresh achievements."

Motherhood clearly draws on new skills and involves goals that matter intensely. But throughout children's development, parenthood offers new avenues for growth too. We intuitively grasp how flow experiences add complexity to the personality when we spend the day building sand castles together, for instance, absorbed in excavating a moat that will protect the castle from the encroaching tide. We return from the day tired from sun and salt, enriched by our shared absorption and happy because those shared interactions harmonize with our larger goal of contributing to our child's enjoyment, creativity, and growth.

Although family life can sometimes feel sluggish, *anti-flow*, we have more control over creating the context for flow experiences than we think. Minimizing distraction (e.g., turning off your phone), unstructured weekend and evening time, and getting down on the floor with your kids are all conducive to cultivating flow. It's easy to imagine that you need a cocktail or Netflix to unwind, but becoming absorbed in flow states by building a LEGO spaceship or making art with your kid can be more rejuvenating. Even doing household chores or yard work with little helpers endows these otherwise menial tasks with intrinsically valuable goals of teaching, guiding, and companionship.

On a macro level, flow in family life would be enhanced by a social contract that honored the freedom to pursue flexible work schedules and safeguarded time for children in the family-building phase of people's lives. In Csikszent-mihalyi's model, the external conditions that facilitate flow include social opportunities for free time and leisure, work schedules that do not dictate what we do when, and work-places that foster stimulation and experimentation. This is a far cry from most people's job conditions. In the United States, policies that would help foster flow conditions in work or family domains are treated as frills rather than necessities; the problem of work-family balance is thrown back on individual families to solve instead of being addressed by systemic changes in our laws and businesses.

If, as Csikszentmihalyi writes, every flow experience has in common "a sense of discovery" and "a creative feeling of transporting a person into a new reality," parenthood provides myriad opportunities. My school-age children and I used to listen to the Beatles in the car. I loved to have them guess who was singing lead and backup, to listen for the bass line, to discover the added instrument on "You've Got to Hide Your Love Away" (flute) or "You're Going to Lose That Girl" (bongos?). Our shared enjoyment connected me to my early childhood, to my love for my older brother, to the feel of summer in my garden with "Day Tripper" wafting out the window. I brought the intense emotion from my early life into the present interaction. They observed my enthusiasm, rooted in interest and memory, and in learning something concrete about the Beatles, they identified with my process of loving something in the world. Between me and my children, between versions of myself, between us and the music, there was a flow back and forth, a sharing of pleasure and engagement on many different levels. These exhilarations are not unique to parenting, but parenting is one place we can find them.

Motherhood and Meaning-Making

The question "What will bring me happiness?" lies at the heart of many women's decision to have children. But happiness, and the sense of wholeness it implies, is what many mothers feel they lack. They feel chronically torn, never able to feel they are doing any job well. I remember hearing a single mother with grown children speak on a radio call-in show in the early 2000s. Impassioned, she said that what matters in mothering children is not whether you work or not, not whether you are baking cookies or winning court cases or driving a truck. What matters is whether you feel joy in being with your kids when you are with them. She said it had taken her twenty years to realize this. Then somehow, by the end of the call, she wound around to saying that motherhood is "hell."

It can be both joy and hell at different times. Part of the hell is not being able to hang on to the joy that occasionally refreshes and then slips through the fingers like water. "Hell" can be the dissonance between the potential for joy and the obstacles to its fulfillment. It can be about the anxiety that you are insufficient somehow, that you are not doing enough, or being enough, or giving enough to your children. "Hell" also arises from our ambivalence about pleasure itself, our socially ingrained suspicion that if an activity brings joy, it might not be the kind of results-oriented, goal-directed endeavor that has value.

We bring to mothering the illusion that we should, or could, do or be or give everything to our children, and when we can't, which is inevitable, we blame ourselves (or our partners or the culture). But those attempts to lay blame fundamentally misapprehend what mothering is. The poet Jorie Graham remarked, "In poetry, you have to feel deeply something inchoate, something which is coming up from a place that you don't even know the register of." With her child, a mother necessarily engages in a similar process. We can't know or be or do everything; we can only listen, notice, and feel our way into who our children are, who we are, and what each of us needs.

Motherhood puts women in a different relationship with themselves; not as some sort of pale "shifting of priorities," but as a new relationship with experience. It can lead them to unknown reservoirs of emotion and prompt them to rethink their identity in light of what they discover. Kristeva writes that the artist's doing his art is necessary for "creating" the artist: "If he doesn't work, if he doesn't produce his music or his page or his sculpture, he would be, quite simply, ill or not alive." Mothers can feel this way about mothering as well.

A mother's sense that caring for her children engages her at this level of vital meaning—that it is something, as my friend said, she "can't not do"—I've seen met with everything from satisfaction to resentment to confusion. Many factors conspire to obscure the effort to make meaning that motherhood expresses. One is our confusion about what frame of reference to apply. Mothering is work, but of what kind? "Work requiring great skills and . . . done freely refines the complexity of self," writes Csikszentmihalyi. On the other hand, "there are few things as entropic as unskilled work done under compulsion." Mothering work can seem like both of these at different times, though it's often unthinkingly lumped in with the second category.

The belief that mothering requires no special skills says more about how we conceptualize skills than it does about motherhood. The skill set on which mothers draw in nurturing their children is rarely identified as such. For instance, the ability to use empathy and intuition to understand inanimate things—as does the repairman when he asks himself, "If I were that toaster, and I didn't work, what would be wrong with me?"—has been held up as an example of a work-related "flow" experience. But this same skill, when applied every day by a mother to understanding her very animate child, tends to elicit neither wonder nor respect.

Some of the conditions provided by work situations, including the sense of control and the opportunities for clear feedback, promote feelings of effectiveness, growth, and "flow" in relatively unambiguous ways. The goals of mothering activity are more open-ended, and the application of skills less quantifiable and more improvisational, than those usually provided by jobs. This is one source of the "I'm so glad it's Monday morning" feeling of many working mothers. When your job gives you some control and measurable achievement, being with children can seem chaotic, exhausting, and Sisyphean by comparison. I once read that the journalist Meredith Vieira purposely kept her office messy so she wouldn't be tempted to spend too much time in it away from her kids. When work is a haven of order, the only place we can complete a thought, it is easy to see why we might linger in our professional world.

The relative lack of structure in staying home with a small child can also give rise to frankly painful mental states. Left alone with children, mothers can feel anxious, sad, lonely, or at loose ends. When I was at home with infants and small children, at times I noticed that my need to neaten the house would escalate in direct proportion to how little time I had to myself to read, think, or attend to my own tasks. Aside from obtaining unexpected insight into the fabled compulsive-housekeeping pathology of fifties housewives, I gained renewed appreciation of my own need for some domain of self-direction.

The way that accomplishments are measured and rewarded, and the way work is structured, means that many mothers find themselves at the intersection of two competing and somewhat mutually exclusive reward systems. We must divide our energy and emotional resources, but being conflicted is the greatest "flow killer." When we interrupt our involvement either at work or at home with a litany of doubts and concerns—"Should I really be doing this? Is this the best use of my time?"—we drain our experience of pleasure, cohesion, and depth. Some mothers feel this conflict over their work and mothering roles as a constant burden, crushing the rewards of both. One woman related to me her experience of going back to work after a vacation and not wanting to call her children because it was "easier just to block it out." "How," she asked, "do you keep the sense of joy going, and at the same time accept that you have to disconnect from a certain kind of feeling with them when you leave home every morning?"

A sustainable and sustaining approach to this kind of conflict begins with respect for, and true curiosity about, our inner lives. If we want to be fully present in relating to our children, we can't usually get there by suppressing one set of feelings or another; rather, we have to remain open to awareness of the multiple strands of need, motive, and feeling. If I feel guilty leaving my child, for example, and I simply suppress the feeling, I lose an opportunity for self-knowledge. If I can sit with it, I may learn something. I may notice that the guilt doesn't vanish when I see my child happily playing with the babysitter. I may realize that the knot of feelings I have labeled "guilt" also includes my own sadness at not being able to stay. It undoubtedly also includes my happiness at being free to leave. Whether I use this information to adjust my outward arrangements or not, awareness of my feelings gives me a more complete picture of the emotional situation. Cultivating awareness means I will feel my sadness, but it also gives me more freedom to experience my pleasure. I am then also more likely to be able to tune in to my child's full range of feelings as well.

Awareness also entails recognizing that we are entitled to our complexity. When a friend arrived at work after a fight with her preadolescent daughter, she was stung by her daughter's criticism of her ineptitude over a trivial matter. Resisting black-and-white thinking, she instead sat with how she, like her daughter, had a deep and complicated interior world, a history. She did not know everything, and it was all right to tolerate not knowing. By including herself in the circle of her compassion, she could think more clearly about what was going on within herself, her daughter, and their relationship.

As mothers, we should give ourselves the room and the dignity to discover what we think and what we want. Each of us must think through these questions for ourselves so that we engage in our lives as personal creations rather than resigned-to realities. One place to start is by embracing maternal pleasure as a worthwhile and meaningful goal. Understanding its sources in communication, attachment, memory, and flow states can help us promote satisfying relationships with our children and ourselves and calm us in moments of parental frustration. It is hard to hold on to all the threads of our lives while we are mothers, but mothering carries within it an extraordinary thrust toward happiness. We must find the words to articulate this happiness, and we owe ourselves the freedom to explore it. We might then begin to envision pleasure as a touchstone for a truer model of maternal motivation and identity.

5

Ambivalence

The meanest I ever was to any of my children was one evening when my husband was out, and I was ruminating about the success of a colleague. Something in the comparison of her jet-setting as a professional while I was housebound gave my life an almost suffocating sense of thanklessness. An unbridgeable divide opened between the seemingly simple tasks I was unable to accomplish (cleaning the house, washing my hair) and the seemingly difficult ones (getting promoted, fielding interviews) that she pulled off with ease. Had I been holding a vase, I'd have thrown it; as it was, I had a ten-month-old who was sitting on the bathroom floor crying because he couldn't see me in the shower. Pulling back the shower curtain, I yelled at him for crying. He only cried louder, his desolation compounded by terror. I must have looked like a drenched witch. I was in the grip of something on which I had no perspective. Having begun innocently enough as a bout of professional frustration, it was now a black hole sucking up every particle of my effectiveness as a mother, my compassion, and my sense of myself as a reasonable human being. I finally collapsed on my bed in tears, holding my son close and saying I was sorry.

When I had calmed down enough to think again, this incident showed me something useful about the psychology of bad moments in caring for children. The way we feel toward our children and the way we behave are shaped by the internal balance we strike at a given moment between all of our desires, judgments, expectations, and frustrations. That inner landscape—everything from wanting recognition to reliving painful events from our past to worrying about our job, marriage, or money—plays a big part in how we manage the ups and downs of mothering.

The writer Anne Lamott articulates the mechanism behind our sudden, surprising bursts of rage:

> When we blow up at our kids, we only *think* we're going from zero to sixty in one second. Our surface and persona is so calm that when the problem first begins, we sound in control when we say, "Now, honey, stop that," or "That's enough." But it's only an illusion. Because actually, all day we've been nursing anger toward the boss or boyfriend or mother, but because we can't get mad at nonkid people, we stuff it down; we keep going without blowing up because we don't want to lose our jobs or partners or reputations. So when the problem with your kid starts up, you're actually starting at fifty-nine, only you're not moving. You're in high idle already, but you are not even aware of how vulnerable and disrespected you already feel.

Once you recognize the mechanism Lamott describes, you see it everywhere. You're getting ready to go out in the evening, and your three-year-old keeps hovering around your legs. You feel dissatisfied with how you look and—

boom—"Could you *please* stop getting in my way?" The kids are squabbling in the backseat of the car while you review an upsetting interaction with your spouse, and—boom— "Stop it! You kids are *driving me nuts*!" You are stewing over a judgmental comment your mother made, your child upsets his cereal bowl, and—boom—the spilled milk on the floor suddenly feels like a completely justified focus for your rage.

My own particular well of misery that night gave me renewed respect for the psychic conflict that is endemic to the lived experience of motherhood. It could not be otherwise, given all the elements that are constantly in play: inevitably conflicting goals and desires, our own child-hood experiences, and the lack of self-control that arises in moments of frustration, ineffectualness, or fatigue. For me, at that moment, the focus was professional achievement, but the more profound issue was a sense of competence, value, and self-worth. It is hard to feel recognized for the value of our day-to-day work of mothering. Anything that makes our sense of competence more tenuous—a baby who can't be soothed, or a preschooler who can't behave in public, or a school-age child who cannot learn—evokes self-doubt. I could have reasoned that I was basically doing what I wanted to do. But in the moment, exhausted from endless bedtime demands, my self-esteem precarious, that knowledge was no bulwark against a wave of ambivalence about my role as a mother.

What is remarkable about these moments is not that they are a rarity or a crisis, but rather that they are so rou-tine. If we can reliably assign any one feature to mothering, it is that it will encompass extreme states of feeling. The weathering and working with those states are not incidental blips or exceptions; they are central moral, emotional, and aspirational problems that motherhood poses.

On the simplest level, we are susceptible to extreme states of feeling because we are fleshly beings, with restless minds and emotions, and we get tired. A friend and her husband tried for years to conceive a child. Finally they were fortunate to adopt a baby boy. Later, after several miscarriages and much pain and suffering, my friend found herself pregnant. In her first trimester of pregnancy, another newborn baby became available for adoption, whom my friends also adopted. Shortly thereafter, I visited my friend, now the mother of an adopted four-year-old and a two-week-old and also ensconced in her nauseous tenth week of pregnancy. She and her husband were trying valiantly to curb the aggression of their none-too-pleased eldest child. My friend was beyond exhaustion. Without question she felt satisfaction in being a mother, but without question she also felt overwhelmed with being pregnant, caring for a newborn, and dealing with her four-year-old. A sense of meaning, happiness, and gratitude proceeded alongside abject fatigue, nausea, and a sense of ineffectualness as a parent.

Bone-tiredness, the endless round of viruses, and even the inability to make a dent in one's lists can dampen or temporarily extinguish the pleasure to be had in mothering. But often, the greatest effect of such states is their power to intensify our existing conflicts. If our psychic equilibrium depends on orderly surroundings because we grew up in chaos, then fatigue and lack of time to straighten up will tend to make us more on edge with our children. If we're upset about decreased income or professional status, these problems can make our reaction to our child's demands more extreme. If our self-esteem comes from doing one job well, then the taxing demands and divided attention of motherhood can make us feel as if we do everything badly. I was astonished to find, when I had infants, how closely extreme exhaustion resembled clinical depression, with all the feelings of inadequacy, irritation, and lack of energy that go with it. In my case, the feelings subsided after I got some sleep, but not everyone is so lucky; roughly 15 percent of new mothers suffer from diagnosable clinical depression postpartum.

Irritation, boredom, frustration, and ineffectiveness are inevitable passing states in a day of mothering. But how we interpret these states is influenced by the social values and life choices of our peer group and larger social milieu. In a vulnerable state of mind, our heightened insecurity that other moms are "doing it better" can intensify the normal emotional challenges of the day-to-day care of children. There are pressures to be continually available, devoted, and patient, as well as to feel ashamed if you can't. There are also pressures to be "perfect"—adorable children, beautiful home, toned body, successful business—that have only become more acute in the era of social media. The pressures never end. There's always another Instagram image of homemade Halloween costumes, a proud social media shot of a triumph on the soccer field, or a Facebook post showcasing a college acceptance, a lavish wedding, or a stunning grandchild.

Becoming a mother puts us into a new relationship with almost everything: our bodies, our partners, our parents, our social world, our work, our concept of self, and, of course, our child. Psychologically, there's an internal tension between the reality that motherhood has the potential to transform us and our complex reactions to that. In my drenched-witch episode, I felt a weird sense of pressure not to be emotionally susceptible to, or professionally derailed by, the inconvenient passions or practical exigencies of hands-on engagement with my children. I didn't worry that I was inadequately devoted, but rather that I was weak or overly emotional precisely *because* I was unable or unwilling to invest my energy in professional achievement like my colleague. In a more reflective, big-picture frame of mind, I could recognize the value in what I was doing, even when it included anger, which it inescapably did. I could also reaffirm that I wanted to do what I was doing and that a momentary longing didn't cancel that out. (A mother at work all day is in a different situation but faces a similar psychological task. A sad day of missing her child at work, even if compelling, does not imply that she should instantly quit her job and go home.) Yet in the moment, my conflict was between how emotionally invested I was in caring for my children and how frustrated I felt about the change it had wrought in my universe of choices.

As a therapist, I spend hours every week with mothers who fear that their ambivalence signals personal or maternal failure. To the contrary, I tell them, maternal ambivalence is a *universal* phenomenon. Childbirth expert and anthropologist Sheila Kitzinger, herself a mother of five, writes, "If having children is all about love, it's also about passion, and once you have passion, there's always this other side—of feeling desperately frustrated, perhaps feeling depressed, angry, all the other side of the intensity of love." Under the anxiety and stress of motherhood, we all have our equivalent of "drenched witch" episodes, where our capacity to think or act in a caring way is wiped out by intense emotion. The problem is not that we have a momentary burst of hatred (welcome to the club); the problem is finding a way to manage the guilt and anxiety that these episodes bring about. After the fact, being curious and compassionate about what gave rise to your emotional distress can help soften self-blame and pinpoint areas in need of change.

Becoming a Parent and Ambivalence about Roles

Becoming a mother involves losses and gains, and the question for any given woman is whether the losses outweigh the gains or vice versa. There are many things that a woman might imagine losing if she becomes a mother, from her "little tummy," as the film star Julia Roberts remarked, to her life. But present-day worries about the costs of motherhood tend to cluster around the loss of independence, economic security, opportunity, achievement, and a sense of equality in relationships and the workplace. The worries are valid. On virtually any measure of professional achievement—pay, power, prestige, even job satisfaction—investing time and energy in caring for children is a recipe for marginalization.

For young women, motherhood and concrete issues such as work-family trade-offs or the household division of labor can seem a long way off, too abstract to think about in the particular. This, combined with whatever subterranean anxiety might be triggered by trying to foresee one's future, may steer young women away from thinking about these issues. The economics professor Nancy Folbre asked her undergraduates to fill out a questionnaire estimating future earnings. She found:

The overwhelming majority of women express no doubt that they will, at age forty, earn the same amount of money as men with similar education credentials. Yet they also plan to have two children, and (unlike the men in the same class) they plan to take time out from their careers in order to raise them. When I point out that something is wrong with their calculations they aren't entirely surprised. But they seem almost embarrassed by having to consider the issue.

These intelligent, thoughtful young women are embarrassed because Folbre's questions force them to confront a conflict between career and maternal aspirations that they have not yet probed.

They may also be wary of discussing their maternal aspirations for other reasons. For one, their embarrassment may indicate discomfort at having attention focused on how their parental goals differ from those of their male peers. After all, men are rarely called out on how they mesh career and parenting goals; women, however, are expected to shoulder the conflict and are also routinely deemed less "serious" or "competitive" when they prioritize motherhood. Society gives women the message that desiring career success confirms your independence and grit, whereas desiring a child (or worse, a husband) reveals you to be woefully contingent. As the journalist Vanessa Grigoriadis writes of her own coming-of-age, "[I] grew up in Manhattan, attended a competitive private high school and a liberal-arts college, and at no point did anyone bring up the notion that the sexes were anything but equal. To me, it seemed like ideology was going to triumph over biology. . . . It was just a matter of steering clear of bathetic girly pathologies [like] making time-sensitive 'life plans' that revolved around a phantom boyfriend."

Women might also recoil from thinking about motherhood in order to better conform with our society's core values. In our neoliberal era, we have a love affair with competition in the marketplace, seeing it as the means to freedom, autonomy, and economic success. We also feel a slight revulsion from anything that might mire us in dependency and an anxiety about the value of private experiences and interpersonal bonds that can't be quantified. Motherhood connects us to others in a dependent relationship, and it is all about private experience. It demands that we relax control over our time and bodies and emotions, a mental attitude people too easily demean as "weak."

Perhaps for these reasons, some girls and young women are vocal in their devaluation of women who design their lives around a maternal role. Bemoaned one stay-at-home mother after Take Our Daughters to Work Day, "My kids came home and shunned me. They said, 'All you're good for is schlepping us around in the Navigator.'" Years ago, college seniors at Wellesley protested the choice of First Lady Barbara Bush as a graduation speaker on the grounds that her only qualification was her husband's political success. As economist Shirley Burggraf observed, the students "seemed not to understand . . . the extent to which their lives were literally built on their own mothers' contributions. Many of the protesting students probably would have never made it to Wellesley, or even have been born, if their mothers and grandmothers hadn't done the kind of work that Barbara Bush did." The students appeared to accept the basic terms of a hierarchy that treats women's caring work as somehow "passive" and devoid of accomplishment; in so doing, they espoused social attitudes every bit as oppressive as the ones they purported to critique.

Many mothers attempt to get around this conflict by assimilating the experience of motherhood into the familiar framework of competitive achievement. If fertility provides a sprinkling of competitive opportunities ("When I meet someone older than me, maybe even a year older, I somehow can't help but feel a little superior—I've got more eggs than she does!"), motherhood produces an even greater bounty. Birth weight, Apgar scores, developmental milestones, academic precocity, and athletic or musical aptitude can all be co-opted for establishing motherhood as an achievement that offers clear-cut measures of one's worth. Certainly, social media's ever-present fantasies of flawlessness and perpetual self-branding also have a part to play in the exhausting standards of maternal success. In the "'You Got This, Girl' culture that is pervasive in the Pinterest era of modern motherhood," it's hard not to feel inadequate by virtue of being a simple mortal.

But the two-for-one gambit of trying to eke out the meaning of mothering in the mode of perfectionism or competitive achievement doesn't address the underlying problem or resolve the basic ambivalence we feel about child-rearing. That is because the conflict mothers feel is between fundamentally different ways of being in the world. The kind of "being with" that grounds our deepest moments of joy in connecting with others can't be done with an eye to the outside or while looking over one's shoulder to see who is watching or winning. Letting the relationship with one's child truly affect and change one is an internal, creative process that is essentially at odds with a model of child-rearing as Mommy Olympics.

Ambivalence and Relationships to Our Mothers

Whether by positive or negative example, we look to how our mother lived her life and interacted with us to map our own maternal course. If our mother was often angry, we wish to exude calm. If she was nonchalant about leaving us, we are fanatical about finding the best care. A friend's mother was chronically torn about work and family; my friend has carefully crafted her life around stay-at-home motherhood. A colleague remembers her mother as depressed; my colleague bends over backward to be upbeat. If it's true, as I've suggested, that every woman's feminism is a love letter to her mother, it's also true that daughters have a powerful desire to repeat the good parts and repair the bad parts of their relationships with their mothers through their relationships with their own children.

In her book *Woman: An Intimate Geography*, Natalie Angier writes, "Women need their mothers. They blame their mothers, they dream of killing their mothers, but they keep coming back for more mother time. They want something, even if they can't articulate the desire. They expect something. They expect their mothers to be there for them, for years and years after they have become adults." As Angier reads the anthropological data, this need is anchored in our evolutionary past, specifically in lactating mothers' reliance on elder female kin to forage the necessary food for her other children. "We need touch, and as a rule the appetite serves us well. In a similar vein, I would argue that a woman's mother-lust, her need for the older female and for other women generally, is also ancient, and also worth heeding." In studying women becoming mothers, the psychiatrist Daniel Stern finds it "eye-opening" that with the birth of a baby, women increasingly turn to maternal figures in their lives as reference points for forging their new identities. They become "more interested in women and less in men, more psychologically involved (consciously or not) with their mothers and less with their fathers." In practical terms, new mothers seek out "benign mother figures," whether their own mother, a mother they remember from their past, or other women in their current life, to teach and affirm them on their journey into motherhood.

When we take account of how important, intergenerationally and even evolutionarily, the mother-daughter bond is, it helps put our intense and contradictory emotions in perspective. Our blame and need of our mothers, their prickly coexistence, may simply be how things are and have always been. Perhaps the idea that we need to get away from our mothers to find ourselves was a little naive, or at least incomplete. It's one side of the story, a reasonable hypothesis, and it makes sense of the facts as long as our project is to become independent and self-sufficient in twenty-first-century America. But, as Angier and Stern show, once children arrive on the scene, we yearn for our mothers' help and support and their (not too overbearing) voice of experience. We are less preoccupied with their limits and more grateful for their abilities. Blame and need switch places.

We also begin to empathize with them and to understand them better, more viscerally. A fifty-five-year-old friend of mine said she'd recently reached a point in her life where she felt she understood her mother almost completely. Over my own years as a parent, I noticed my various criticisms of my mother fell away. I came to feel the same enjoyment of her that I remembered feeling as a child, just from a different position. We are two grown women who care about our children and each other, and these common values add new notes to our mutual sympathy.

Yet some women had mothers who did not enjoy being mothers or who approached motherhood with competitiveness or narcissism or coldness. All children need loving responsiveness to their need in the form of help, care, and interest, and if a mother can't give of herself in this way, the deprivation is primal. When a daughter of such a mother herself becomes a mother, she doesn't have a healthy internalized role model on which to draw. A therapist in my community offers a support group, Adult Daughters with Difficult Mothers during the Holidays, focused on "maintain[ing] your own sense of self and preserv[ing] healthy boundaries when these events activate deep longing for the mother that was not there for you emotionally and/or physically." Sometimes difficult mothers become doting grandparents, and their daughters can't help but be ambivalent—happy for what their mothers give the grandchildren, but sad and resentful about what they didn't get themselves.

One particularly painful way this ambivalence can manifest itself is through the dynamics of envy, when mothers and daughters (and by extension, sisters or women friends) become locked in a zero-sum game in which if one of them has "something," the other is doomed to have "nothing." Troubled mother-daughter relationships have a keen potential for breakdown into the psychological roles of the "have" and the "have-not"; this divide is the very drama of who will command the riches—whether beauty, power, or food—that is reiterated in countless fairy tales. This rivalry can also play out between women in procreation, where specifically female capacities are prized and treasured. A pregnant woman I knew was in a standoff with a good friend, also pregnant, because each felt the other owed her a call to acknowledge and congratulate her on her pregnancy. Each subtly vied to be acknowledged as the queen her pregnancy made her feel she rightfully was.

A professional colleague of mine says that every time she sees a new book about mothers, she feels mingled dread and hope as a question instantly pops into her mind: "Is it for me or against me?" She experiences these books not as reasoned argument, but as primitive attack. When we strive to "outdo" the mother who preceded us or a friend who is doing things differently, a fear may lurk that we will be proven "all wrong," chastised and humbled. This dynamic of triumph and comeuppance plays out not merely intergenerationally, but often between individuals and as an internal conflict. The only way out of this painful cycle is to recognize that we will feel free and secure in having "something" only if we allow the other person to have "something" too. The wish to deprive the other and the fear of being deprived are two sides of the same coin. It can take effort to remember there is more than one right way to be and that motherhood will be more fulfilling if it's collaborative rather than competitive.

Eating, Control, and Ambivalence about the Maternal

In our society, perhaps especially among those who have been groomed for achievement and success, women need to work at not developing a controlling attitude toward their eating and their weight. This effort becomes even more daunting for pregnant women and mothers. It's common for my therapy patients who are prospective mothers to fear the pain of childbirth and the stresses of parenthood, but some also envision the postpartum maternal body as a horror they are desperate to avoid, either because of fears of losing their sexual attractiveness or because they derive a sense of intactness, power, and identity from their current body type.

Karen was one such patient, a thirty-two-year-old woman at an impasse with her husband about having a child. Her younger sister already had one-year-old twins, on whom Karen lavished love; however, the children also stirred her envious and competitive feelings toward her sister. As we worked together, it became clear that she wanted to have a baby but was terribly afraid of how pregnancy would aesthetically alter her body. Over time, we explored the ways that, while she was growing up, her competence and athletic prowess had been ways of "holding herself together" given her largely absent father and self-absorbed mother. As the older sister, Karen had provided nurturance to her younger sibling, but had felt "seen" and rewarded by her parents only for her independence and lack of need. In her teen years, eating became a test of her self-control and self-discipline. If she could control her body, her subconscious bargain went, she could control her sense of emotional need. No wonder the prospect of pregnancy was so destabilizing, opening as it did both the reality of profound body changes and the conflicted emotional terrain of need, dependency, and nurture in family relationships.

Our cultural devaluation of female capacities, including motherhood, contributes to why eating becomes so loaded for women. The philosopher Susan Bordo writes about American women's widespread obsession with thinness in terms of "contradictory ideals and directives." The ideology of femininity "requires that women learn to feed others, not the self," and "construe[s] any desires for self-nurturance as greedy and excessive." To succeed in the terms set forth by the culture, women must "also learn to embody the 'masculine' language and values" of "self-control, determination, cool, emotional discipline, mastery, and so on." The result of these pressures can often be a complex about eating that tends toward unhealthy self-denial or ashamed indulgence.

Body fat and eating take on meaning not only through the clash of "feminine" and "masculine" ideals, but also through women's conflicted relationship to reproductive and nurturing femaleness. One of the latest trends in maternity clothes, the skintight spandex tank tops and form-fitting jersey dresses, offer not only a positive recuperation of the pregnant belly but also another arena of "mastery" since they demand disciplined attention to being sculpted and toned everywhere else. After having babies, women continue to live out the "contradictory ideals" Bordo identifies. They feel pressure to "get their bodies back" both to be sexually attractive to their mates and to reestablish some sense of control and self-esteem. Yet the challenges of new motherhood—the need for more calories, the inadequate amount of sleep, the unpredictable and unruly emotions—all make it hard to make weight reduction a priority.

I'll never forget my annoyance when my first, birdlike obstetrician insisted that twenty-four to twenty-seven pounds was the desired weight gain in pregnancy. Beyond the obvious issue of maternal and child health, it seemed oddly, ascetically preoccupied with self-control at just the moment when one should have the freedom, the joy, the permission, finally, to feed one's baby and to feed oneself. This is not to say that I was exempt from the occasional fantasy that getting thinner would give me more power. When my children were tiny, if I felt irritated or inadequate in some conflict with my husband, I was not above indulging the thought "Okay, I'll get really thin and always look great, and I'll be busy and not be home to cook dinner, and I'll be totally self-sufficient, and then he can see how he likes it!" In other words, at times I co-opted thinness into an illusory project of perfection and control.

These "I'll show you" fantasies always include a strong dose of anger. They are also fueled by the wish to establish one's superiority by being impervious to attachment or need. The problem with fantasies of control is how unrealistic they are, especially with children to consider. You can maintain the illusion for a day or two, but then something happens. Your child gets sick. Your babysitter quits. The washing machine overflows. You have a worrisome mammogram. You have the choice of escalating and becoming a control freak of truly disturbed proportions or loosening up and finding a way to peaceably live with unmatched socks, green phlegm, and life's inherent entropy. Perhaps most central, you find a way to live with—even embrace—all the ways your attachments to others completely condition your life.

We can hope that, even as the market is moving toward ever-more-demanding maternity clothes, the culture as a whole is moving toward a more pleasurable embrace and celebration of the nourished, mothering female body. As the advice columnist Heather Havrilesky writes to a woman afraid of all the physical, emotional, and life changes of having a baby, "We aren't used to accepting what our bodies were apparently, at least partially, built to do. We've been fighting against our bodies for decades, pushing them to be smaller and cuter and better. Letting your body be what it is and keep a human alive is fascinating and relaxing as hell."

The Upside of Maternal Ambivalence

The psychotherapist Rozsika Parker observes that although maternal ambivalence tends to provoke anxiety and an attempt to suppress conflict, it should instead arouse "a recognition of the creative potential of the ambivalent state of mind for maternal development." The notion that powerful negative feelings toward our children might offer a creative force rather than a destructive one is quite alien to our usual way of thinking. Our first impulse is usually to try to get rid of our negative feelings, whether by denial, projection, or going to the gym. But these strategies attempt to banish or disown bad feelings rather than putting them to use. In Parker's view, ambivalence can prompt mothers to know themselves and their child better; it can encourage them to grow. She writes:

> It is in the very anguish of maternal ambivalence itself that a fruitfulness for mothers and children resides. . . . The conflict between love and hate actually spurs mothers on to struggle to understand and know their baby. In other words, the suffering of ambivalence can promote thought—and the capacity to think about the baby

and child is arguably the single most important aspect of mothering.

The hardest part of being in a rage with my child or feeling resentful toward him is that in the moment I can't think. In my drenched-witch episode, I was completely gripped by emotion. But Parker suggests that once we calm down, our feelings of resentment, frustration, failure, impatience, or ineffectiveness can spur us to think about what is going on and why our buttons are being pressed. That thinking can lead to an understanding of what might need to change and to a more compassionate view of ourselves and of our child.

Parker and others have argued that social taboos against maternal (and female) hate and unhappiness pressure women to dampen their ambivalence and insist on an overly sunny, even sentimental, view of motherhood. They have shown how cultural ideals of the "good mother" can intensify mothers' guilt and anxiety, heighten their self-doubt, and drain them of confidence. The most exhaustively examined such idea, the "all-giving mother," puts pressure on mothers by minimizing how hard maternal giving can be, especially without sufficient family or social support. Such writings provide a welcome lifting of the stigma associated with maternal frustration, anger, and boredom.

While we can all agree that an idealized image of mothering obscures a darker reality, it's also worth asking what a focus on that darker reality might itself obscure. Critiques of "sentimentalized" images of devoted motherhood appear dismissive of, and at times almost phobic about, the notion that women might seriously aspire to the connection, fostering of growth, and shared pleasure that are also at the heart of those images. In our effort to support women by acknowledging the difficult aspects of maternal experience, we sometimes misrepresent its opportunities for enjoyment.

If "sentimentality" is one way of dismissing the complex arena of maternal devotion, the idea that consenting to care for children is somehow "masochistic" functions in much the same way. Mothers sometimes feel confused about whether their daily run of child-centered activity sinks them toward doormat status. Even for the most self-assertive mother, it is always a balancing act. But when we eye service suspiciously as one more problematic or socially engineered manifestation of female submission, we mischaracterize the active desires involved. In the absence of another framework with which to evaluate it, mothers often fear that their very wish to care for their children means they are insufficiently self-affirming; they wonder if something is "wrong" with them or criticize themselves for not having enough "self-esteem" to have dodged the role of putting others' needs first, which mothering often demands.

Both the idealization and the devaluation of the rewards of motherhood tend to distract us from the much more individual and creative finding of a way to live that is true to ourselves and responsive to our child. That involves connecting to our private experience, as opposed to the clamorous yardstick-measuring of the Mommy Olympics. The pediatrician and psychoanalyst D. W. Winnicott coined the term "the good enough mother" to work against anxious perfectionism and to help parents see that hovering intrusiveness can be almost as problematic as neglect. A good enough mother (or parent) provides sensitive responsiveness most of the time, while giving her child the space he needs to discover his own impulses and initiative. In Winnicott's view, the capacity to live creatively and become one's own person begins in a private experience of self. When we are babies, relaxed and purposeless in the presence of a trusted caregiver, we are free to discover an impulse of our own. We discover what we want and how we feel from the "inside out," rather than in reactive compliance to the external world. Experiencing ourselves as authentic and creative depends on what Winnicott calls "the capacity to be alone," which, paradoxically, only develops through the presence of a loving other: "The infant is able to become unintegrated, to flounder . . . to be able to exist for a time without being either a reactor to an external impingement or an active person with a direction of interest or movement. . . . In this setting the sensation or impulse will feel real and be truly a personal experience."

Winnicott's observation about the baby's development can be seen in a mother's development as well. We discover who we are as mothers partly through our own "floundering" in the presence of our baby. When we accept ambiguity and fluidity, when we stay open to new experiences and relax our rigid need for certainty and control, we discover a place of initiative within ourselves out of which we can creatively respond to what we perceive as our own and our baby's needs. Attuned to our own experience, we are also less oriented to complying with external pressures, standards, and ideals.

A similar possibility exists while mothering older children as well. I think of that archetypal parent-child battleground, homework, in response to which I operated in two distinct emotional modes. Sometimes, when my school-age children were not "getting it" or were procrastinating, the specter of failed standardized tests and bad character loomed, and I became demanding in response to my own anxiety. At other times, I was able to get "inside" their thought processes and observe their individual styles. When I was open to their process of learning and shared my own, I tuned in to a different level of experience and was able to be more creative and helpful.

Whatever the conflicts that besiege us as mothers, it helps to acknowledge our whole range of feelings, not siding with one and rejecting the other, but accepting that we contain them all. If we can accept contradictions and use that equanimity to initiate creative thinking, we can ultimately understand ourselves and our children even better.

BEING A "GOOD ENOUGH" mother is, finally, not about image but about process. In her novel *Still Life*, A. S. Byatt gives a beautiful rendition of this distinction. Elinor Poole, a graceful Bloomsbury matron with three charming children, has every appearance of being the perfect mother. She bakes scones, she makes her own yogurt. She and her children create things together: a dragon collage, a cake, a papier-mâché dolphin. Observing Elinor, Alexander, a houseguest who becomes her lover, begins "to feel sometimes as though these careful surfaces, like the unbroken shell of the riddling egg, like the silk balloon with no door in which spiderlings live and grow, were impenetrable." It is ironic, though not surprising, that in the novel's sequel, Elinor abandons her family altogether. Although she has done everything "right" with her children, she has never let them in.

Another of *Still Life*'s characters, Stephanie, has recently given birth to a son, William, when she tentatively tries to

resume her scholarly work on his namesake, the poet Words-
worth. Though she "seemed to hear, to feel, to smell, powerful calling sounds, rufflings of the air, odors, which wanted
her back, insisted that she must return," she manages to
"put down rational foot after rational foot, with difficulty,"
on her way to the library. Once there, she attempts to work:

> It took time before the task in hand seemed possible,
> and more before it came to life, and more still before it
> became imperative and obsessive. There had to be a time
> before thought, a woolgathering time where nothing hap-
> pened, a time of yawning, of wandering eyes and feet, of
> reluctance to do what would finally become delightful and
> energetic. Threads of thought had to rise and be gathered
> and catch on other threads of old thought, from some
> unused memory store. She had snatched from Marcus
> and Daniel's mum, worse, from William, whose physical
> being filled her inner eye and almost all her immediate
> memory, barely time for this vacancy, let alone the subse-
> quent concentration. She told herself she must learn to
> do without the vacancy if she was to survive. She must be
> cunning. She must learn to think in bus queues, in buses,
> in lavatories, between table and sink. It was hard. She was
> tired. She yawned. Time moved on.

Stephanie's child has changed her utterly; he fills her
time, "her inner eye and almost all her immediate memory." She has also "with some pain cleared this small space"
to allow for the vacancy, the "woolgathering" (Winnicott's
"floundering") that precedes the creative moment. Her son's
need of her and her preoccupation with him have made

it difficult to work; yet, at the same time, his birth triggers her growth as a reader, giving new depth to her perspective on her objects of study. Stephanie is like a new story whose cadences draw on an ancient text; she must find a way to carry forward who she was before, though in a totally new way. It is hard. She is torn. But she keeps faith with herself, her son, the poetry, by letting it all in and not letting any part of it go.

6

Childcare

One winter morning, our babysitter comes downstairs and says that she is moving to Florida in a month. Her new husband is having trouble finding work, and they can no longer afford to live in the San Francisco Bay Area. At first, tears roll silently down my cheeks; then I start to sob. I feel badly for my children, my littlest boy particularly, whose mornings are spent in her company. I feel anxious for myself—how am I going to find a good new situation? I completely understand her decision; I know it is painful for them. But I feel angry and hurt too, as if she is abandoning me.

These dramas of separation were a huge issue in my experience of childcare and in the experience of many others I know. One of the most difficult moments in my life as a parent was when I decided I had to fire a caregiver whom the children loved but who was chronically late. She adored the kids, she was helpful to me, but she was rarely on time. First I tried to work around it. Then I tried to talk with her about it. Things improved and then got worse again. I began spending the first hour of my day trying to overcome my anger, sometimes calling my sister in Washington, DC, to have her talk me down.

Finally I knew I couldn't manage the lateness or my feelings about it anymore. The day I told the caregiver I felt dreadful. I took a long walk. I came home and slowly showered and dressed. I tried to be levelheaded and composed, but I was helpless to control the power of my emotions. After she left, I didn't look to hire any help for several months. I felt our family had lost someone and needed time to heal.

When childcare arrangements are working, life feels as if it makes sense, even as if it sings with balance and purpose. When they don't, we are pitched into desperation, where the foundations of life feel askew. When it goes well, we easily, perhaps sometimes a bit smugly, take credit. But when it goes badly, the precariousness of the entire system is revealed, and we often want more than anything else not to have to deal with it anymore. In my first nine years of motherhood I hired eight part-time caregivers; three were unequivocal shining successes, three were mixed, and two were downright bad. In-home childcare has risks and benefits, but problems can arise in any arrangement. My friend Sarah, a college professor, was thrilled by the university childcare center's services for her two-month-old daughter and felt her whole family was supported by the collaborative relationship they had with their daughter's main caregiver, Lynn. When Sarah's daughter was twenty months old, Lynn left the center, and Sarah told me it took both her and her daughter "months to recover." A colleague of mine employed au pair after au pair, and each hire was as difficult and wrenching as the last, but she took on the task each time with the stamina of a long-distance runner. Another friend, once her children were finally past the childcare stage, melodramatically opined to a pregnant acquaintance that dealing with childcare makes you want to "kill yourself." It would be easy to view these stories as atypical except that some version of this ordeal has bedeviled practically every mother I know. It's an issue for mothers across the economic spectrum and takes on even more urgency for single parents.

The problems of continuity and reliability would be drastically diminished if we had a national system of childcare centers like France's. These issues are also eased for those families who can provide high pay, benefits, and good in-home working conditions to hired caregivers. But the problems cannot ever be completely controlled or solved. Most parents must face that even the most dedicated, well-compensated, loving childcare workers can, and often do, leave. And so do most others, at their initiative or ours. Disruption is the rule rather than the exception.

As childcare arrangements fall apart or fall short, we repeatedly confront the same round of painful questions. What does it mean to our children when their caregivers leave? How do such departures affect their emotional lives? Should the fact that caregivers leave affect our own life choices? And how do we deal with childcare being so *expensive*, and when does paying less result in worse care? These dilemmas, born out of political reality, economic necessity, and individual happenstance, are so important because they cut to the heart of maternal self-esteem. Our sense of being good mothers depends on providing good care for our children and on taking their well-being to heart, feeling it to be inextricable from our own. The problems presented by the run-of-the-mill unpredictability of childcare land us, over and over, smack-dab in the middle of what it means to be a good parent.

The Central Role of Caregiver Turnover
in the Work-Home Conflict

It's heartbreaking to read the poet Sylvia Plath's letters to her mother about her need for help with her children. "I got this nanny back for today and tomorrow. She is a whiz, and I see what a heaven my life could be if I had a good live-in nanny" (September 24, 1962). "If I had time to get a good nanny, possibly an Irish girl to come home with me, I could get on with my life" (October 16, 1962). "I adore the babies and am glad to have them, even though now they make my life fantastically difficult. If I can just financially get through this year, I should have time to get a good nanny" (October 21, 1962). Plath's need was larger than that of most: her husband had left her, she was broke, and she was inwardly compelled to express her poetic gift. Tragically, she was also suicidally depressed. Few of us deal with anything approaching Plath's terrible difficulties. But at our worst moments of adversity in finding or affording the childcare we need, our feelings can resonate with Plath's note of desperation.

At the most basic level, childcare is about whether you have coverage or not, whether you are gripped by panic that there is "no one" or you are flooded with relief that there is "someone." If we were to put it in terms of Abraham Maslow's hierarchy of needs, taught in Psychology 101, the need for coverage might be likened to the basic need for food and shelter. Once that need is met, however, we quickly move to a concern about how good the care actually is. That appraisal strongly affects our effectiveness, concentration, and satisfaction at work. Any formulation of day care policy that urges us to still our anxieties on this score is at cross-purposes with our inclinations as parents. Our unwillingness to engage in a dispassionate cost-benefit analysis, trading off our own welfare against our child's, is one of the things on which people base their parental self-esteem. When we admit or discover that things are not going well, we are likely to try to look for alternative solutions, even rethinking our careers.

When we find a good childcare situation, though, our concern shifts to sustaining that arrangement. Whether one is hiring an in-home caregiver or a childcare center, turnover is too high. Everyone, including day care advocates, agrees that high staff turnover, other things being equal, is not good for children. A prerequisite of continuity is often reliability. As I found with our good but chronically late caregiver, unreliability can become almost as stressful as no care at all.

The ups and downs of childcare availability, quality, consistency, and reliability play a more basic role in mothers' conflicts between work and home than we usually acknowledge. For a mother with economic means, the unpredictability of childcare may mesh with her ambivalence about how much her job keeps her away from her children and tip her toward finding a way to spend more time caring for them herself. For most others, no matter how much difficulty and unpredictability childcare arrangements add to their lives, the alternative is worse. They need to work, and they do what it takes to make it possible.

At any level of the hierarchy of childcare needs, differing individual pressures cause people to opt in or opt out of work at different times. That's one reason why politicized dichotomies between "working" and "stay-at-home" mothers don't ring true. Conservative spokeswomen in particular scold women for the very thing they themselves engage in (work), adopting the role of "faux stay-at-home mom," in Katha Pollitt's phrase. A competitive "my maternal devotion is bigger than yours" muscle flexing is afoot, but without the attendant commitment to a role that one would expect from someone asserting that superiority.

In reality, the self-designation as *working* or *stay-at-home* is subject to change as mothers continually evaluate the economic, practical, and emotional dimensions of family life. Mothers often find rigid role descriptions superficial because they so often find themselves on both sides of the issue. One book group in Brooklyn became exasperated by the pile of texts on working mothers that a *New York Times* reporter asked them to read because they felt the categories offered were artificial constructions irrelevant to their lives. The women moved between roles; they identified themselves less as "stay-at-home mothers" or "working mothers" than as mothers who tried to find ways to respond to the needs and desires of their children, themselves, and their entire families.

The Childcare Paradox and the Realities of Class

Public discussion of maternal work and day care so rarely grapples with how the well-being of mothers is inextricably entwined with the well-being of children and the quality of the childcare available and within means. In proposed solution after proposed solution, some part of this phenomenon is missed. Turning the care of our newborn, baby, or small child over to another, nonfamilial person, someone we often have known only briefly, is complex emotionally and psychologically. It is fraught with a combination of relief and fear, hope and sadness. That web of emotions obviously affects our sense of comfort and success as parents. But it also contributes to shaping the underlying themes in the larger debate about day care policy.

On the policy level is the question of how to reduce caregiver turnover so as to protect more children and their families from its practical and psychological effects. The solution generally advocated is sound: better working conditions, education, pay, and benefits for childcare professionals. As the authors of the leading study on childcare staffing put it, "Taking care of children requires taking care of their teachers." The people caring for "our nation's most precious resource" should not be trapped in low-wage, low-prestige jobs. The best way to confer respect on these jobs and make them attractive as long-term, stable career options is to reward childcare workers with compensation appropriate to the high value of their work. Virtually everyone can agree in principle on this urgent and necessary goal. But Americans remain curiously intransigent about improving the childcare system. What accounts for this paradox? To answer, we need to recognize a basic conflict at the heart of the childcare dilemma, a conflict that is structured by dynamics of economic opportunity, maternal desire, and social class.

Consider a mother who is well paid and professionally committed and who wishes to continue working while her children are little. For her, the benefit of a stable, highly trained, well-remunerated childcare infrastructure is clear. She will outearn hired childcare workers by a decisive margin, and greater stability in her childcare arrangements and better training of staff can only work to her and her children's benefit. If we consider a mother lower on the socioeconomic scale, however, who receives relatively lower gratification, prestige, and pay from her job, the cost-benefit analysis may be quite different. She may feel that as child-care workers' wages increasingly approximate her own, the added benefit that her income provides is eroded, and the incentive to earn money at the expense of time spent caring for her children is decreased.

Scholars have described a preference among many working-class mothers to care for their own children at home. According to Ann Crittenden, "uneducated married mothers are the least likely to be employed, having the least to gain from a job. They calculate, quite correctly, that as long as the family has one breadwinner, their presence at home can create more value, and be more satisfying, than much of the (under)-paid work they could find." A family that ends up keeping only a sliver of the mother's salary after it has met its childcare costs might justifiably feel doubly penalized by their position: constrained by the high cost of childcare and deprived of the ability to care for their children themselves.

The seemingly obvious solution to these inequalities is for the government to subsidize day care or to provide a day care system that lowers the financial burden on individual families. But that goal meets with a similar lack of political will. Given how enormously expensive a government-funded day care system of highly trained, well-paid staff would be, many people would rather put their money toward funding their own "high quality" care of their children than toward a publicly funded system.

Another facet of the childcare paradox is revealed by examining the "best case" day care scenario, where parents have access to impeccably consistent, reliable, loving caregivers. Such a world has been envisioned by the primatologist

Sarah Blaffer Hrdy, who offers a utopian solution to the day care issue in her call for day care centers to employ "well-paid and highly respected 'allo-mothers,' a cadre of 'as-if' mothers, who can be either male or female, so long as they are stable, conscientious, and treat the children like their closest kin." The obvious question is where day care centers might locate a population of "as-if" mothers who hadn't already decided to deploy their energies caring for their own "closest kin." Certainly no longer, as the economist Shirley Burggraf has observed, from the huge population of gifted women teachers, nurses, and other caring professionals that previous generations could draw upon, a population that existed because women were largely excluded from most "masculine" professions and that has since dispersed into a wider array of jobs throughout the economy.

But over and above these recruitment challenges is the question of *who* would be amenable to funding this well-paid cadre. For a parent to be able and willing to pay for a surrogate as good as herself, she would have to be both sufficiently well paid and sufficiently unambivalent about trading the rewards of caring for her children for the rewards of her work. Many economically advantaged mothers, such as Hrdy, find themselves in this situation. But most mothers do not have both interesting work and high pay, which affects the viability of allo-mothers as a societywide solution.

The main weakness of Hrdy's well-meaning proposal may not be its impracticality but the assumptions about maternal motivation on which it rests. In *Mother Nature*, her exhaustive book on the evolutionary biology of motherhood, Hrdy turns to her area of expertise, primatology, to put forth a model for understanding mothers' competing goals. Among chimps such as Jane Goodall's Flo, Hrdy argues, a mother's ambition—to command resources, territory, and power—is not at odds with, but is instead an inherent part of, good mothering behavior. Flo combines nurturing and ambition, but her ambition is also a kind of nurturing. In Flo, Hrdy sees something like an inspiration for how to think about our own motherhood.

But Flo's situation and our own, as Hrdy acknowledges, are crucially different: Flo can maintain proximity with her offspring while she pursues her ambition. By contrast, the specifically human conflicts about mothering and work arise largely from the spatial split between the workplace and home, as well as the mental focus required for professional responsibilities. Human mothers of young offspring today, unlike their primate and Pleistocene-era counterparts, have to make various trade-offs between ambition and proximity because of the absorbing nature of both work and child-rearing.

One virtue of the idea of allo-mothers is that it allows mothers facing a conflict between ambition and proximity to imagine siding with their ambition without sadness or guilt. It suggests that if you've solved the problem of providing a consistent, loving caregiver, then you've solved the problem of maternal proximity and freed maternal ambition. But for many mothers, the problem is a prior one: it is the reluctance to surrender their *own* proximity to their child, *regardless* of how loving or consistent their replacement is. Mothers' desire to care for their children, and their ambivalence about structuring social life in a way that decreases the possibility of that care, subtly undermines support of large-scale day care solutions, even idealistic ones of the sort that Hrdy proposes.

When mothers forgo proximity in exchange for ambition, they still feel fiercely protective of, and deeply invested in, their central importance to their children. This investment can manifest in parents' ambivalent feelings about their children's bonds with their hired caregivers, even if, as Susan Chira reports, this insecurity is empirically questionable: "Despite parents' worries, the results of studies are virtually unanimous: children's relationships to other caregivers do not surpass the one with their parents in emotional intensity or influence. Study after study has found, with only rare exceptions, that children overwhelmingly prefer their parents to their caregivers."

While assuaging of one kind of anxiety, though, this statement is troubling in other ways. It seems to encourage parents to reassure themselves by diminishing the importance of the caregiver's role, and it strangely detaches the quelling of their worries from their children's "overwhelming preference" for them. Considering this "overwhelming preference" plays a key role in how we decide upon the right balance in work and family time, because responding effectively to our children's desires is part of how we feel good about ourselves as parents.

The Absence of Maternal Desire in the Day Care Debate

When the discussion of childcare fails to recognize what it means to mothers to care for their children and to delegate that care, it misses the impact of maternal desire on the societywide search for day care solutions. For the psychologist and day care advocate Sandra Scarr, for example, public policies that interfere with women's equal participation in the workforce operate to the detriment of most women's interests. She rejects the advantages of family-friendly policies, such as those in Sweden, that "help mothers to balance work and family life by granting paid, job-guaranteed maternity and parental leaves, child allowances to supplement family income, and part-time work for mothers when their children are young," because they "support maternal absences from the labor force" and thus have negative effects on women's careers. Scarr implies that such arrangements are imposed on women by those who wrongly imagine that women would want the opportunity or flexibility to be at home with children. "Unequal child-care responsibilities lead mothers to be less invested in career development and less motivated to maintain continuous, full-time employment," she writes. These innocently declarative phrases "lead mothers to be less invested in career development" and "less motivated to maintain continuous, full-time employment" treat the mother as a completely passive actor, somehow "led" to certain actions by her "unequal" time caring for children. Her own desire is acknowledged only as it relates to work. That a mother might *want* to shoulder greater responsibility for her child's care is not considered.

Believing that the key to gender equality is the removal of women's unequal childcare responsibilities, Scarr proposes that childcare center regulations should be relaxed to make the price affordable for working parents. The regulations as they stand increase childcare costs, with the danger of "driving most families into the underground market of unregulated care." Scarr was CEO of the for-profit day care chain Kinder-Care Learning Centers, Inc., which may account for her use of this shadowy, "gray-market" imagery. But her formulation legitimizes only one aspect of mothers' interests: that of maintaining employment. Scarr's response to fiscal conservatives' "logically obvious" question—"What is the minimal expense for child care that will allow mothers to work and not do permanent damage to children?"—is to argue for government standards that "prevent terrible care." Avoiding "terrible care" for one's child is not the standard most people consider adequate in seeking childcare. When parents feel their children are in substandard care, that is when parents question how they are structuring their lives, if they have the means to do so. For many mothers, leaving their children in mediocre care or worse is a recipe not for maternal freedom but for maternal despair. And the recommendation is particularly insensitive to single mothers, since they are likely both to need more parenting support and to be more economically vulnerable.

At the heart of the issue is the interdependency of the mother and the child's well-being. One day care advocate entitles her book *Children's Interests/Mothers' Rights*, as if the agendas could be so clearly separated. Parents have important interests distinct from their children's, but they also take their children's well-being to heart in a way that overtakes self-interest. (When my children were young, they were fond of asking me, "Who would you rather have die first, you or me?" I responded without a moment's hesitation, "Me." Never mind that they then added the cat to the list and wanted to know why I'd save myself before I'd save her.)

Once when I looked into family day care for my youngest son, I visited a nice woman in my town who had six two-year-olds under her care, including her own. She had a lot of neat toys and some fun activities, but the kids kept having little accidents. One kid fell out of his booster seat at snack. Relentless fighting over toys ended in fisticuffs and hair pulling (two-year-olds aren't into sharing). The caregiver's own daughter was whiny and aggressive toward the other kids, and she seemed angry to be sharing her mom all day with so many other children of similar ages. In making these observations, I may sound like a perfectionist, but I don't believe children need "perfect" environments, and I even think a little boredom and adversity are good for kids. If my two-year-old boy had spent his mornings at that family day care, I know he would have adjusted and that he would have been neither completely miserable nor emotionally damaged. But I didn't feel it was a place I wanted him to have to adjust to.

Was this decision based on a consideration of his needs or mine, his well-being or mine? Would he have been unhappy, or was it my problem? With day care, the two cannot be easily teased apart. How you feel as a parent affects how your child feels. Whatever makes you uncomfortable has a good chance of somehow affecting your child too. When you are unhappy, the whole purpose of day care—to allow you to accomplish your work—is marred by your discomfort and preoccupation with how your child is feeling and doing.

One knee-jerk reply to these emotional concerns is that they are the luxury of the few and that for most people economic realities preclude a prolonged engagement with such concerns. Indeed, economics are always central to needing to work and paying for day care; however, it sometimes feels as if economic "reality" is invoked to shut women up. The message that we "can't afford" to feel what we feel, so we should corral our feelings into existing categories and arrangements, obscures that "reality" is constructed, socially and individually. As the writer Marilynne Robinson remarks in *The Death of Adam*, "We act as if the reality of economics were reality itself, the one Truth to which everything must refer. I can only suggest that terror at complexity has driven us back on this very crude monism." When mothers' interests are defined only in terms of their economic interests, it tells us less about "reality" than about values, values about money and time that exclude many of the things that are most important to actual mothers.

Mothers' "Choice"

All sorts of ungenerous attitudes toward mothers are rationalized through the contemporary rhetoric of "choice." Since it is a woman's choice to have a child, the reasoning goes, it is her responsibility to bear all professional and economic costs associated with that choice. Such judgments are visited especially harshly on single mothers. In response to this rhetoric, and to safeguard whatever gains they've made, women may observe a code of silence regarding maternal desire, lest the pleasure they derive from their children be marshaled as further evidence of the purely voluntary and personal nature of the enterprise.

The issue of choice with respect to work and mothering is a lot more complicated than this view of self-determination would suggest. The legal scholar Joan Williams argues that in the American workplace, the "ideal worker" is someone who can put in long hours, conform to inflexible professional schedules, and relocate if necessary. These characteristics, Williams points out, require the background presence of someone who takes care of the "flow of household work." As family caregivers, women are often responsible for administering or executing this task. The norm of the ideal worker thus tends to draw men disproportionately toward those vocational roles and women toward lives focused on caregiving. As a result, men overwhelmingly miss out on time with children, and women are marginalized in the workplace for fulfilling their parental obligations.

Williams reminds us that all choices come about within an economic and ideological force field. In particular, a mother's "choice" to care for children is affected by norms that sanction fathers' time-consuming jobs and mothers' orientation around caregiving. Mothers who quit their professional jobs and stay home because "'it just wasn't working'" are not simply making a free and voluntary decision; they are responding to what Williams calls the "stiff headwinds from domesticity," an ideology characterized by a sharp, and highly gendered, split between home and work.

The choice to care for children (and to put up with the losses and trade-offs associated with it) is certainly affected by the ideology of domesticity, but it also connects to feelings people experience as personal, feelings they may see no virtue in ignoring or minimizing. Whatever roles mothers assume, their feeling that their lives make sense often includes a feeling of connection to their children. Parents vary in how much time and attention they need to give to their children to achieve a sense of connection, but this connection is often the single most decisive issue in whether they feel their situation works. An employed mother may well declare, "It just wasn't working," because she realizes she can't handle both being an ideal worker and accomplishing the flow of household work. But she might also come to that conclusion when performing as an ideal worker works "too well"; when, for example, she has the thought, "*I'm the mother, I* want to give them a bath," when she comes home and sees her children all toweled off by the nanny and readied for bed.

In Williams's view, a solution to the split between male ideal workers and female marginalized caregivers would be a social agreement on the amount of parental care children need. Once we agree on this, childcare could and should be divided equally between partners. A social agreement on the norm of parental care has virtues, chief among them the agreement on a minimal level necessary for children of *all* backgrounds. But at the heart of some of our most divisive disagreements is the question of what kind of parental care children should have. People can even espouse the same goal but believe that it is best met in different ways. Some parents conceptualize the amount of paid work they do as the only, or best, way to give their children advantages, whereas others see their availability at home as conferring essential benefits to their kids. Among my urban professional patients who are mothers, one of the most consuming dilemmas is whether it is better for their children if they work so as to provide them a private-school education or stay home to offer them guidance and companionship. For these mothers and so many others, the question of "choice" is not simple, as they constantly strive to recognize ideological pressures, personal feelings, ambitions, and social values that pull them in many different directions at once.

Childcare, Work, and Sensitivity

Because our concern for our children is so strong and the stakes feel so high, we're often anxious for the world to tell us unequivocally what is "right" about day care. Statistics often function like modern-day tea leaves, providing inconclusive information that we overinterpret in our fretful need to know something. And there is no shortage of experts willing to proffer ready-made formulas: you should be at home, you should be at work, day care is bad for children, day care is good for children. In our insecure moments, it's easy to hang on to the latest trend or talking head.

One place we look for objective information to guide our thinking about our childcare decisions is psychological research. The vast National Institute of Child Health and Human Development (NICHD) Study of Early Child Care followed 1,364 children ages seven and up from diverse families in ten locations between 1991 and 2006. It tracked a host of variables related to children's outcomes, familial structures, and childcare characteristics, and it strived to move beyond the simplistic question of whether day care "hurts" children to consider the interaction of formative factors in children's lives.

The study's overarching message is one of complexity: no one factor in a child's upbringing has any one effect. What light does the NICHD study shed on the impact of day care on the mother-child relationship? Concerning attachment, the study showed that infants who had extensive childcare experiences in the first fifteen months of life were no less securely attached, on average, than children who had not. Time spent apart from parents did not in itself appear to affect the security or insecurity of the mother-infant bond. What did appear to make a difference was the sensitivity and responsiveness of the mother. Low scores in measures of maternal sensitivity or responsiveness, when combined with more than minimal amounts of childcare, poor-quality childcare, or more than one care arrangement, related to less secure attachment scores for children. More time spent in childcare for children ranging from six months to three years was also found to correlate with lower scores in maternal sensitivity, though the strength of this connection was fairly weak.

A question these findings prompt is whether the mothers' lower sensitivity was more situational in nature, reflecting the amounts of time they spent working and their children spent in childcare, or more dispositional, reflecting their personal caregiving approach. Looking at the lower sensitivity scores among mothers who worked more than thirty hours per week by their child's ninth month, the researchers found that even when these mothers' prior level of sensitivity was held constant, they still scored significantly lower in sensitivity measures at thirty-six months than mothers who did not work at all when their children were nine months old. In other words, their lower sensitivity scores were not explained by personality characteristics or prior behavior. Working more than thirty hours in their child's ninth month appeared to exert a causal effect on mothers' lower sensitivity to their children.

This finding gives us some insight into what can be so painful to mothers about being apart for significant amounts of time from their babies and small children. It can make it harder to read behavior, to respond aptly, and to foster mutually satisfying interactions. As we saw in chapter 4, states of shared pleasure come about through attunement and the achievement of "flow" states, both of which are compromised when mothers are self-conscious or worried about achieving a fulfilling interaction. For example, a patient of mine has a toddler who is frustrated easily and often inconsolable. There is often a ready-at-hand reason ("She's hungry," "She needs a nap"), but privately my patient fears that she doesn't know how to comfort her daughter as well as the full-time nanny does. Her self-consciousness about whether she can read her daughter accurately, her worry about the effect of her absence, and her sense of inadequacy about her capacity to comfort all make her feel even more tense when things don't go well, which makes her feel more stilted in their interactions. Her best path to relaxation and "flow" would be self-acceptance, but that is hard to attain.

The question in the back of many a mother's mind, whether she is at home or at work, is whether she and her child have enough opportunities to tune in to each other. A mother who is apart from her child many hours a day may strive to be particularly conscientious about tuning in to her child afterward precisely because she was away so long. A mother who is home, whose paramount concern is getting through the day with her young children without completely losing it, may find that her sensitivity to her children is not exactly finely tuned. An occasional lament of mothers who have stopped working to stay home with their children is that, instead of reveling in the slower pace and responding to their child, they get ensnared in an endless round of needs and chores with little ready relief.

I was on both sides of this dilemma when I was a mother

of young children. The feeling I needed more time with the kids was usually accompanied by pit-in-the-stomach sadness. Feeling I didn't have enough time for work was usually accompanied by a sense of frustration and anxiety. At different phases of my life I experienced startlingly different realities. When my first child was a baby, I couldn't bear to leave her. When my second child started preschool, I felt I wanted to stay for all of "circle time," to know what school was like for him, to feel connected to his new world. My third child had more childcare than the others and developed a close relationship with his babysitter. When he was two, I began to become more involved with my work. It was the first time as a mother that I had allowed myself to feel that I could happily have stayed in my office all day. Sometimes I'd feel a sharp sense of loss when I wasn't sharing experiences with him. Still, I was at a different point in my development as a mother when he was two, five and a half years after my first child was that age. Though I could both relish what was exciting about this phase and regret what I was giving up, I couldn't turn back the clock. It seemed the best I could do was try to take the long view, to look at the big picture of what was important to each of us individually and as a family.

If we discover that the hours a mother spends with her small child have anything to do with that child's readiness for school, or complexity of thinking, or anger-management skills, or anything else, it will not be because mothers are holding up flash cards or teaching their kids chess; rather, these data will reflect something about the way the mothers and children relate. Today's psychological and neuroscientific research overwhelmingly demonstrates that children develop emotional regulation skills and healthy responses to stress through their caretakers' protectiveness, attention, and attunement to their emotions. Emotional regulation, in turn, is at the core of concentrating in school, resisting temptation, cooperating with others, and sticking with a task, all capacities that comprise a necessary foundation for learning.

That all these crucial life skills emerge out of strong attachment relationships informs parents' interest in finding ways to be present to their children as much as possible. It also makes clear how important it is for children to have supportive, responsive, and sensitive early-childhood teachers as well. Given that, we as a society shouldn't be paying childcare workers a wage somewhere between that of animal caretakers and fast-food cooks. Stressed teachers, like stressed parents, are a problem for children's development, and our government policies and business models need to respond to this consideration.

The Pursuit of Happiness

When we have children, we sometimes crave freedom of movement, and we may even want our old selves back. But we may remain stubbornly unreconciled to what we have to do to simulate that freedom—relinquish the care of our child to another. As in Anne Lamott's portrait of maternal anger, we are not always aware of how ambivalent we are; after all, the relief at having the help we need can be so palpable. Then, suddenly, some emotional line that we didn't even know existed is overstepped—perhaps the babysitter has taken care of everything and we can't quite find where we fit in—and we are returned to an almost primal possessiveness, an agitated sense that we are not where we most want to be. Even mothers who experience their baby's dependence as a kind of prison grieve for the lost singularity of that early bond. "The storm of emotion, of the new, that accompanied her arrival is over now," writes Rachel Cusk. "In her growing up I have watched the present become the past, have seen at first hand how life acquires the savour of longing." Women who experience the immersion of motherhood as deeply difficult are often astonished to find, once that immersion is over, that they yearn to have another child and live it all over again.

Childcare is about social priorities, policy options, the needs of children, and the needs of working parents. But it is also about purpose, human limits, and happiness. Its fraught, politicized nature stems from these deeper emotional roots. We can't possibly understand what stands in the way of what every well-meaning policy recommendation says families need—reasonably priced, reliable, high-quality day care—without looking at some of the emotions that fuel our stasis and our disagreements.

Our whole discussion of day care says next to nothing about the mutual happiness of parent and child, yet that may be the one true measure of its success. Perhaps we don't talk about happiness because individuals can differ so drastically in their views of what brings it about. On the one hand, the psychologist Sandra Scarr appears unable even to perceive the possibility that a woman would be made happy and liberated, rather than dejected and imprisoned, by staying home with her children. The only hypothesis Scarr formulates regarding why mothers might want to "remain in close contact with their newborns" is for rest after childbirth and the need to establish a nursing schedule. On the other hand, the baby-care-manual author Penelope Leach assumes complete symmetry between a mother's and a baby's happiness: "Your interests and his are identical. You are all on the same side; the side that wants to be happy, to have fun." Scarr treats a mother's and baby's happiness as completely separate; Leach treats them as completely fused. But the reality for most mothers is somewhere in between.

Yet, happiness is the entry point to the territory we need to explore. The journalist Susan Chira describes a moment of sublime integration: "Cradling my nursing baby in one arm and the phone in my ear, conducting an interview with some serious personage, I could hardly contain my happiness. I don't really advocate trying to interview with a baby on one arm. But that one moment, ridiculous as it sounds, stands out because it was the first time I felt both my selves fit together with an audible click." Notice the self-consciousness, almost the embarrassment ("I don't really advocate," "ridiculous as it sounds"), with which Chira shares having lived such a moment; its raw power makes her bashful or afraid she will not be understood. When we have these moments, our lives make sense. Maybe everything suddenly fits together when our children are in a day care center downstairs from work, where we can visit them, instead of across town; maybe a moment of illumination occurs when all our fretting over our schedule pays off, when things are in balance; or perhaps we feel fully alive as parents when we realize the work of caring for our child is the work we want to do. However it appears to us, this experience of wholeness is something to follow, observe, and describe. Becoming intimate with these experiences of happiness and figuring out what they mean for our lives, and even the life of the culture, is our childcare dilemma's private face, its personal frontier.

7

Fertility

Once many years ago, while visiting some friends, I spied a book on their shelf called *How to Get Pregnant* by Sherman Silber, MD. In it, I came across a statistic that astonished me. In any given month of trying to conceive a baby, a normally fertile couple has a 20 percent chance of success. That meant that in a group of one hundred women, twenty would likely get pregnant in the first month of trying, and eighty would not. The next month, sixteen of the remaining women would likely get pregnant, leaving sixty-four who did not, and so on, until after one year, six women would not have conceived due to chance alone. The 20 percent statistic surprised me in two ways. First, I hadn't realized that the probability of a healthy woman's getting pregnant in a given month was so low—a fact that could not help but reassure if one was, say, in the fourth month of trying to get pregnant. Second, I was taken aback by my own ignorance; how could I not have had even a ballpark sense of these rates of conception?

My reaction took me back nine years earlier, to when I was first planning to try to become pregnant myself. I thought I would take the opportunity to educate myself a bit about the biology of conception, so I bought a slim book called *The Fertility Question* by Margaret Nofziger. Graphing my temperature on my ovulation chart was one of the more exciting and nerve-racking science experiments I'd ever conducted. But the temperature-taking, graphing, and noticing of changes in cervical mucus (learning there was *such a thing* as cervical mucus), even as it made me marvel at the workings of my female body, also left me with a feeling of feminist irritation. How could it be that these basic facts of my biology were *new information* to me at the age of thirty-three? Had I been actively avoiding knowledge that was readily available in the world around me? When I'd read *Our Bodies, Ourselves* as an adolescent, the topic of conception was probably far too remote to excite my interest. Still, I felt wronged somehow not to have been thoroughly tutored in these aspects of the female reproductive cycle in my high school biology class. The immediate, observable monthly cycles of our own bodies, as well as their day-by-day correlations with our fertility and even with our moods, were surely as worthwhile an object of study as the ecology of a nearby creek.

I suppose I also took a discoverer's pleasure in happening upon a pocket of science about sexual reproduction that I had not even known existed. But my stronger feeling was that something was weird about my ignorance of my fertility, and something askew about the fact that most women learn about their fertility only when something goes wrong. Today, the website of the International Council on Infertility Information Dissemination (INCIID.org) is one of the few places where women's thorough scientific knowledge of human reproduction is dazzlingly on view, offering an abundance of forums on topics such as in vitro fertilization

(IVF), reproductive health, and fertility after forty. Yet, in the precincts of despair where women confide their miscarriages and their failed IVF cycles, it is hard not to feel that something is backward about our before-the-fact ignorance of our fertility and our after-the-fact expertise.

Fertility and Age

It seems little has changed when it comes to young people's ignorance of fertility. In a 2017 survey of over twelve hundred Australian college students, about a third of both men and women thought women's fertility starts to decline at forty, and many overestimated the likelihood of a forty-year-old woman's having a baby after one round of IVF. Only 38 percent of men and 45 percent of women knew that a woman's fertility declines in the midthirties; less than 20 percent of men and women knew that men's fertility declines in the midforties. Many women told the researchers that they planned to postpone childbearing until they had completed their education, launched their careers, had had a chance to travel, and were able to combine work and family flexibly. The students wanted to fit in a lot before having children, and the researchers worried "that they seemed to be making these choices without being informed about the effects of age on fertility."

Certainly, the students had more immediate and pressing concerns than having children (studying, supporting themselves, sex), and their consciousness was shaded by the normal delusions of youth ("I'll never get old"). But staying fuzzy about fertility is also fueled by anxiety, the kind of anxiety we surmised among Folbre's economics students described in chapter 5. Thinking about fertility can be scary. It's uncertain how and when and with whom we might ultimately actualize our reproductive potential, and it's hard to imagine how we'll cope with difficult choices in balancing our conflicting interests and goals.

Although both men and women struggle with these questions, fertility and age tend to be more loaded issues for women. Women's "biological clock" is widely heralded, and everyone seems to think the burden of fertility belongs on the shoulders of women, despite that 33 percent of cases are due to men's infertility (this number has been growing—from 1973 to 2011, the sperm counts of men in Western countries declined a whopping 52.4 percent). Women will likely spend more of their time caring for children, and concerns about fertility and age weigh on them for that reason too. Their lives will be more dramatically changed by the arrival of children, and as a result they're understandably ambivalent about the pressures of a fertility "deadline."

Age is like a seemingly innocuous thread that, once pulled, begins to unravel a skein of issues in women's lives. We're aware of the extraordinary opportunities—educational, professional, creative, and sexual—that can be realized in a life unencumbered by children. With life spans hovering around eighty years, many people who ultimately want children also want to prolong the child-free phase of life. This dilemma is not all about the expectation of "having it all" or a millennial "sense of entitlement," two stereotypes the press has mobilized over the years to tut-tut women. Rather, negotiating these contradictory positions is about trying to realize various important, and sometimes conflicting, human goals. It is also about our perpetual struggle to align our individual development with the timetable of our bodies and the structures of social life. Fertility challenges us both to embrace possibilities and accept limits, but it also provides an occasion for considering how we might best organize our lives to pursue the values and ambitions we find most fulfilling.

Because childbearing decisions are so personal and lend themselves to the language of "choice," it is easy to overlook the powerful social forces that shape women's decisions about whether and when they have children. The sociologist Kristin Luker argues that the social factors that pressure less economically secure women to have children early are similar to those that push more privileged women to have them late. Both groups are "devising individual solutions for a massive social problem"—namely, the lack of a social structure that offers support for women attempting to combine child-rearing with education and paid work during their prime childbearing years.

The pressures Luker pinpoints are visible in the stark geographic and educational lines that divide women who have children at different ages: 2016 statistics indicate that women with college degrees have children seven years later on average than women without. In coastal cities such as San Francisco and New York, a woman's average age at first birth is thirty-one; in rural areas in the Great Plains and the South, it's closer to twenty-two. There's no evidence that one group enjoys motherhood more or less than the other, but a mother's education can have a significant impact on children's future prospects. Women with college degrees (who bear children later) are more likely to be married, less likely to divorce, and more able to provide economic and educational resources to their children. In terms of economic security and opportunity, the children of late childbearers are the haves and early childbearers are the have-nots in our increasingly divided class landscape.

Luker astutely argues that both poor and affluent women's strategies for childbearing entail social costs, but "only the costs of early childbearing have been the occasion of public handwringing." Educated, higher-earning women delay having children to solidify their financial situations and create opportunities for their future children, but they are also more likely to incur costs on the back end for fertility treatment and medical complications. The economic costs of assisted reproduction technology (ART) are high, and because insurance coverage is woefully inadequate, affluent, older mothers are most able to afford it (the advertising strategies of fertility clinics are also geared to capturing this overwhelmingly white, pay-out-of-pocket market). The medical costs of late childbearing are well documented and include the mother's increased health risks, her use of expensive technologies, and the health needs of the babies, who are more likely to be multiples (e.g., twins, triplets) and therefore more susceptible to prematurity and low birth weight.

Conversely, the alarm sounded about high birth rates among younger, poorer women (often of color) has a moralizing, even sinister, tone. In the dominant narrative, such women lack other sources of meaning so they fall back on motherhood as a "stand-in for status." They're viewed as lacking the ability to delay gratification—though similar "indulgence" by the rich, famous, and beautiful, whose fertility is celebrated and gushed over on gossip sites, is exempt from such judgments. As with so many narratives concerning female desire and choice, especially among the economically disadvantaged, maternal desire is the problem and its control the solution. Women sometimes tie their self-esteem to how well they've internalized this narrative, meaning how fully they've embraced goals other than motherhood. In a world where it is increasingly difficult to achieve financial security, economic pressures conspire with psychological ideals to make women feel they must consign themselves to somehow "fitting in" maternal desire around the edges.

On the Clock: Fertility versus Changes in Maternal Desire

Concerns about fertility are obviously not a problem when women know they do not want children. That women have this freedom of choice ranks as a resounding technological achievement and social good. The choice not to have children is increasingly articulated and championed in the culture at large. The writer Meghan Daum, who edited the anthology *Selfish, Shallow, and Self-Absorbed: Sixteen Writers on the Decision Not to Have Kids,* suggests that the epithet *selfish* might more accurately be applied to the "underthinkers" who have children "not so much because they want to but because it's what you do . . . people who have children to improve their marriages, to please their families, or out of fear that they'll regret it later if they don't." When a recent *New York Times* article quoted experts fretting about the falling US birthrate, hundreds of comments poured in from women and men who were happy not to have had children. They deemed the decision to remain childless rational and responsible, particularly in light of the world's overpopulation, the extraordinary expense of children, and the lack of government support for parents. One twenty-seven-year-old woman specifically thanked the older childless women who'd sent in comments, writing, "It's so good to hear from you all about how fulfilling your lives have been and how confident you feel in your decisions despite societal/family/etc. pressure. Those of us who wish to forge our own paths but face doubt from external sources need to hear your stories."

A heartrending problem arises when a woman who'd felt that the choice not to have children was settled finds, too late, that her feelings have changed. In her younger years, such a woman may feel more kinship with women for whom motherhood had never held much appeal and who will remain contentedly child-free. Psychological development clearly plays a role in whether a woman reopens the question about whether she wants children. "I never thought I wanted children," writes Karen Collins. "My mother died when I was 13, my father when I was 17. The idea of 'family' for me was linked to the terror of loss." Later, though, when Collins was in a secure relationship and had resolved some of her feelings about past losses, the desire for a child came to inform her hopes and goals. I've sometimes been told similar stories by therapy patients who spent their childhoods taking care of sick parents, or who, as oldest siblings, shouldered parentlike responsibility for younger ones. It can take time to claim one's own life, and it's often only after moving past childhood wounds that people can make fully deliberated decisions about wanting children or not.

The varied timetables of our psychological development do not always synchronize with the biological clocks that affect our fertility, and this reality is an often-overlooked complication for young people considering (or ignoring) the likelihood of their futures as parents or otherwise. One of the major challenges for young women, along with becoming educated and gainfully employed, is to sort out enough all the emotional effects of their childhoods to make a wise choice in a partner. Even if one's parents didn't divorce, the high rate of divorce, not to mention the specter of an unhappy marriage, is something most earnest young people soberly contemplate. People who marry young divorce at a higher rate than others, and a period of critical thought and emotional self-exploration is often crucial before establishing a strong life partnership. However, the possibility of utterly changing one's life and goals during this period should also remind young people to be skeptical about whether their attitudes toward parenting will remain constant.

Though it seems young to me now, I remember being twenty-eight and feeling not young at all. Single again after another collapsed relationship, I did what any self-respecting psychology graduate student who knew she wanted children would do: I went into therapy. Luck always plays a role in questions of love and fertility, and going into therapy doesn't directly create luck. But it can help us to perceive how we are unconsciously working at cross-purposes with ourselves. A youngish woman, caught in a confusing or unsatisfying pattern of relationships, or unable to consider the question of children with a person she loves, is in a particularly urgent, edgy situation. She may be more or less aware of the closing of the reproductive window—not right now, but someday in the not unimaginably distant future. The stakes for figuring out how to choose the right kind of person, how to make a relationship work, and how to approach the issue of children (with or without a partner) begin to feel increasingly high.

The uncertainty about whether one will find someone to love is not unlike the uncertainty about whether one will have children. Women who want these things are up against aspects of life they cannot fully determine or control. They are inevitably vulnerable. Women have highly conflicted feelings about this predicament, especially since today we exert greater control over so many more aspects of our lives than ever before. The writer Agnes Rossi captures what it was like to admit how desperately she wanted a baby:

> There's great vulnerability in desperation. How much safer you are if there isn't anything you want too badly. And how much cooler. Cool is, I suppose, the absence of desperation, of urgent desire, of neediness. I had wanted to believe that I was somehow different from all the women who were undergoing one high-tech procedure after another in pursuit of pregnancy. I'd hoped that I was more highly evolved, less sentimental, less traditional. I wasn't. I wanted a baby as badly as anybody did.

That "urgent desire," that "neediness," is in part what women's expanded life choices are supposed to have freed us from. Something is almost unseemly about a raw desire's eruption right in the middle of a perfectly civilized, reasonable life. Our qualms over acknowledging it might be akin to how women in an earlier era might have felt about bringing a diaphragm on a first date. It feels at once too vulnerable and too brazen to admit one's desire in advance of the sure chance of fulfilling it. My forty-five-year-old friend told me of the difference between her younger and current self: "If you'd asked me in my twenties about having children, I'd have said, 'No problem, if we can't have them, we'll adopt.' I was completely caught unawares by the primal rage I felt at being infertile. I felt like a cavewoman. I remember feeling that if I can't have a baby, I'm going to burn this house down."

Changes in a woman's subjective experience of maternal desire can also be influenced by partners' attitudes toward having children. For some sensitive men, deference to the hard-won nature of women's freedom, belief in the value of desired motherhood, and a respect for women's other aspirations all contribute to the gingerliness with which they discuss children with their spouses. On the other hand, some men formulate explicit or implicit strategies to urge children on their partners. The writer Phillip Lopate admits that one of his wife's many attractions when he married her was that she was of childbearing age. When she said she wanted time alone as a married couple before having children, he responded, "A reasonable request, I thought. I could wait. Not indefinitely, but . . . 'What if I never want to have children?' she asked. 'Would you still love me? Stay married?' I swallowed hard, said yes, and meant it. In the back of my mind, though, I gambled that she would come around eventually." Lopate's "gamble" surely registers his standpoint, subtly (or not too subtly) influencing over time his wife's attitude toward motherhood.

In a more painful case, the writer Bob Shacochis chronicles his wife's and his efforts to conceive in a haunting essay, "Missing Children." Early in their marriage, when he raised the issue of children with his wife, "more than wanting the freedom to anchor herself in a career, she simply didn't wish to be pregnant, she told me, ever; pregnancy was synonymous with trauma, perhaps even self-destruction. And although I was alarmed by her rhetorical absolutism, I was also willing to tell myself that this was not her final word on procreation." Further on in his account, we learn of his wife's traumatic second-trimester abortion at the age of sixteen, when she waited alone for three days in a hospital room until her "womb evacuat[ed] its voluminous contents onto the tile floor." Decades later, after numerous fruitless attempts to conceive, his wife is almost prostrated by grief as it becomes virtually certain she will never be able to bear her own biological child.

When the choice to defer pregnancy arises from trauma, a woman may close the door on babies even if what she needs most is help in processing her experience. If her desire to forgo children or pregnancy is respectfully unquestioned as a matter of her right to self-determination, it may delay the possibility of considering whether her rejection of motherhood is self-protective. If she waits too long and pregnancy is no longer possible, she stands to lose twice over. Yet, to ask whether a desire to mother is being suppressed or ignored, even to wonder aloud about this possibility, feels strangely forbidden, as if one is reducing the selfhood of women by claiming they are only happy if they are barefoot and pregnant.

Egg Freezing as Liberation

Given all the emotional, medical, and economic benefits of bearing children neither very early nor very late, it seems we should be stumbling over ourselves trying to rearrange society, rather than women's reproductive biology, to accommodate those timetables. But in this domain of central, passionate import, we are caught in a web of pressures and taboos that move us toward certain solutions and away from others.

In careers, powerful incentives exist to try to work within, rather than oppose, the status quo, even though the status quo tends to disadvantage women reproductively and economically. It is accordingly not hard to envision a world where, in the presence of inflexible work structures and aggressively marketed fertility treatments, we accept fertility interventions as more and more of a norm. Already, fertility technology is coming to be viewed not as a last resort but as an "opportunity" to postpone childbearing into one's forties. Grimmest of all—shades of the futuristic movie *Gattaca*—by degrees we're finding that assisted reproduction is acquiring a sheen as the newer and better "option," glimmery in its vague association with celebrities and cutting-edge technologies, pointing somehow in the right direction because it's about "freedom" and "choices." Yet all the while, we are finding ourselves increasingly unable to analyze the constraining set of assumptions that got us into this way of thinking.

The normalization of these phenomena can be discerned in the way some critics recast the pain, unpredictability, and risk of fertility treatment as women's ultimate opportunity. Over twenty years ago, the law professor Jane Cohen, who became a mother of IVF twins at age fifty, envisioned a "vanguard feminism" and the "dawn of a new consciousness" when eggs can be "frozen and put on the shelf." That day has arrived, with companies such as Google, Apple, and Facebook paying for their employees' egg-harvesting and freezing procedures. Despite the only 2 to 12 percent chance that a frozen egg will ultimately result in a birth, egg-freezing businesses such as Extend aggressively market their services by warning that "eggs are a nonrenewable resource," and some clinics offer "let's chill" egg-freezing parties, complete with champagne.

Behind the egg-freezing industry's pretensions toward empowerment ("free your career," "preserve your options") lies another, more complicated story. The consumer advocate Judith Steinberg Turiel asks, "If the choice were up to them, how would women and their partners prefer to experience childbearing?" If they have the option, people prefer the lowest-tech method possible, preferably through having sex, preferably with someone they love. Research suggests that most women freeze their eggs not to prioritize their careers, but rather because they have not yet found a partner or don't have a stable relationship. These goals are not always easy to achieve, but achieving them depends more on self-awareness, self-acceptance, and self-compassion than the illusory hyper-control that egg-freezing companies purport to sell.

Whatever the commercial motives of the fertility industry, ART is of extraordinary value to prospective parents who cannot or do not want to conceive babies in other ways— among them same-sex couples, single people, and couples wherein one or both partners are trans—and has been crucial to enabling more people to create the families they desire. ART has weakened the association between the desire to parent and categories of gender and sexuality, and along with the expanding range of accepted family structures, it has led to a fuller appreciation of the desire to parent as a shared human impulse. When the role of caring for children loses its automatic association with our concepts of "female" and "mother," we're freed from the idealizations, judgments, and ideas of "normal" that these concepts have historically evoked. That ART can disrupt cisgender and heteronormative attitudes toward reproductive health and family structure is an important quality to note. Perhaps this quality can remind us that the highest goal of our social policies and technological advancements regarding sexual reproduction is not to validate the normalization of reengineering young women's reproductive biology, but to expand inclusivity and build strong, loving families.

The Problem of the Pregnant Body

In 2017, Beyoncé dazzled the world with her spellbinding performance of expectant motherhood at the Grammy Awards. She was gorgeously fecund, her voluptuous form draped in sun-goddess splendor. Beyoncé knows how to shine her light, and she has an amazing amount of light to shine. Every woman who bears new life within her body is living a miracle. Yet, among the rank and file, pregnancy is often a pretext for discrimination.

The pregnant bodies of the rich and famous are endlessly vaunted. "It's what sells magazines," remarks one longtime celebrity journalist. Sanitized and photoshopped images of tanned and toned celebrities spirit away the fleshly struggle of pregnancy. They also pay homage to the edict that women must be sexy to be valued. The Instagram feeds of supermodels with their baby bumps fuel the obsession and silently persecute the uncomfortably pregnant women in the supermarket checkout line. Then, once the celebrities' babies are born, said supermodels persecute said women with their now magically restored bodies and careers.

It seems okay for a woman to be pregnant only if she's also rich, beautiful, famous, and making money for other people. If she's a regular pregnant woman who is working in a regular job, she may well be demeaned. Among professional women who become pregnant, stories are routine of being forced out for it, even when the ostensible reason isn't pregnancy. A friend who edited a newspaper was asked to leave when she became pregnant. Another was told by the president of her company, after she returned from maternity leave, that he didn't like "her style," though he had voiced no previous complaints. Those hardest hit by such biases are low-wage workers. When a pregnant woman who lifted fifty-pound trays of food at Walmart asked for light duty due to bleeding, her female boss told her no, saying that she'd seen "a pregnant Demi Moore doing acrobatics on TV" (it was a stunt double).

It's almost as if people are cruel toward pregnant women workers because they can be. Spotting vulnerability, the impulse to crush the weak is excited. On a primal level, pregnant bodies induce envy. The swelling belly, the ample breasts, even the self-satisfied contentment on some pregnant women's faces, can arouse anything from annoyance, to malice, to feeling vaguely deprived or left out. If a woman lacks power or means, if she is of color or unpartnered, the unleashing of resentment is even more automatic. In a pregnancy-discrimination suit against UPS that reached the Supreme Court, Ruth Bader Ginsburg challenged the firm's lawyer to cite "'a single instance of anyone who needed a lifting dispensation who didn't get it except for pregnant people.' The UPS lawyer drew a blank." Laura Brown, the founder of First Shift Justice Project, writes, "The cultural narrative that devalues women for having children will be disrupted only when all pregnant women are able to assert their workplace rights." Could this truth be said any more simply or damningly?

Having Children, Caring for Children

In Nicole Holofcener's film *Lovely and Amazing*, the heroine, Michelle, keeps telling her story of natural childbirth to anyone who will listen. A frustrated artist in a rudderless marriage, Michelle is insecure, and she clings to her unmedicated childbirth as her one accomplishment—a political statement, claim to specialness, and icebreaker rolled into one. In Michelle's endless rehashing of her birth experience, Holofcener captures a kind of narcissism that easily attaches to producing a child. I remember when I was pregnant with my first child, I felt startled and indignant when cars did not stop at crosswalks. Couldn't they see that *a pregnant woman* was trying to cross the street? The writer Agnes Rossi describes similar feelings about being able to bear children: "Our language needs a word for the feminine equivalent of machismo. *Feminisa*, or something. Just as the ultimate symbol of machismo is the erect penis, the essence of *feminisa* is the ability to create a living, breathing human being in the space between one's hipbones." Or, as in the reflection of the French writer Colette, "I am tired of hiding what was never mentioned—namely, the state of pride, of vulgar grandeur, which I enjoyed while ripening my fruit."

The feelings of specialness and entitlement surrounding pregnancy and bearing children may pack an additional kick in our culture by virtue of the high value we place on ownership as a sign of worth. Children, aside from being people we love, are our ticket to the future, our hope, our royal bloodline. No toy, no darling outfit, should be spared. In the Facebook and Instagram era, exhibitionism has become a social norm. Our love for our children is sometimes difficult to keep separate from the fantasy of narcissistic completeness that our competitive culture continually excites. An orthopedic surgeon boasted to me in idle cocktail-party chatter that his wife had gotten pregnant *right away*, though he evinced no shame that he and his wife were astonishingly absent from their children's day-to-day lives. One cannot help detecting in this disconnect a sensibility that is supremely keyed to the racking up of kudos and assets but neglectful of the actual presence required for nurturing relationships. This sensibility may come more easily to those who reap great material or professional rewards for endorsing it, but its diffusion throughout the culture ends up permeating the air that all of us breathe.

Women today are right in the thick of this issue, trying to make sense of ourselves as "producers" and "nurturers." In some ways, physically birthing her own baby seems to make a woman both producer and nurturer in one fell swoop. Yet, if we consider the bond with a child as arising from the practice of caring for him or her, perhaps we would not be so inclined to interpret having a baby within a framework of individual accomplishment.

The psychoanalyst Julia Kristeva draws a distinction between the psychology of pregnancy and of parenting a child. In pregnancy, a woman can experience "a fantasy of totality" that is "a sort of instituted, socialized, natural psychosis." The arrival of the child, on the other hand, calls the mother to "the slow, difficult, and delightful apprenticeship in attentiveness, gentleness, forgetting oneself." There can be a high to getting pregnant, being pregnant, and having a baby; one could almost call it manic, for the sense of power and expansiveness it brings. This expansiveness is utterly appropriate to the miracles of pregnancy and childbirth. But it has little in common with the states of mind that go into the daily care of children.

A searching discussion of having versus caring for children has arisen among women who have gone through the agony of infertility and emerged childless on the other side. A forty-six-year-old friend who was divorced in her midthirties and spent much of the next few years frantically pursuing pregnancy on her own through various procedures said:

> At forty-three, I was still completely in the grip of needing to have a baby. At forty-six, I feel over it, and it is a relief. I finally got to the point where I said to myself, "This isn't only about having a baby." The pull to do that is very strong. I think it comes from somewhere deep in our primitive brains. I came to a point where I realized it was really ultimately more about caring for a baby and child. And in my case I realized that once I got past the intense desire to have a baby, I didn't feel I was really cut out for caring for my own child, and I do much better caring for other people's children.

Melissa Ludtke, the author of a study of single motherhood, *On Our Own*, describes a similar process in her own development. In her midforties, she revisited the question of whether to become a mother, a path she had previously pursued through artificial insemination. She notices that "the powerful emotions that once dominated my decision-making were now partnered with concrete evaluations about whether adopting a child was the only, or even the best way, for me to express my 'mothering' desires. . . . This time around there is an absence of the constantly churning internal and external pressures I felt when I was in my thirties and driven by 'baby hunger.'" Then, at the close of her book, Ludtke anticipates adopting a Chinese girl in the coming year.

Some observers have pointed out the hierarchy of value that's built into how we conceptualize adoption and infertility treatment. For example, resolving feelings about not being able to have one's own biological baby is commonly viewed as a prerequisite to pursuing adoption. But as the legal scholar Elizabeth Bartholet observes, "It may be impossible to know what part of the pain of infertility relates to a desire to parent, and whether this desire will be satisfied by adoption, without knowing what adoption is about. An understanding of adoption may thus be essential to resolving feelings about infertility." Subtly and inadvertently, the astounding, tantalizing advances in fertility medicine direct our attention toward the importance of having our own biological children and deflect it away from our confused ambivalence about how the practice of caring fits into parenthood. Even as fertility medicine is all about women's desire to mother, its predication on the biological mother-child connection cannot help but contribute to our societal emphasis on having, as opposed to caring for, children.

Alongside the public discussion of all the risks of adoption is another compelling and moving discussion by adoptive parents about their experience. They speak both of the incredibly chance nature of having become a parent to this child and their profound sense of its "rightness." Herself an adoptive mother, Bartholet writes, "I could not have anticipated that this family formed across the continents would seem so clearly the family that was meant to be, that these children thrown together with me and with each other, with no blood ties linking us together or to a common history, would seem so clearly the children meant for me." Researching adoption, the adoptive father and journalist Evan Eisenberg encounters similar testimony of "rightness" and fit: "In workshop after workshop I heard parents attest, with wonder still fresh, that their adopted child seemed meant for them from the start, and that they could not imagine loving a 'biological' child more." Some stepparents describe a similarly intense and involving journey into parenthood, adding further evidence that "naturally" birthing biological children is no prerequisite for experiencing parenting as a "natural" means of fulfilling one's purpose in life.

In her memoir *The Art of Waiting*, Belle Boggs details the proliferating options for couples who want children—IVF, egg donation, embryo donation, surrogacy, adoption, fostering, and more. In one case, her friends Gabe and Todd consider the practical and ethical quandaries of international gestational surrogacy. In their proposed situation, the sperm would be Gabe's, the egg would come from a South African donor, and the surrogate would be a woman in Nepal, the whole operation coordinated by an Israeli international surrogacy agency (one irony for prospective parents who have endured "months and years of waiting and planning" is that they are "often met by professionals who have a financial interest in moving things along"). Commenting on the complexity of the considerations involved, Boggs contends that "ART requires a decision, a commitment," and an inspirational message of her book is that a tumultuous journey to parenthood spurs deeper reflection on one's parenting desires, motives, and needs. The waiting and effort involved demands a level of discernment that isn't required when couples get pregnant the low-tech way, and that kind of discernment contributes to the core of being a loving parent. I have been a therapist to couples for many years, and I've listened to many patients discuss how, as their children grow up and cause them to worry and stew, they ultimately relinquish the fantasy that they have control over who their kids will become. Watching parents struggle and endure and celebrate their children in the day-in, day-out practice of care, I am continually moved by their devotion. That devotion is the same whether the children are fostered, adopted, genetically related to one parent, or genetically related to both.

One of my therapist colleagues likens the nurturing and raising of children to what the psychoanalyst Melanie Klein calls the *depressive position*. The term refers not to depression, but rather to the developmental achievement of being able to love another as a whole, separate person. It involves the capacity to cope with the feelings of loss, disappointment, and guilt that real relationships inevitably bring, and it demands the relinquishment of the illusion that others exist for one's own gratification or as projections of one's own mind. For a mother, feelings of totality, specialness, or omnipotence surrounding having a baby must give way to the daily recurring needs for attentiveness and empathy as well as to the acceptance of inevitable daily failures. There is the high of having the baby, and then there is the rest of life. I have sometimes thought that there is something significant about the lavish bestowal of gifts at the arrival of a child, about the way their beauty exceeds their functionality, which captures this heightened, expectant moment of miraculous specialness, setting it apart from every moment of parenthood that follows.

It is no wonder that women who want children want all of this, that they want the whole experience; they want it in their bodies, in their minds, in their hands, and in their hearts. But as a society, we should strive to be as ingenious at providing people with tools to care for their children as we are at helping people to have them.

8

Abortion

When my husband picked me up after work during my first pregnancy, I would vomit before I could even say hello. I had to admire, in the glazed aftermath of yet another bout of puking, the sheer will to life displayed by the small cluster of cells growing inside me. It seemed it would do anything short of killing me to ensure its own survival. I remember learning during my third pregnancy, when I suffered an endless string of flus and colds, that a pregnant woman's immune responses are partly suppressed to lessen the chance her system will react against her own baby. It seemed that as long as I stayed alive, nature didn't much care how sick I felt.

Many women, including me, were unprepared for how abstract their happiness at being pregnant became in the face of those first-trimester physical surges—the midsentence stuporous sleep, the racking waves of nausea. But in that brutal and awe-inspiring contest of bodies, I also sensed the genesis of a relationship at the core of which was the struggle for growth in earnest and in which my love—already too ethereal a word—was expressed, and even strangely defined, by my strength and resilience in the face of that struggle. That stage of pregnancy was my best lesson in the unsaccharine nature of mother love and its intimacy with creation and destruction.

Pregnancy begins a *relationship*. Most essentially, it launches a relationship between a woman and the potential child she carries within. It also initiates a new relationship between a woman and herself—her body, her history, and her future. For these reasons, when a woman considers abortion, the question of whether the fetus should continue to develop does not stand alone. It also involves a question about whether the relationship should continue to develop between herself as a potential mother and the fetus as a potential baby.

Some believe that the fetus is a full-fledged person from conception. I do not. But the belief that the fetus is not a full-fledged person does not make abortion emotionally easy or morally simple. Awareness of the potential relationship set in motion by pregnancy is one of the most heartrending and ethically fraught issues for a woman considering abortion. Pregnancy's inescapably relational nature means that once it begins, it can never be completely negated. A baby comes to term or it doesn't, through choice or chance. It comes to term, and it is kept or relinquished. In any case, in any outcome, the woman has to *do something with* a relationship—mourn it, celebrate it, try to forget it, embrace it, accept its loss. When a woman feels she must not allow the child and the relationship to develop, it is almost never a physically or psychologically simple decision. Yet women sometimes feel that as difficult, painful, even tragic as it is, they must make it to survive or to respect themselves and their situations in life.

This aspect of the abortion dilemma illuminates a facet of maternal desire. The desire to mother involves the intention and commitment to enter into a relationship of love and care with a child. It represents an attempt to integrate our deepest personal longings and highest human aspirations. In some situations a woman does not want to enter into that relationship or she recognizes she does not have the ability to responsibly commit to it. In such a case a woman confronts the same basic realities as the woman who chooses to keep a pregnancy. First, each grapples with the enormous importance of her desire for a child and to that potential child's flourishing and fulfillment as a human being. Second, each confronts the reality that whenever a woman bears a child, she channels her emotional and physical energies in new ways that are hugely consequential in defining the person she will become. In light of these facts, what a woman wants with respect to having a child is of absolutely decisive, even sacred, importance.

Desire and Selfhood

There is a stark, almost shocking difference between how one feels when one wants to be pregnant and how one feels when one doesn't. The same physiological event can be experienced as a blessing or a catastrophe, as being in harmony with one's body or as being assaulted by it. Women's lives are often described as contextual, but this may be the most contextual aspect of all, "the mother of all contexts." The extremes of women's responses in the face of pregnancy, and every ambiguous point in between, puts us face-to-face with how central the issue of *wanting* is to the abortion dilemma.

We have difficulty knowing how to weigh the mother's desire for a child; by its very nature, it seems too capricious, too emotional, and too devoid of principle. Perhaps because this desire is so hard to evaluate, its complexity is flattened both by abortion rights' opponents and proponents. Among abortion conservatives, the mother's desire is too often dismissed as a selfish interest in "convenience," a touchy-feely, morally insignificant wisp in comparison with the sober matter of fetal life. For abortion liberals, it seems desire is best not probed too energetically, for fear that women's ambivalence about abortion might be used to discredit their decisions and undermine the legitimacy of their right to decide.

In fact, maternal desire is absolutely central to the morality of abortion, even though the ways we tend to talk about these concepts have not always helped us understand the importance of that connection. In the wrong hands, the notion of "wanting" is simplistically lumped in with a "we are empowered and can do whatever we want" strain of moral nihilism. But desire is actually more complex than the casual notions of feeling or preference imply. The critic Adam Gopnik describes desire as a "thought-through feeling," a conceptualization that aptly points out that this aspect of the human experience is not simply about what we want, however complicated or conflictual; it is also about intentions, the coordinated movement of feeling, thought, and action toward a self-chosen purpose. The freedom and responsibility to form the intentions most important to us are central features of what we believe it means to be a person. A woman's desire with respect to something so consuming and momentous as carrying a pregnancy to term involves just this sort of meaning-making activity.

In *Fruitful,* a memoir of her life as a mother and a feminist, the writer Anne Roiphe reflects on the folly of trying to ground the ethics of abortion in defining when life begins, as she and her friends had tried to do in the days before *Roe v. Wade.* "We should have drawn the line on whether the fetus was or was not wanted and shaped the debate on that issue," she writes, "instead of getting mired in metaphysics or theology about the beginning of life." Roiphe speaks of whether the mother wants the fetus, but the political contention that grounds her discussion is that the potential mother is the person in the best position to assess her desires and make judgments about them. Whether a child is "wanted" functions as a shorthand to convey two related but distinct meanings: first, a woman's intentions for herself as a person and potential parent, and, second, her prerogative to evaluate these intentions to come to her own decision.

This work of self-reflection is rarely straightforward because a woman's feelings about an unintentional pregnancy are almost always mixed. Even when she is deeply distressed to be pregnant, she may feel remorse about having an abortion. She may imagine pleasure at mothering but see no practical way to support a child. She may have no interest in caring for a child but feel swayed by her family's wishes for her to keep it. She may ultimately hope for a child with her partner but feel that to have one now would threaten the viability of their relationship. She may ambivalently decide to continue the pregnancy and one day find herself happy about it. When a woman considers her intentions, whatever they are, she also likely considers them in light of her values. It is almost impossible to think about abortion without one's feelings involving ethical concern.

Yet, whatever a woman feels about an abortion—whether she feels bereft, suicidal, liberated, that she will go to hell, or all of the above; whether she has an abortion half-awake, half-asleep, or completely confused about what she wants— her entitlement to make her own decision does not derive from the *content* of her feelings. It derives from her ultimate authority to weigh her desires, intentions, and values and to undertake her own course of action based on them.

In this sense, decisions about continuing a pregnancy confront us with the connection, in its most naked form, between a woman's claim to personhood and her reproductive freedom. To take to term a pregnancy to which one does not consent is a traumatic violation of one's integrity as a person, just as having a baby that one desires is a fulfillment of oneself as a person. Not being able to have a baby when one wants to do so is experienced as a great injury to the self, while ending a pregnancy due to practical or medical concerns is experienced as a wrenching but necessary act of self-preservation. Each instance bears out just how deeply our reproductive fates are enmeshed with our identities as human beings.

The trivialization of the connection between a woman's integrity, her full selfhood, and procreative choice has problematically found expression in legal arguments against women's reproductive self-determination. In her article "Are Mothers Persons?" (note the pointed reversal of the more usual question, "Are fetuses persons?"), the philosopher Susan Bordo demonstrates the stunning desecration of women's personhood that occurs right under our noses in the realm of reproductive law. Bordo notes, first, that the legal principle of a person's right to physical inviolability has been strenuously protected in cases concerning such issues as whether someone can be legally compelled to donate bone marrow to a dying relative. The import of this protection is not simply physical; it constitutes, she writes,

> a protection of the *subjectivity* of the person involved—that is, it is an acknowledgment that the body can never be regarded merely as a site of quantifiable processes that can be assessed objectively, but must be treated as invested with personal meaning, history, and value that are ultimately determinable only by the subject who lives "within" it.

When this "meaning-bestowing function is in danger of being taken away," the law tends to interpret "the situation as a violent invasion of the personal space of the body."

Yet, when the legal matter involves women's reproductive decisions, this core ethical value, which would appear to be a sacrosanct human right in our society, is violently circumscribed. As Bordo writes, when the body in question is a woman's pregnant or reproductive body, the right to physical integrity and the protection of subjectivity gives way to the abrogation of a woman's will for the sake of an unborn child. Courts do not order people to make the personal sacrifices of a transplant or marrow donation, even to save their own child's life; despite that a child's life hangs in the balance—a full-fledged person's life—the potential donor's right to inviolable subjectivity overrides the potential recipient's need for life-saving support. In contrast, courts have ordered caesarean sections, intrauterine transfusions, and the delivery of babies of terminally ill women against their will. With these legal precedents, we see in sharpest relief a particular bias directed not simply against women as people but specifically against women's autonomy in pregnancy decisions.

Furthermore, if a woman is poor, pregnant, and of color, she "comes as close as a human being can get to being regarded, medically and legally, as 'mere body,' her wishes, desires, dreams, religious scruples of little consequence and easily ignored in the interests of fetal well-being." Bordo cites a 1987 study that found that 81 percent of court-ordered obstetrical interventions involved African American, Asian, or Hispanic women. (In criminal cases of "fetal endangerment" between 1973 and 2005, 52 percent of the pregnant women were black.) In the case of Ayesha Madyun, a woman who resisted a caesarean on religious grounds, the judge ruled that "for him not to issue a court order forcing her to have the operation would be to 'indulge' Madyun's 'desires' at the expense of the safety of her fetus." This sort of dismissal by the judicial system is, as the legal scholar Stephen Carter has argued, part of a general cultural tendency to treat religious convictions as optional and expendable. But even beyond that, such legal opinions essentially deprive the pregnant woman of the right to informed consent, paternalistically declaring how she should interpret the meaning and value of a given procedure. By so doing, they preempt the very act that forms the core of her entitlement to informed consent: that is, her own subjective determination of what a given intervention means to *her*.

Bordo helps us appreciate that coercion in reproductive decisions undermines not simply what individual women want but also their entitlement to subjectivity itself. A woman's personhood cannot be cleanly disentangled from her reproductive life. "The nature of pregnancy is such," Bordo correctly observes, "that to deprive the woman of control over her reproductive life . . . is necessarily also to mount an assault on her personal integrity and autonomy (the essence of personhood in our culture) and to treat her merely as [a] material incubator of fetal subjectivity." In this powerful argument, Bordo makes clear that to regard a woman's maternal intentions as an expendable aspect of subjectivity is to erode the integrity of her full personhood as such.

Pregnancy as Relationship

The reason freedom in reproductive decisions is so important to women's integrity has to do with the kind of relationships pregnancy and motherhood are. If requiring a woman to carry a baby to term were on the order of insisting she pay a parking ticket, we wouldn't bat an eye; no morally weighty abridgment of personal freedom would be involved. Our sense that coercion in reproductive decisions jeopardizes women's important and legitimate interests in self-determination reflects what a woman commits to, psychologically and emotionally, by carrying a baby to term.

It helps to consider the unique character of pregnancy. Most obviously, pregnancy is unique in that there is no counterpart in male experience. For the woman herself, it is unique in that it involves a new relationship between "me" and "other," between "my body" and "not my body." Women rarely experience pregnancy as a clear matter of "me the mother" and "you (or 'it') the fetus." Instead, we are intimate with the fetus's otherness early on, and this otherness is instantly able to alter our *own* reality. When we are tired or nauseated, we feel taken over by a stubborn force wresting life from our flesh, our bone, our consciousness. Individual women experience this situation in their own ways, which are inflected by psyche, tradition, history, and circumstance. No universal norm guides a woman's experience of it; every pregnancy is different, every woman is different, and each pregnancy for a given woman is different. But each pregnant woman faces a basic situation and has to make sense of it in her own way, and that is the relationship between herself and the developing fetus.

The reality of pregnancy is that it is a relationship of great, and progressively greater, physical and psychological investment. That is abundantly clear when a pregnancy is wanted; it is why women can become grief-stricken after even an early miscarriage and why women who choose to have prenatal diagnostic testing want to do so as early as possible. Yet even when a woman does not want to be pregnant, she almost inevitably becomes increasingly involved psychologically and emotionally as the pregnancy continues. To insist, then, that all women carry their pregnancies to term and then give the baby up for adoption if need be is to make deciding against involving oneself in the relationship virtually impossible. By the same token, if a woman is compelled to have an abortion, she is wrongfully barred from deciding to involve herself in the life of her potential child.

Even when women respect the potential of fetal life, one reason they choose abortion over giving a baby up for adoption is their awareness of how deeply attached they will become to their developing fetus as pregnancy progresses. For some, the idea that they would have to relinquish the child at birth becomes increasingly unbearable. During my second pregnancy, I had amniocentesis around halfway through the pregnancy. The baby was already kicking. I walked around in a moral fog, not even quite sure if it was right to have taken the test, since I could barely allow myself to think of any outcome but keeping the baby, no matter what the test revealed. My experience, which I don't think was unusual, underscores just how emotionally and physically involving the relationship of pregnancy is. For that reason, among others, many women faced with an unwanted pregnancy decide that ending it while it is still mostly a potential relationship is the more endurable choice.

In the view of many of abortion's opponents, the ethical remedy to an unwanted pregnancy is for a woman to carry the baby to term and either find a way to care for the baby or put it up for adoption. Both of these are honorable, even noble, solutions when they are chosen by a woman herself. But the moment either solution is coerced, by law or overbearing emotional pressure, troubling implications follow for both the woman and her relationship to the child. Consider, for example, a relational "worst-case scenario" in which continuing a pregnancy is forced on a woman. In a case described by Bordo, a man was granted an injunction against his girlfriend's abortion by a judge who ruled that "since the woman was not in school, was unemployed, and was living with her mother, 'the continuance of her pregnancy would not interfere with either her employment or education.'" The judge continued, "The appearance and demeanor of the respondent . . . indicated that she is a very pleasant young lady, slender in stature, healthy, and well able to carry a baby to delivery without an undue burden." What does it do to the development of one's relationship with a child to have it forced on one, not simply by biological fate, but by one's boyfriend and then by the law? It seems certain that the mother will feel robbed of her will and compromised in her ability to share parental responsibilities with the child's father. And what does it mean to a child to be born into a universe of such contention and the total absence of shared goals?

The likely result of such forced childbearing is misery for mother and child. This will appear even more morally urgent if one considers not just "the life of the unborn" but also the conditions that the "born" require to flourish. The judge in the case focused on the former and ignored the latter; by his lights, if the woman was "well able to carry a baby," why shouldn't she also be "well able" to devote her life to that child? For the potential mother, by contrast, her ability and desire to devote herself to caring for the child are absolutely central issues of ethical self-reflection. Caring for the child will require an enormous share of her emotional and practical resources; the relationship with her child will become central to who she is. A woman who rejects a pregnancy cannot be forced to find room in her soul to embrace it. And if there is a path of discovery that could allow a pregnant woman to transform her resistance into acceptance, only she herself can uncover and tread that path.

Only when we understand the centrality of a potential *relationship* to the abortion decision do we see that a woman's deliberations involve her prospects for caring for a child in the *context* of her responsibility to other people in her life, herself, and the wider community. When the abortion dilemma is framed solely in terms of the fetus's right to life, consideration of this responsibility drops out of the picture.

But the fetus's alleged right to life is completely inseparable from another human's commitment of enormous resources, time, and energy. Taking into account a mother's complex and sometimes conflicting orientation toward parenthood and care, we quickly leave the black-and-white world of anti-abortion certitude. We enter into the more ambiguous, complicated domain of what obligations a woman has to nurturing this potential child and supporting this potential relationship, in light of her other responsibilities and the incontrovertible reality that her resources for caring for others and herself are not limitless.

One of the many complexities women face in weighing decisions about pregnancy is that, even if legal coercion is not at issue, psychological pressure can exert an enormously powerful force. One college student sought therapy with me because she was still suffering from a traumatic experience of pregnancy and adoption two years earlier. When she became pregnant at seventeen, her devoutly Catholic parents never discussed it with her but silently assumed that she would live at home, carry the baby to term, and give it up for adoption. The young woman described her pain at seeing her biological daughter in the care of the adoptive mother. She felt the mother was well meaning, and the family provided all the signs and symbols of a good home, but in her eyes, the adoptive mother seemed somewhat superficial. The young woman was plagued by thoughts of how the adoptive mother wasn't doing things as she herself would have done.

Relinquishing a child in adoption can be extraordinarily painful in any circumstance. But this young woman's trauma was intensified by her lack of opportunity to talk honestly, sort out her feelings at the time, think them through, and come to a decision for herself. Likewise in cases of abortion, coercion complicates already difficult emotions. In any unintended pregnancy, there is no pain-free solution. But whatever confusion, regret, or grief a woman feels in making her own decision, a compulsory decision compounds these emotions and brutally transgresses her senses of self-determination and self-respect.

What Is Sacred?

One of the mysteries of abortion is that, while at times unspeakably sad, ending a pregnancy can also involve love. A woman can feel strongly that to have a child in a compromised situation, in which she is not prepared to devote her full attention and commitment, is not something she would want to do to someone she loved. This paradox is captured in Gwendolyn Brooks's poem entitled "the mother," which describes how abortion does not put an end to thinking about one's unborn children or imagining what their lives might have been and closes with the line "Believe me, I loved you all." By dint of their biology, women are charged with the knowledge that life involves ruthlessness, even sometimes toward those we love or those we could love. We bear children, and we are faced at times with terrible decisions about how to value a life—our own and the one growing within us. We rear children, and we become intimate with the psychological realities of relationships, including their pain and conflict and moral complexity. Recalling her illegal abortion in 1938, the activist Lana Phelan remembers, "I was lying on that gurney just sobbing my heart out, and I'll never forget that woman [her abortionist], she was wonderful. She came around, big black lady, she put her arms around me on the gurney, and she put her face down near mine, and she kind of put her cheek up next to mine. And she said, 'Honey, did you think it was so easy to be a woman?'"

The paradox that we can feel love for a potential life that we choose to end becomes suspect, even incoherent, if we believe that the fetus is a person just like ourselves. For if we regard the fetus as a full-fledged person entitled to rights, the notion of loving a potential life we choose to end becomes indistinguishable from the delusional or grim claim of the murderer to have loved her victim. The passionate disagreements between people about abortion appear to revolve around the rights of the fetus to life on the one hand, and the rights of the woman to self-determination on the other. But perhaps there is a way to think about these issues that does justice to our intuitions both about the sanctity of life and the dignity of the individual.

The philosopher Ronald Dworkin has argued that few people actually believe, even if they think they do, that fetuses have the right not to be killed and an interest in remaining alive. Most abortion conservatives, for example, permit some exceptions to their antiabortion stance, in cases such as rape or incest. Yet if a fetus had a right to life on par with already-born individuals, ending that life could never be justified on the basis of a crime of which the fetus itself was innocent. Instead, Dworkin suggests, the objection to abortion is grounded on something else: the belief that individual human life is sacred.

According to Dworkin, people with widely divergent views on abortion hold in common a belief in the sacredness or intrinsic value of a human life. We revere the "natural miracle" of "any human creature, including the most immature embryo, [as] a triumph of divine or evolutionary creation, which produces a complex, reasoning being from, as it were, nothing." Likewise, we honor the human creative investment, both "the processes of nation and community and language through which a human being will come to absorb and continue hundreds of generations of cultures" and "the process of internal personal creation and judgement by which a person will make and remake himself." The sacredness of human life lies in both natural creation—of the natural world, the species of the earth, our human bodies—and human creation, the human creative force that feeds art, culture, and human personality. In Dworkin's view, the difference between abortion conservatives and liberals often lies in the aspect of sacredness they deem most important. Abortion conservatives tend to rank the natural creative element above the human, though they acknowledge the latter's importance. Abortion liberals, while recognizing the value of the natural, tend to give greater weight to the human creative contribution. Different positions on abortion can thus be understood as lying along a continuum of the relative value people place on the natural and the human creative contributions to human life.

Any woman considering abortion who regards the embryo not as just a bunch of cells but as a biological wonder and a potential human being believes both the natural and the human forms of creation to be meaningful and worthy of reverence. For many women, it's the integration of natural and human creativity that is itself a sacred feature of bringing a child into the world. To require women to carry all pregnancies to term is to thwart their aspiration to this integration. If women do not have reproductive choice, they are frustrated in their ability to exercise their specifically human creativity. This is not because having and caring for children itself frustrates creative aspiration. Rather, it is because preventing women from making their own reproductive decisions curtails their choices with respect to their own human investments. Determining the meaning of having children for women, deciding for them when they will have children and when they will not, effectively takes the choice about how they will use their bodies and what work they will do out of their hands.

Women must obviously be in a position to decide for themselves how they will value the natural and human contributions represented by an unborn child. But their powerful sense of the connection between natural and human creation is exactly what makes an abortion decision so complicated and so painful. Women throughout history have experienced that connection in an immediate way because it is they who have both birthed and nurtured babies. "Conceiving children is not enough for the continuation of human life," writes Annie Leclerc. "It is also necessary to feed them, care for them, cajole them, talk to them; it is necessary to live them so that they live." The primal, psychological truth of relationships is that babies are conceived from sex, but unless they are nurtured and brought into the human community, they die. They need the passionate commitment of another human to become fully human. Women know that if they are able or willing to provide that nurturance, to commit huge amounts of their own energy, talents, time, and emotion, the fetus will indeed, under most circumstances, become a fully human child. That is part of the difficult context they confront.

That a woman needs to invest herself for the child to grow is treated as dispensable and all but morally weightless when the natural and the human contributions to life are cleanly separated and placed in a hierarchical relationship, with "nature's miracle"—conception—defined as the highest pinnacle. The moral clarity with which some argue the pro-life position depends on a perspective that treats women's investments of their humanity, their time, and their love as part of "nature's miracle," thereby effacing the reality that women actually have to work hard and undergo personal transformation on many levels to enable the flourishing of another human life. In this scheme, any intuition women might have about the value to a child's development of their own desire to mother is deemed completely irrelevant. Yet if our aspiration is to create humans in the highest sense, people who can love, reflect on the world, and bring understanding and compassion to their relationships with themselves and others, we should acknowledge and honor both the natural and the human aspects of creating a child and view their integration as itself sacred.

Pro-life Feminism and the Problem of Saintliness

There are those who fully endorse the sanctity of the connection of natural and human creativity but are passionately against abortion. "Pro-life feminism" has been one label used to refer to the view that a stand against abortion is a stand for respecting women. The position is exemplified by the pro-life feminist Sidney Callahan's statement "I can't see separating fetal liberation from women's liberation. Ultimately, I think the feminist movement made a serious mistake—politically, morally, and psychologically—by committing itself to a pro-choice stance, a stance which in effect pits women against their children."

Almost everyone can agree that as a society we devalue caring for children. We can also acknowledge that pro-choice rhetoric has by and large avoided dealing with the common intuition that conception and fetal life have a sacred dimension. We can even concede that a spiritual opportunity might be posed by an unplanned pregnancy or can admire women who are truly able to put the life of a potential baby on par with their own. This admiration is not far removed from how I feel about James McBride's mother in his memoir, *The Color of Water*, who overcomes the trauma of her early life and her own loss and depression and is able, through faith and love, to raise eight children. Similarly, we tend to regard as virtuous and even enlightened those people who adopt or foster troubled or disabled children, sometimes many of them.

Pro-life feminists legitimately question whether a permissive or even cavalier approach to abortion works to the detriment of women's interests. Their concern derives from a belief in the value of women's reproductive capacity and extends to a vision of society organized around recognition of that value. In that sense, their view converges with that of some ardently pro-choice feminists. Both consider what society might look like if women's concerns were given the same centrality and respect that men's have traditionally enjoyed. Both find fault with a society that condemns abortion but does little to make the health and welfare of children a primary goal.

However, I find it problematic when pro-life feminists argue backward from the sanctity (and the rights) of fetal life to a prescriptive, utopian view of women's reproductive lives. They don't always acknowledge that the key intermediate step must always be women's ultimate responsibility to make their own abortion decisions. We cannot go directly from an opposition to abortion to a certain vision—even if a freer, more respectful vision, according to its advocates—of women's lives. We can only proceed through a respect for women's personhood. It is not enough to insist that women will find their sense of greatest meaning and value in a society that opposes abortion; it is necessary to create a society where women are free to discover and assess the potential of that source of meaning for themselves.

Recognizing women's rights to self-determination entails accepting that society cannot compel saintliness. It is fundamentally unfair to oblige women to be Good Samaritans with respect to their pregnancies. Throughout history, women have often not been free to make and take responsibility for decisions about sexuality and motherhood, and it has been easy enough to create identities for them, to make them stand for good or evil. When we finally accept that women must be their own mediators of their conscience, we lose a fantasy about the purity of women and clarity about their rightful destiny. But we gain a fairer, more truthful, more complex view of each other.

9

Fathers

In 1903, my maternal grandmother's father was fatally shot in a barroom in Lawrence, Massachusetts. My grandmother Helen was four years old. Michael Moher, her father, was a twenty-six-year-old bartender and amateur boxer who had sailed from Ireland with his four brothers and two sisters eleven years before. As the Lawrence newspaper recounts it, an Italian patron, angered at not having his pail filled with more beer, later returned to the bar and shot my great-grandfather. From the front-page story, you can take in at a glance the ongoing tensions between the Irish and the Italians in the industrial mill town. It also conveys with astonishing intimacy the tragic human cost: "Mrs. Moher is a frail little woman and is almost prostrated by the blow. . . . 'Poor Mike,' she said, . . . 'did not count on so cowardly an attack. He could defend himself in a fair fight but to be shot in such a treacherous way; oh, it is awful, awful' and she burst into tears." She died three years later from what my grandmother would call "a broken heart," leaving her seven-year-old daughter and four-year-old son behind.

In 1935, my mother's father, Helen's husband, died of a bleeding ulcer. My mother was eighteen months old. She doesn't remember him. He worked for the American Tobacco Company. My mother and her brother speculated that smoking or drink may have led to his demise, but she never quite felt comfortable asking her mother to spell things out. The image of her father that she conjured up from her mother's stories was of an easy-tempered man and a good dancer who watched over her from heaven. Till the end of her life, my grandmother sprinkled her rose-tinted tales from the past with allusions to "your father" to my mother, or to us, "your grandfather," in her Boston accent.

My parents divorced in the late sixties, when I was in second grade. I was listening to Petula Clark's hit song "Downtown" when my father came into our living room, turned off the record player, and convened a family meeting. My mother had told us earlier in the day that we couldn't have friends over that evening because she and Daddy were going to have a talk with us. My siblings and I were nervous, giggly. We thought maybe they were having another baby. They told us they were getting divorced. Remembering that arc from eager expectation to world-altering sadness can still make me cry.

My personal twist on the cherished American idea of progress has had a lot to do with fathers. From quite a young age, I discerned a trajectory from my grandmother, who lost her father and mother, to my mother, who lost her father, to myself, who lost living with my mother and father together. Progress in my own life revolved around creating an intact family in which father and mother were both alive, present, and involved. This is the "better life for my children" that most preoccupied me as a young woman, my particular American Dream.

The legacy of these paternal losses has given me some insight into how fathers get "written out" of the psyches of women. The loss of the father (death, divorce, abandonment) can be passed down through the generations, with grief, confusion, and denial of need often filling the void. In my clinical experience, I far more commonly hear divorced mothers say "Why would the children have any need to see their father?" than hear divorced fathers voice that view of mothers. The critique of patriarchy, intended to dismantle injustices and restructure limiting gender norms, can inadvertently minimize the importance of flesh-and-blood fatherhood to the well-being of children. We pay a lot of attention to the irresponsibility of fathers, whether documenting deadbeat dads or the tenacious "second shift" burden on mothers, but there's comparatively little discussion of paternal desire and the journey to fatherhood that young men face.

My topic is mothers—their relationships to their children, themselves, and the wider culture. But in my work as a therapist, mostly to heterosexual couples of cisgender partners, I see some of the ways that mothers view fathers and how that affects the constellations of fathering and mothering we see today. How do the dynamics of maternal desire, lived on a cultural and personal level, influence women's understanding of the role of fathers in children's lives and the role of husbands in their own? And how do men's pathways to fatherhood in today's society affect how women themselves approach parenthood?

Men's Journey to Fatherhood

Julie, a twenty-eight-year-old artist, said to me in a therapy session, "It's so *easy* for men to say, 'Of course I want kids one day.' It doesn't cost them anything! They have years and years to wait, and when they're good and ready, it'll happen, with some woman who will rearrange her entire life in the process." Julie had recently gotten involved with a new partner, and when they had a "Do you want kids?" discussion, she felt keenly aware of how different it was for each of them to contemplate parenthood. "I feel so much more pressure on my identity than he does. I think, 'If I'm going to be a mother, I have to really *take this on.*' For him, it seems much more abstract."

My impression talking to young men is that Julie isn't off base. Nat, a twenty-seven-year-old neuroscience grad student, said, "My friends aren't ultramasculine at all, but we're definitely conditioned or encouraged to think that wanting to be a parent or spend time taking care of kids is akin to feminization. Maybe one day being a father will be the greatest experience ever. But on this side of it, no one is saying, 'I want to be a really highly engaged, attentive, present dad.' And being a stay-at-home father is definitely not a validating identity or an acceptable aspiration."

The gist of Julie and Nat's comments is carried forward when couples anticipate their first child. In the classes I teach to couples about how to stay connected as partners when the baby arrives, couples talk a lot about not wanting their closeness to be swallowed up by the role of parent. Yet, male and female partners express different concerns about the ways this parental absorption might affect their experiences of freedom and agency within the relationship. Prospective fathers rarely worry aloud about having too little time with the baby. They are much more tense about their partners' potential frustration with them for "not doing enough." Prospective mothers fear that their temporarily housebound status will subtly demote them in the power dynamics of the relationship. I sometimes feel that the couple is united in their shared minimization or misunderstanding of what's to come. For now, each is focused on how the baby will compromise their independence, equality, and shared couple interests.

When the baby arrives, I witness a repetitive bind in couples where one parent is more "work centered" and one is more "home centered." The parents at home feel physically and emotionally taxed, sometimes overwhelmed, and naturally desire their partners' help and support. Work-centered parents come home and are held to a standard of "fairness" on evening chores that feels insensitive to their stresses and responsibilities. Each parent acutely needs help and support, and both experience an empathy gap. The dynamic can play out in any couple with this role division; it comes up frequently as well in the same-sex couples I see in my practice. But in heterosexual couples, it can turn into a politicized battleground about the respect accorded to "male" and "female" roles.

Jacob, thirty-three, was a new father. He and his wife, Tina, came to see me when their daughter, Louisa, was six months old. Jacob had grown up with a single mother. He'd met his father twice. He worked as a lawyer, had a bully for a boss, and was working long hours while his wife was on maternity leave. He had a loving relationship with his wife, but he seemed to accept without question that his role as a husband was to deliver on what she expected. One day he became visibly upset. "It's almost as if Tina expects me to be two places at once. She's mad that I haven't done the dishes, but I'm actually at work." Tina loved being home with Louisa, but was touchy about being seen by Jacob as "the maid." He felt he was in a bind. To prove he respected her role, he had to commit to doing things that he couldn't possibly be home to do.

In my clinical experience, Jacob's story is not all that unusual. He never lived with his father or with two adults in a healthy relationship with each other. He comes to marriage and parenthood with a fervent wish to do things right and an anxious sense that being a good husband means putting his wife's needs first. It makes it hard for him to hear his inner voice and reflect on what he himself wants. Between performing at work and responding to his wife's need for help, he hasn't a lot of room to discover his own feelings or articulate his own vision of fairness.

A friend said to me once, "Men take ten years to become fathers." I don't know if the interval was precise, but he was trying to capture that becoming a father is a process, usually a more-or-less private one, that involves development, experience, and time. Your average man is not socialized to analyze feelings with his friends or to give voice to the doubts and dilemmas that women routinely discuss regarding relationships, including motherhood. In this respect, men are "behind" women on the path to parenthood. Certainly women can feel burdened or offended by the expectation, internal or external, that their lives or concerns are focused on children (as a prominent female academic sniffed to me, "Of course my children aren't at the center of my life!"). And women do not necessarily gravitate toward feelings-oriented self-investigation of relationships and parenting identity. But as the world of mother blogs confirms, many women do bond and find community in the discussion of children, emotions, and relationships.

This asymmetry in the way men and women conceive of parenthood, as well as the fact that desiring parenthood is "feminized" in some young men's minds, relates to the lack of cultural space men have for exploring their own journey into fatherhood. The stardom of Jordan Peterson, the Canadian professor and clinical-psychologist-turned-You-Tube-phenomenon, has been traced to his role as "virtual father" to a generation of lost young men. Part of Peterson's appeal is that he talks about gender differences in a way that feels viscerally true to many people. Regarding parenthood, for instance, he insists that a man's path to fatherhood, even the nature of being a father, is fundamentally different from a woman's path to motherhood and the nature of being a mother. In Peterson's view, both are needed and valuable, and neither is "better" or "worse" than the other, but qualitative differences exist between the two. In his writing, these differences structure and delimit the possibilities and responsibilities of both parental roles in the home.

One of Peterson's structuring differences between motherhood and fatherhood derives from his argument that real, adult men must remain steely in the face of the whims of their children: as he writes, "If a father disciplines his son properly, he obviously interferes with his freedom [and] if the father does not take such action, he merely lets his son remain Peter Pan, the eternal Boy, King of the Lost Boys, Ruler of the non-existent Neverland. That is not a morally acceptable alternative." Peterson in turn instructs the maturing son to establish an oppositional stance against the matured father, creating an ostensibly generative, though disciplinary, relationship that stimulates growth. Peterson enjoins sons, "Become your own person. By rejecting your father's vision, you develop your own. And then, as your parents age, you've become adult enough to be there for them, when they come to need you." Without recourse to psychological reasoning or empirical evidence, Peterson imagines the adversarial father-son stance is shed like an exoskeleton simply by dint of the son's maturation and arrival into an undefined realm of adulthood. There's little guidance or reasoning about how a nurturant, flexible paternal identity might develop, one that embodies the melding of warmth and firmness that is the hallmark of *all* healthy parent-child relationships. In fact, Peterson emphasizes that the paternal role is to toughen up children once they are no longer infants, taking a fairly dim view of men's potential to contribute or bond in the first years of life (his business partner "spent a lot of his time taking care of his kids when they were little. . . . He's a pretty masculine guy, and it was hard on him, man, like it just about killed him").

Peterson's views may hearken back to an imagined era before gender-equality movements began to destabilize traditional parental roles, but it's unclear just how far back in the past his model for parenthood reaches. Even in the benighted, "sexist" 1940s, Dr. Seuss offered a more nurturant view of fatherhood in his children's book *Horton Hatches the Egg*. In that tale, Horton the elephant is recruited to sit on the egg of a mother bird longing for a tropical vacation. The sincere Horton agrees, and he endures storms, drought, and hunters' attempts on his life to fulfill his commitment. Meanwhile, we see the mother bird sunning herself, blissfully forgetful of those she left behind. As the egg is about to hatch, she swoops back into the picture and tries to take possession of her baby. But when the bird hatches, it is a baby elephant with wings. Horton becomes a parent by faithfully caring for the baby bird.

Men's journey to fatherhood is complicated by misunderstandings and stereotypes about the character of paternal love, some of which receive support in Peterson's "tough love" model. Fatherly love is not only protective and providing—a love from a disciplinary remove—it is also tenderly nurturing and intensely felt, a love from "close in." Fathers' love for their children remains a glaringly underdeveloped narrative, and pursuing a deeper understanding of this aspect of parenting is a crucial task for couples seeking to make productive life adjustments and grow together when raising a child.

Letting Men In

The author Emma Brockes chronicles her choice to have twins as a single parent, and among the benefits she notes, "In lots of ways it's easier than the alternative. You make decisions more quickly. (There is nothing more satisfying to single parents than watching a couple with a baby try to arrive at a decision: 'Should we take his temperature? What do you think?' 'No, what do *you* think?')." As a couples therapist, I'd be the last person to minimize the discomfort of couple negotiation or the sentiment of many mothers (and fathers) that "it's easier to do it myself." But when children observe two adults who care about them talking to each other, listening to each other, and meshing their points of view, they internalize a useful model of close relationships. Virtually all partnered adults attempting to achieve a coparenting alliance struggle to hold on to their individuality, and most have been known to curse the need for compromise. Still, children benefit from having parents who desire a relationship with each other and can disagree, even if a bit loudly and messily, and then come together on their behalf.

In other words, both parents are important to children in their own right, but also in their relation to each other. In development, a baby moves from her early intense relationship with a caregiver to an enlarged circle of relationships with other people, ideally one of whom loves the primary caregiver as well. A child finds her place in the family partly by wrestling with a basic limit with which all humans must contend, the boundary between the generations. A child comes to recognize that no matter how much she loves her two parents, she will never be either's mate; she will always be their child, and they will have a special relationship to each other from which she is excluded. This is a painful but necessary psychological reckoning. Accepting generational limits is part of the difficult but necessary acceptance of the reality of the "outside world"—the reality that other people have relationships to each other that you cannot control and to which you must adapt. The triad itself is more central than the sex of the parents. A nonheteronormative couple equally provides an opportunity for children to observe and accept their place within a family in which two adults have a relationship with each other. Contra Peterson, this function is not solely performed by the disciplinarian father.

Once they become mothers, women sometimes find it hard to include their male partners fully. An occasional topic of discussion among new mothers is that while their husbands feel they've lost their relationship with their wives, the new mothers feel burdened by their husbands' need for attention. Social scientists have observed that historically, mothers have had a stronger tendency to turn to their children to gratify emotional needs for intimacy, warmth, and pleasure, whereas men have sought to gratify these same needs primarily in their relationships with women. (Clearly the model was based on heterosexual couples.) They argue that this asymmetry was based on the social fact that both male and female children are predominantly cared for by women.

The solution to this asymmetry, second-wave feminist theorists argued, was to be found in equalizing men's and women's caregiving roles. To a striking extent, we're moving in that direction. Dads today nurture children in many of the same ways moms do. Men with newborns strapped to their chests are a completely normal sight; fifty years ago it would have been as "emasculating" as a man putting on an apron. The website Fatherly.com "empowers men to become better parents so they can raise great kids and lead more fulfilling adult lives," and many of the articles are indistinguishable from what you would find on a parenting website aimed at mothers ("How to Avoid Dangerous Bath Habits," "How to Comfort a Child After Mom or Dad Gets Angry"). The Good Men Project website offers an ongoing critique of biases against stay-at-home dads, standards of financial success that leave many fathers feeling like failures, and the "Man-Box," which creates pressure to be the "ideal man" and punishes anyone who deviates from that norm. In my clinical work, I've seen that fathers are as passionate about being good parents as mothers are. The main reason given by both men and women for not wanting to dismantle a difficult marriage is that neither can bear living with their children half of the time.

Yet, women's psychological barriers to including men fully in family life are complex, having to do with their relationship with motherhood, their partners, and their own parents. If a woman feels her partner ignores or devalues or finds her maternal investment threatening, she can have the disillusioning experience of feeling she is not really known, or loved, or that she has less in common with her partner than she thought she did. That moment of alienation might tempt her to cede her terrain and join him on his: "Okay, if you don't get what's so important and precious about caring for the kids, let's compete over who needs to spend more time at work." New mothers also have to be careful not to fall into the expectation that men will be transformed in just the same ways they themselves are. They are sometimes prone to seeing fathers as mothers manqué, becoming exasperated when fathers fail to act like mothers. As a result, the potential for breaking ground on new, fulfilling models of selfhood—of both people actualizing themselves as parents and parenting spouses—remains underexplored. A shared transformation of parenthood is not about dissolving difference; it involves, instead, a heightened attention to the experience of each individual.

Ideally, principles of gender equality should help us articulate to ourselves and our partners what we aspire for in our familial and domestic routines and practices, including how we envision a fulfilling distribution of responsibilities, physical contributions, and emotional work. And they should also help us to critique notions of masculinity that tend to gather excessively around competition, status, and sexuality.

This critique should help us to say to our next generation of young, prospective fathers, "Open yourself to the changes of parenthood. Be receptive to the transformation of becoming a parent."

Father as Caregiver versus Father as Provider

One evening when my kids were young, some friends and I were out to dinner, intently discussing a career choice that needed to be made by one of the women's husbands by the next day. As the wife laid it out, one job was close to home, required only a year's commitment, was low pressure, and was relatively low paying. The other job required a forty-five-minute commute and a five-year contract, and it offered higher prestige, higher pay, and various seductive perks. The jobs were equally interesting. "The first job has everything we've been saying we're looking for," she said. "He'll have more time for the kids, we'll live at a slower pace. It's a step toward a more spiritual life. But then every time he says he's leaning toward that job, I think, 'Wait a minute, what about saving for retirement, what about our mortgage, what about our standard of living?' I feel like a total hypocrite."

No one at that table felt completely innocent; we all recognized the basic contradiction. It is easy to believe that partners should share childcare equally or that men should not be immersed in the rat race. Easy to believe, that is, until the moment when the plan might actually go into effect. Each of the mothers at the table worked at a job that meant a lot to her: one was a teacher, one was a data analyst, and two were therapists. Each was married to a man who worked longer hours and made more money than she did. Two of the women's husbands were unhappy in their current jobs, but none of the four husbands resented shouldering a larger share of the family's financial burdens, and only one was actively lobbying to be home with the children more.

In therapy it is not uncommon to hear a woman patient, while considering the good and bad points of a new love interest, wonder aloud at his ability to support her if they have children, even if she herself has an advanced degree and a highly paid job. Her concern can be understood as a rational calculation of whether she will sustain a demotion in living standards or class status if she takes time off to raise children. But it also relates psychologically to her notions about masculinity and femininity, her own maternal goals, and the meaning she associates with being provided for.

Even if men and women endorse gender equality in principle, they often have powerful preconceptions about how providing links up with being a successful man or woman. A sobering sociological finding is that men's unemployment or underemployment is one of the major risk factors for divorce. Marriage ideally provides more than what you could get in the strict exchange economy of the marketplace, but most of us know people whose marriages follow the "cost center" model. Insisting that both members of the couple pull their own economic weight at all times is a buffer against unfairness, but it also constricts the aspirational opportunities that can be furthered by marriage. One spouse's desire to go back to school or change careers must not cost the family time or money; another spouse can take an extended parental leave only if it doesn't decrease his or her contribution to the family pot. A common and thoroughly straitjacketing example is that a mother's salary must offset all childcare expenses for her job to be "worth it." All these arrangements come at a price to flexibility, closeness, and trust.

In long-term relationships, a sense of justice is closely tied to love. If one or the other person does not feel treated fairly, it corrodes the bond. If they insist on literal dollar-and-cents equity in all things, the feeling of generosity can be diminished, which can also be destructive. Before we have children, we can fairly easily evaluate fairness in our partnerships: if he is cooking, I am doing the dishes; if I am working more, he is cleaning the house. But when children arrive, the calculus of fairness becomes more complicated. Parents often fill different roles, and they also often have different feelings about those roles. Many of the mothers I see as a therapist feel more conflicted than the fathers I see in their dual roles of provider and hands-on parent. Fathers feel less guilt ridden going to work on Monday morning than mothers, but fathers also feel less entitled to cut back on work in order to care for children.

On a practical level, how can we handle these differences? Most obviously, it must be worked through on a personal level, one couple at a time. But a central component of success is what the sociologist Arlie Hochschild characterizes as "the economy of gratitude" in intimate partnerships. A couple's satisfaction with their division of labor is deeply tied to what counts as "a gift" in their relationship. "When couples struggle," Hochschild writes, "it is seldom simply over who does what. Far more often, it is over the giving and receiving of gratitude." When my husband and I were parents of babies and young children, our division of labor worked in part because we each felt we were giving and receiving a "gift." Between us, caring for the children was a good to be prized, and because of that we both agreed that my husband's paid work was a gift to me. He, in turn, felt that my desire and willingness to care for the children was a gift to him and to the family.

Certainly it was not all sweetness and light. At times we each felt exhausted, put-upon, overworked, ungratified, and generally underappreciated. I felt inhibited in my right to complain since we had tacitly agreed that, all told, I had the better deal. In my gloomier moments, I would wonder whether looking like a slob, spending my days in a messy house with no hope of cleaning it up, and finishing washing the dishes from one meal only to start in on the next *did* constitute the better deal. I would darkly imagine my husband's pleasure at dressing for work, strolling down the street for a solitary cup of coffee during a break, and greeting friends and colleagues at various professional meetings.

I was most often restored at those times by a good night's sleep. But perhaps just as powerful, acting as a subterranean stream to refresh and replenish me, was the value my husband placed on what I was doing and, significantly, his interest in doing the very things I was doing. He was hungry to hear what the kids had done all day and couldn't wait to get down on the floor and play with LEGOs or read *Harry Potter* to them. He was not a man who "couldn't possibly imagine" spending his time taking care of the children, or who "wondered what I did all day." In our family culture, my job had all the value, all the "prestige" that his did, maybe a bit more. I felt appreciated, and just as importantly, I felt understood. Likewise, he felt my gratitude for his work role and was glad to do what he did, even if at times he felt more distant from home life than he would have liked.

In their study of marriage and the transition to parenthood, psychologists wonder why some couples deal with the arrival of a baby so smoothly and others suffer so acutely. They find that the transition goes better when the father joins the mother in undergoing a transformation, when he consents to share the world of parenting and she allows him in. When that sharing doesn't happen, some common problems get in the way. The general level of stress and depletion that naturally attends the arrival of a baby, not to mention the raising of children, makes it hard for couples to consistently "grease the wheels" of their relationship with expressions of affection and gratitude. More deeply, some couples find it hard to move from a twosome to a threesome. One therapy patient became infuriated when her husband didn't "get with the program" of weekend plans she made for family activities. She only gradually acknowledged her own problems sharing parenthood with him. She could only see life in terms of "my way" or "his way," rather than "our way." She also tended to seeing him as a "source" that provided for the family, rather than as a person who suffered with his own stresses, deprivations, and conflicts.

Divorce: Economic Equality, Caregiving Equality

One way of exposing and reevaluating our ingrained, gendered biases about parental roles is to examine legal and cultural discourses of divorce. Laws regarding the equitable distribution of property, spousal support, and child support after divorce have been on the books for decades, though problems still abound. Historically, the economic asymmetries have been documented, wherein women are disadvantaged by divorce settlements that treat the money earned by the family's major breadwinner, most often the father, as legitimately "his." Comparatively little attention has been paid to the emotional asymmetries between parents, and the marginalization of fathers in caregiving, after the divorce is finalized.

This marginalization, and the sense of disaffection it can fuel, plays its own role in the characteristic American patterns of family dissolution. When a marriage is intact, each partner benefits from the other's services. The breadwinner gains from the caregiver's care of their children, and the caregiver gains from the breadwinner's work. Ideally, each experiences some vicarious satisfaction from the other's efforts. In a divorce, however, what was once perceived as working for the good of the family is now perceived as a source of inequality. The economic inequality derives from the primary caregiver's relinquishment of paid work. The emotional inequality derives from the primary breadwinner's relinquishment of caring for the children. No one can do everything, and in a satisfactory marriage each partner is usually willing to sacrifice something for the sake of the whole. But divorce often exhausts that goodwill, and the systems of cooperation and compromise degrade into accusations of unfairness and inequality.

The high incidence of divorce has generated much discussion about the need for women to stay competitive in the workforce and well employed throughout marriage to buffer the potentially devastating financial effects of marital dissolution. But we hear comparatively little discussion of men's need to "stay competitive" in caregiving, to remain intensively involved in parenting to guard against being marginalized in their children's lives. Given the value we place on economic clout and the relatively demeaned status of caregiving, this lack is not particularly surprising. But it also reflects and maintains a bias, apparently shared by women and men alike, that men's involvement in fatherhood need not be actively pursued or carefully protected.

Many reasons might be offered for the virtues of a division of labor in families. Some may argue, for instance, that maternal care is preferable when children are very young because they are more dependent on the mother, or because the father can earn more in the workplace. But we should acknowledge how closely intertwined and mutually reinforcing these conditions are, and also what fathers risk losing out on as a result of this emotional situation. Research by the sociologist Lillian Rubin in the 1970s observed that mothers were often quite relieved, even happy, when their children left for college, whereas fathers tended to take it much harder. As she understood it, fathers were more pained because they felt they had never really "lived" their children's childhoods. In the decades since Rubin's research, social norms have raised the standard for how involved fathers should be with their children. A father today is in a much better position to feel and articulate his desire to care for his children than previous generations of fathers were. But with socially defined parental roles still favoring men as "ideal workers" (in Joan Williams's phrase) and women as caregivers, some aspects of the situation Rubin described remain in place. Fathers spend more time with their children than in the past, but over 60 percent feel they spend too little time with their kids and less than half feel they are doing "a very good job" raising them.

Fathers sometimes actively collude in their own marginalization. Postdivorce, their fear of not doing "a very good job" may be justified if they suddenly revel in their freedom from the "drudgery of everyday life," take up with new partners, have kids with new partners, and leave the heavy lifting of parenting to the ex-wife. But even within an intact family, fathers can become overly identified with their work, detached from relationships in general, fearful of entering the demeaned female arena of caregiving, or complacent about their partners' taking care of the family. Social and workplace norms constrict fathers' participation in family life, influencing the construction of masculine identity by conveying that successful manhood involves being a provider. Men often do not consciously think through these pressures, but they unconsciously enact them.

However, that men sometimes seem to "choose" their marginalization neither relieves us of the need to consider the effect of the caregiving inequality on men's involvement in family life, nor does it absolve us of the need to understand better the assumptions that underlie it. Both men's and women's thinking about this issue is affected, for example, by the pervasive assumption that children need mothers more than fathers. A colleague of mine, a child psychologist who conducts mediation in high-friction custody cases, says she notices a consistent gender breakdown in which mothers say, "My children need me," whereas fathers usually say that they "want" to be with their children (until they remember the coaching that their attorney has given them and assert that it is "good for" the children to be with them). It is significant that mothers often do genuinely experience their children as needing them more and themselves as needing their children more. Do fathers actually feel their children need them less? Do they feel they need their children less? Or has ideology shaped feeling, such that fathers have a hard time claiming that children need them as much as children need their mothers?

Answering these questions in an honest and probing fashion is crucial for parents in thriving marriages and dissolving ones. "In mediation," a colleague told me, "I far too often hear the mother in the divorcing couple insist that children are upset because they aren't spending enough time with her. Her solution to every problem is 'they need more time with me.' My thought is usually, we need to figure out a way to get them away from you more so that they don't have to take care of you." Perhaps such mothers have insight into their children's needs; after all, they've made a "profession" out of caring for kids. But women strongly identify with the role of mother for many complex reasons, and not all of them are necessarily of benefit to the children when it comes to divorce. Similarly, fathers identify with the breadwinning role for many reasons, but divorce is a particularly important time for those reasons to be recalibrated and for fathers to invest emotionally in their children's lives, both for their children's sake and their own.

Fairness and Generosity

Given all I've said about the benefits of sharing parenthood and the need to include fathers, a question emerges: Is it sexist for a woman to feel she should be the primary caregiver for her baby or child? In answering that question, we must recognize, first, that for many women, this feeling is based on an authentic, powerful, passionate wish. Such women are obliged to be aware of that wish; to do what they can to make certain, in the terms of Buddhist teacher Jack Kornfield, that "their path is connected to their heart." The error is then to insist that this feeling is based on an essential truth that dictates what should happen. Maternal desire should not be a platform from which to make a power bid or a decree about how things should be arranged. Recognizing maternal desire should work as a springboard, a starting point for uncovering, sorting, and communicating about how we want to live our lives. A father or prospective father needs to go through a similar process.

This requires doing what scares many people about role division in parenting: namely, having a conversation. Not simply about logistics, but also about feelings, doubts, and uncertainties about one's feelings. Voicing fears and hopes is hard not only because traditions run deep and because parenthood is hard to anticipate, but also because decisions about how to raise our children relate so centrally to our identities and what we each want from life. Some women get the message that they are weak or irresponsible to miss a beat or to want to miss a beat when children come along. Others are disappointed when their husbands expect them to stay home. Whatever the issues for a given couple, in parenthood unconscious, "default" frameworks can hold enormous sway without our full critical awareness. Consciously considering these frameworks can frighten and disorient, and even upend, basic assumptions about the relationship.

Fearing adjustments and knowing so little about what to expect, couples can temporarily delude themselves that they will return to "normal" soon after the baby is born. Yet, destabilizing as it can be, expecting a child is also a time of hopefulness, possibility, and transformation. If love is "the will to extend one's self for the purpose of nurturing one's own or another's spiritual growth," new parenthood presents an opportunity to engage in an infant's growth alongside one's own and one's partner's.

To take one example of a couple who pursued this opportunity productively, I worked with a husband and wife who were both researchers in the same field. When they had a baby, they were committed both to sharing the care of their child and continuing to pursue their work at a similar level. When the baby was five months old, the mother was invited to a conference in another city. She was still nursing, and she assumed, without really thinking, that she would take the baby with her. Her husband initiated a conversation about this arrangement. They had decided to share the baby's care. If that was what they intended to do, he felt their baby should stay home with him, where he was available to care for her in familiar surroundings with no disruption to her routine. This took an adjustment for the mother, but on balance she agreed. It was fairer; it did not deeply or lastingly impinge on the basic structure of her relationship with her baby. She would still nurse, though perhaps not quite as often, when she got back. She would be strengthened in her sense of her husband's parental competence and in their sense of shared enterprise.

The couple therapist Daniel Wile has pointed out that couples having arguments sometimes "employ powerful, irrefutable, culturally sanctioned complaints to try to get across points they are having difficulty getting across." People are tempted to use slogans (her: "You never help with housework"; him: "You're a nag") to justify feelings that they don't quite understand. The heart of a couple relationship, in Wile's view, is "saying what you need to say and feeling that it has gotten across." In this sense, we can see that many of the standard, genderized arguments between men and women—including about parenting—are a way not to know, or not to risk expressing, our greatest vulnerabilities. If the woman in this couple had insisted on bringing the baby on her professional trip, it might have both enacted and obscured her fear that if she shared care with the father, she would feel less close to her baby or she would feel worse about herself as a mother. Being able to talk about the underlying issues provided the couple their best chance to feel close and connected.

At a time—early parenthood—when gender roles are both conservative and contested, it can be hard to rouse oneself from the fatigue, the petty resentments, and the stress of childcare to articulate what one really needs and wants. Yet during this time, couples also yearn for appreciation of the gifts they are giving each other. We live at a cultural moment when women feel conflicted about how involved we want to be in the care of our children and about the role of men in the same. In some ways the two are connected. Women feel conflicting things, and so we give complex messages. We can feel exasperated and unsupported and lonely when men are not our full parenting partners, but we may implicitly demand that men provide for us or acknowledge our parental primacy. For women in heterosexual partnerships dealing honestly with the competing impulses we feel and the messages we send can foster more fair and equal parenting participation. One step in this direction is to try to understand and communicate the place maternal desire occupies in our minds and hearts. That process is not about defining our desire in contrast to that of men, but rather about speaking from the heart about our desire in true conversation with them.

10

Time with Children

When our third child was born, it was June. He was a big baby, but he was my first easy birth. He was heavy, and for weeks I'd felt as if he might simply drop out of me. I fretted over the countless possible circumstances of his coming, about where I might be when it started, and with whom, since our second child had come eight minutes after we arrived at the hospital and could well have been born in the car. But in the end, there was no rush. The baby remained securely settled till his due date. I was four centimeters dilated, and had been for days, when we decided to break my water. The grandparents had long since arrived, and my husband was able to leave work unhurriedly. So, at noon on a cloudless spring day, he and I found ourselves driving to the hospital, nervous and almost shy to be alone again with this rite of passage before us, knowing that no words could make a bridge between this luminous, ordinary moment and the fruition, so near at hand, of the deep bloody marriage of our bodies.

That summer, I was happier than I had ever been in my life. I felt calmly ecstatic, in a place of lively rest. Was this the peace that came of having endured the anxieties and strains and excitements of my fertility and having arrived safely at the other side? I remembered my giddy freedom from the first days of pregnancy; now I felt light and heavy in my body at the same time, akin to the repose of sated passion. Yet I felt less drowsy, more alert. I felt at ease with the universe. We were content with each other; we'd done well.

During the first days of my son's life, while relatives were still there to entertain the older children, I read *The Leopard* while I nursed. It is a book of exquisite melancholy, the story of a magnetic Sicilian prince whose waning years coincide with the twilight of southern Italy's monarchic rule. Tomasi di Lampedusa wrote his novel in the last two years of his life, and his descriptions of the parched, unforgiving earth, of the nonchalant cruelties that pass for love, of the prince's last wisps of consciousness, are the product of a mind on intimate terms with life and death. On a still morning when everyone else went down to the park, I sat alone with the baby, listening to his newborn breaths as he slept on my lap and, later, to his hungry suckling sounds. I could hear the cooing of the mourning dove perched on the telephone wire above the street and the crows' cawing farther down the hill. Out the window were drooping sunlit spiderwebs the children would later inspect and destroy, and butterflies, whose darting, bright lives are measured in days. I could not have been more full; life could not have been more sweet. Yet there was also that ache at "the rustling of the grains of sand as they slid lightly away" and at my baby's sleeping breath; that ache of beauty and longing and time and the unbearable fragility and surpassing preciousness of this moment.

Perhaps because I felt such fullness, I could bear to gaze at the naked contours of my yearning. This yearning had no object, at least no visible, earthly one. I have heard it called "the nostalgia for the present." There is the well-known biblical passage from 1 Corinthians 13:12: "For now we see through a glass, darkly; but then face to face: now I know in part; but then shall I know even as also I am known." For me, it captures the expectant yearning, the urge to see behind the veil, that seems to be part of the very fabric of love. When we love, we are never spent, there is always more. Love seems to encompass a feeling of seeking but of never quite reaching. Its yearning is like a question with no final answer; to love life, to love other people, it seems, is to tenderly embrace that mystery.

SEVERAL THINGS MADE the time with my children over that summer and the year that followed so happy. For one, I was able to give myself over to it. For the time being, while we had an infant and two small children, we could afford to live on one salary. As a psychologist, my interests also lay in the same direction as parenthood. I felt grounded and constructive when responding to the children's needs and desires, in the countless acts of diapering, feeding, filling cups, fastening shoes, comforting, and answering questions. One source of pleasure was doing different things while in one another's company. I liked reading a book while I was nursing the baby, the five-year-old was drawing in another room, and the two-year-old was pretending to be Prince Phillip from *Sleeping Beauty* falling off his horse or building with blocks somewhere near my feet. I felt integrated in those moments—physically engaged with the baby, intellectually engaged with my book, emotionally engaged with my son and daughter, in harmony with them and with myself.

As sleep deprivation finally receded and professional engagement returned, I felt increasingly compelled to focus my intellectual effort on understanding the most central thing in my life, taking care of children. I began to write about it, which helped me productively handle the feeling of being pulled in different directions by my children and my work. My particular solution to the dilemma of children and work is obviously not available, or attractive, to everyone. But the basic issues it was intended to address in my own life are central to many mothers' lives. Mothers everywhere want more freedom to be responsive to their children; they want the enormous importance of their nurturing to be acknowledged; and they suffer when they are unable to put together an arrangement that satisfies both their economic and psychological need for employment and their children's need for them.

Women thinkers of previous generations, blessed like me with education and opportunity, cogently anatomized the oppressions mothers face. Adrienne Rich trained the force of her analysis on the transformative potential of motherhood and its corruption by patriarchal culture. My own experience drew me to charting the pleasures of caring for babies and small children and what it could mean for mothers' identity. Certainly the realm of maternal pleasure is much wider than that; some mothers find their keenest delight in conversation with their older children, and others express their maternal gifts in spheres wholly other than familial. But in attempting to analyze my desire to care for my small children, and to place that desire in the broader context of women's aspirations and our social life, it occurred to me that the radical promise of exploring maternal pleasure had remained unfulfilled.

De Beauvoir asked, all those years ago, "What is a woman?" and her answer reverberated in every subsequent treatment of motherhood. "One is not born, but rather becomes a woman," she writes, meaning that the defining characteristic of the social category "woman" is not her reproductive system, but her status as "a person who is not expected to set her own agenda in the world." Ever since, it has been hard to rescue women's proclivity toward taking care of others from the taint of inauthenticity. It has been hard, in other words, to see our desire and choice to care for children as a way we legitimately set our own agenda in the world.

It may once have been true that the price of a woman's social acceptance was that she leave her ambitious, striving self outside the door. But today, she is as likely to be urged to leave outside, or at least politely hide, her intensely emotional concern about caring for her children. Virtually every area of our reproductive and caregiving lives is distorted by the fear that if we prioritize the importance of having and caring for children, we risk losing our opportunities, our freedom, and even our dignity as persons. Over the years, feminist writing has cast a skeptical eye on the meaning to mothers themselves of taking care of children. Psychoanalytic writing has at times implied that caring for children and desire have little to do with each other. Debates about day care warily step around the complicated fact that for many women caring for their children is a way to connect both to their kids and to themselves. An array of psychological and social forces contribute to women's confusion and ambivalence about their desire to mother, which in turn render their attitudes toward fertility and the specter of infertility particularly charged. Maternal desire is all but absent from the arguments on either side of the abortion rights issue, regarded as irrelevant or politically dangerous. And with respect to the role of fathers, our efforts to share parenting more equally are impeded not only by structures of work and entrenched gender norms, but also by the conflicting feelings mothers have, and the mixed messages they send, about the meaning they attach to caring for children.

The project of understanding maternal desire has only just begun. For so long, *maternal* and *desire* seemed contradictory; in conjoining them, though, we can begin to develop a psychological language for the autonomous goals and creative intentions that women have expressed in mothering all along. We may disagree on many questions confronting women, but we can all endorse the fundamental value of women's ability to interpret their own desires and become authors of their own lives. Giving maternal desire the centrality in our thinking that it has in our experience can only help us toward that goal.

I HAVE BEEN SPEAKING throughout about time with children. And I have been speaking of how parental availability to children can facilitate a richer quality of time together. But this is precisely the kind of time that many parents lack. A friend commented that she realized she and her husband fought less about money than about time. "Time-saving techniques" are a parenting-website staple. Surveys document that not having enough time for children ranks highly as a primary source of parental dissatisfaction. Plenty of reasons for this dearth of time are obvious: high costs of living, economic insecurity, longer commutes, our 24-7 internet-connected work and social lives, and the reduction of public support structures, such as pensions or school lunches, that somewhat alleviated sources of the larger time crunch.

Yet, researchers also call into question the widely held perception of our "time famine," observing that workloads have held steady for the last fifty years and, if anything, have decreased. In general, leisure time is up. In a study of eleven Western countries, the average mother spent almost twice as much time caring for children in 2012 as she did in 1965 (104 vs. 54 minutes per day), and fathers' time with children increased almost fourfold over the same period (59 vs. 16 minutes per day). The research and survey data suggest that time scarcity is less an objective reality than a psychological perception. What is fueling our subjective sense of being temporally squeezed?

Considering the nature of child-rearing and mothering might provide one answer. A British study found that women are more likely to feel "always rushed" than men. Time spent in unpaid work (such as childcare) is linked both to greater fragmentation in daily tasks and greater frequency of multitasking. Switching between activities, which mothers who perform both paid work and childcare frequently need to do, is a major factor in the subjective perception of being rushed. In response, we try to increase the "yield" of our time by pursuing strategies of "time deepening": trying to fit more into a given unit of time by speeding up an activity, choosing activities that can be done quickly, or doing more than one activity at once. Time deepening also underlies the notion of familial "quality time," a concept that foregrounds our pretensions toward accomplishing "efficiently" the parent-child closeness and engagement we might more effectively achieve through leisurely companionship. People have become understandably skeptical of the notion of quality time in recent years because they sense that the degree to which people, especially children, feel cared for in relationships is strongly influenced by their loved one's actual presence.

Our imperfect perception of how much free time we actually have also reflects that it is often available only in fragments that are easily frittered away without a second thought. Instead of using fifteen minutes here or there to have a conversation or play with a child, people end up looking at their phones. Indeed, when you have children, phones present a special challenge. You may find yourself pleasantly "alone together" with your child, harmlessly checking Instagram while your little one is doing a puzzle. Then, before you know it, you're absorbed in a work email thread and ignoring your child's bids for attention or irritably stalling her pleas for lunch. As kids grow into later childhood and adolescence, the smartphone can be a marvelous tool of communication, perfectly adapted to young people who have no interest in telephone conversations, never respond to voice mail, and try to minimize parental interference. Later still, parents may find themselves tsk-tsked by their adult children (as I have been) for being "addicted" to their phones. But when children are little, they need a "serve-and-return" style of conversation. The obsessive lure of the phone and of other technologies of absorption and distraction makes it hard to give oneself over to the sustained engagement that children want and need to grow.

Some of our tendencies when thinking about time and how much of it we truly have at our disposal also relate to the age-old dichotomy of "having" as opposed to "being." The having orientation is so basic to how we as a culture think about time, money, things, and ourselves that we hardly notice we are inhabiting it. In the having mode, we define ourselves through our property, including our possessions, our bodies, our egos, our relationships, our feelings, and our problems. We consume material goods, as well as information, educational material, and new experiences. Our economic system operates in part by capitalizing upon the enormous power and self-regenerating nature of human craving. It encourages this voracious appetite for accumulating things through its endless creation of imaginative new ways to incite and satisfy it.

In contrast to the having mode, when we are oriented to "being," our agenda is to be "at one with." We are concerned not so much with possessing things as with participating in noticing, understanding, and responding. An unlikely messenger of the being mode is one of my favorite children's books, *Peek-A-Boo!* by Janet and Allan Ahlberg. As in many books for children, nothing much is accomplished: a baby plays peekaboo with his family throughout the day. What charms me as a reader is how messy the house is. In every illustration, the mother and the father are tending to the tasks of life—washing windows, ironing, cooking, feeding children, bathing the baby—with no illusion of completion; around them are a jumble of children's toys and shoes, heaps of dirty laundry, open drawers, and sponges soaking in the sink. The pictures burst with the processes of living, with the thousand undone jobs that betoken the priority of responsiveness over perfection that makes for a happy family.

Our cultural ethos puts parents in an odd position. Within the paradigm of having, we feel responsible, even virtuous, when we conceptualize our activities according to quantifiable standards of accomplishment. But relating to children is stubbornly resistant to that formula, so the more time a mother spends in the being mode with children, the more some recess of her conscience may charge her with "accomplishing nothing." Thus it is that a general social problem about values and priorities is experienced by individual women as a problem of personal identity.

A high-achieving woman whom I'd been seeing in my therapy practice became pregnant after fertility treatment and was exceedingly happy. But within a few weeks, once past the iffy first trimester, her joyful anticipation gave way to an intense preoccupation with how much time to take off work to tend her baby, and she voiced the fear that a long leave would be "like stepping into a void." Each time she began to sit with her uncertainty and try to honor her genuine conflicts, she would become absorbed with devising ways to forestall the imagined loss of others' respect and to perform a semblance of "staying on track." For her, as for many, work conferred status, power, prestige, and a voice in the world, and these things were central to her sense of identity. Yet, sadly, she wielded that thought as a painful and almost punishing standard, fearing she would no longer have anything of value if she was not at her job and was with her baby.

While sending women the message that they'd better buy into the values of the capitalist marketplace if they expect to garner security, independence, and self-respect, we also demonize "the working mother" and promulgate punitive morality tales about the social costs of her professional choices. This is just one more double standard by which women are co-opted into shouldering the burden of society's incongruous values. Women's paid employment obviously fulfills many purposes in addition to the economic, including the enactment of deeply held values and the expression of care for others. The categories of working and nonworking mother too often function as code for other variables entirely.

The pull of our acquisitive culture is extremely relevant to working mothers, but it also exerts an enormous pull on stay-at-home mothers. Some mothers endorse the value of hands-on, home-based mothering in part as an explicit protest against the dehumanizing aspects of the marketplace. Still, stay-at-home mothers' orientation toward our culture of commodities is also ambiguous. We are all so immersed in metaphors of "productivity" and "results" that the stay-at-home mother must fight the impulse to write herself a job description that defines her effectiveness in terms of her children's measurable accomplishments. The pull for at-home mothers to try to give their mothering work the sheen of productivity is particularly strong, perhaps, because they feel vulnerable, inwardly and outwardly, to the charge that caring for kids amounts to "doing nothing," to a waste of their skills and earning power. The "responsible" stay-at-home mother, then, feels compelled to organize a roster of activities for her toddler, launching him on the path of being "well-rounded" and herself on the path of high-intensity, child-focused chauffeuring. She earnestly evaluates the local baby gym's techniques for enhancing sensorimotor skills, even though she's vaguely aware that children don't need pricey classes to acquire capacities they would develop naturally anyway. The marketplace machinery that creates needs in order to fill them is up and running in babyhood, and therefore one's sense of being a "good parent" often becomes tied to what and how much one consumes on behalf of one's child.

The whole point of those gym classes is for children to have fun. We all know that. But the way they are pitched reveals a facet of the weirdly constraining atmosphere of parenting today, whereby the responsible parent will look with suspicion on something that is "just" for fun. Piano lessons and music classes are routinely advertised as means of enhancing math skills. We have a hard time escaping the dictate of our conscience that all our actions must be means to some other end. When we give our children piano lessons to improve their mathematical reasoning skills, we feel we are being good parents regardless of what this activity actually means to our children or ourselves.

Why is it depressing to measure children's success, or our own, in terms of quantifiable "packets" of experience? What is grating about watching a mother suddenly burst into a lesson about counting integers in the midst of her cooing back and forth with her baby while she changes a diaper? It is something about her overeager intrusion of teaching into a moment of communion. One feels the mother attempting to take their fullest moment of being "at one" and colonizing it in the lesser exercise of skills acquisition. Amid all our talk of productivity, the true waste is this: at the one time in our lives when our children offer us the unconditional gift of being loved beyond measure, we retreat, as if we can't even let ourselves feel it unless we make some gesture toward proving we've earned it. We struggle mightily to turn the miracle of being into having, hoping somehow to stanch the flow of moments that burble by without ever allowing us to possess them.

For mothers, the effect of these pressures is to turn us away from our intrinsic value to our children and our blinding knowledge of our amazing, undeserved importance in their lives. We're tempted to distract ourselves by offering things in our place, as if our human presence were not infinitely more valuable than a stimulating toy. We may manage our anxiety in the face of this awesome reality by grabbing at whatever ideological security blanket best comforts us: by railing against unrealistic models of "intensive mothering" as victimizations of women, by claiming that children don't need all the attention that the softhearted "experts" recommend. Yet whatever position we take, it serves in part to help us cope with the gap between our enormous aspiration and our sense of insufficiency in living motherhood as intensely as we can. The early years of our children's lives give us a unique opportunity to embrace life fully, in all its fatigue, moodiness, laughter, inconvenience, pleasure, and messiness. The list of reasons why such engagement is hard to attain is huge, from conflicts between work and family to the pervasive pressures of a materialistic culture to existential anxiety. But it is worth asking ourselves, What can we do to help ourselves claim the pleasure?

A first step that any of us can take is to sit with the problem, whatever form it takes in our lives. We need to listen to the stirrings of our own souls, take responsibility for all our different feelings, and work toward greater discernment of our desires amid the clamor of voices. How do we do that? First, we notice. We notice the clench in our stomach or the low-level distractedness we feel when we leave our baby for the day. We ask ourselves what we can learn from it. We notice our sense of relief when we get out the door and leave our screaming toddler. We turn that sense of freedom over in our minds, trying to learn all we can about its sources. We notice our thought that we are doing "nothing" in caring for a baby all day, or the way thoughts about what we need to get done tumble forward when we sit down to read our child a story. We notice what the pressure of too little time feels like, the way it scatters our attention, wears away at our sense of effectiveness, and prompts us to try to relocate the discomfort outside ourselves by looking for someone or something to blame. Noticing does not make bad feelings go away, but it creates slightly more breathing space, giving us a moment of honest specificity amid the self-persecuting half-truths that usually clog our minds. Such moments of clarity can make us more compassionate toward ourselves and less lonely inside our own heads.

We try to notice things about our children too. We try to decipher their signs and signals from a centered place, neither reading too much into their ups and downs nor denying their significance. We try to notice what they are asking from us and how they are asking. We try to figure out whether the way they ask (whining, demandingness, tantrums) is making it hard for us to give them what they want or need. A child played on a beach during vacation. He had been there with a nanny for several hours. His mother arrived, and the child soon fell to whining. Minutes later, exasperated, the mother presented him with an ultimatum: "Stop whining, or I'm leaving." This scene was painful to witness, since the child's whining was clearly a plea for the mother's attention. Unable to receive his message, the mother felt ineffective, maybe guilty, and turned her desperation against him. They missed each other by a mile. Sometimes our children ask for things we can't give, such as more of our time. But again, being aware of their feelings and our own has value, as does letting our children know we understand their feelings rather than denying them out of guilt or sadness.

We also try to notice the larger stories we tell ourselves about our lives and the values our choices express. Children can, if we let them, expand our fellow feeling. As a friend said when I revealed years ago my wistfulness at the end of childbearing, "The point isn't whether you keep having children. It's being able to find a way for the experience of love that you have toward your own children, a love that feels like it can't be matched, to widen and deepen your love for others." That is why, once we are no longer drowning in diapers, no longer struggling to compose a shopping list (let alone a letter to our representative in Congress), it is worth considering how we might bring the knowledge we gained from tending children into the larger culture.

There is evidence of such efforts all around us. We see it in the beautiful, rigorous scholarship that has been informed by women's and men's experiences of having and caring for children. We see it in grassroots efforts to ease the way of those who come after, such as the group of older mothers in my community, volunteering their time to improve the day care options for the county's poorer parents. We see it in the effort of a parent who pushes the policies of his or her workplace in a slightly more flexible direction. We find it in ourselves when we respect that there are many ways to mother well, when we refuse to judge our own or others' maternal choices by rigid ideals, and when we live by the knowledge that mothering is not about perfection but about love, acceptance, responsibility, and engagement, toward our children and ourselves.

Finally, it is important to notice when we are "choosing away" from spending time with our children and to ask ourselves what those decisions reflect. I remember that when our children were two, four, and seven years old, the babysitter, one day each week, Tuesday, worked all day, from 9:00 a.m. till 5:00 p.m. Every other day of the week, I ended my workday by 2:00 p.m., or I didn't work at all. I came to notice what I called "the Tuesday effect." On Tuesday evenings after I'd been with my kids for about an hour, I would have the thought, "Oh, boy, it's exhausting to be with these kids all day!"—and then I realized that I was having this thought *only* on the day when I *wasn't* with them for much of the time. I came to wonder about that. What I was noticing with the Tuesday effect is akin to what Arlie Hochschild describes in her book *The Time Bind*. It's not simply that parents "lack time" for children, but rather that parents are "choosing against" time with family by putting in more time at work. Their sense of meaning increasingly derives from their work identity, thereby rendering domestic activities less rewarding. At home, they feel less effective; the emotional needs are more unruly, more confusing, and less easily dispatched there. For me, the more I worked on a given day, the more my center of gravity was in my work and the less I could find exactly what there was to enjoy in taking care of my children.

Our ability to appreciate something, whether it is a person or a pursuit, is affected through the time we give to it. The more time we spend on a relationship (with a child, with nature, with a piece of music), the more we know, the more we appreciate, and the more facets there are to love. In some ways, the speed at which we live our lives is implicated in the degradation of our capacity to appreciate. Paradoxically, though our perpetual busyness can be understood to reflect our ever-rising standard for what is necessary to a good life, we seem less and less able as a society to provide for the true necessities of people's lives, namely health care, a working wage, the comforts of home, good care for our children, and accessibility to restorative leisure.

If we notice ourselves choosing away from spending time nurturing our children, each of us needs to ask, Have I set up my life so as to rationalize shying away from authentic connection? To what extent are my activities oriented toward maintaining my sense of control, or managing my fear of want and insecurity, or stoking my vanity, in a way that leads me away from experiencing the depth of love I could? The theologian Thomas Merton writes, "Love affects more than our thinking and our behavior toward those we love. It transforms our entire life. Genuine love is a personal revolution. Love takes your ideas, your desires, and your actions and welds them together in one experience and one living reality which is a new *you*." This is how people talk about becoming parents. This is how women talk about becoming mothers. This the explosion in one's heart as old as time.

WHEN THE CHILDREN were little, we'd ride bicycles to school in the morning, the oldest on a two-wheeler, the middle one on training wheels, and the youngest in a cart attached to the back of my bike. One day after dropping off the older ones, I remember climbing the hill to the bike path with my three-year-old in tow. As I began mentally carving up my day, wondering how I would fit in my errands and my work, I was suddenly returned to the beauty of the morning—the mist, our chatting, the pumping of my heart. Every time my son asked me a question, it mattered how I answered it, not so much the facts I offered, but the way I listened, the way I kept faith with his earnest effort to make sense of the world. His thirst for knowledge and my power to slake it moved me. It let me notice once again what our time together meant for us both. It felt good and right to hallow this morning, this hour. "The liberation of the heart, which is love," I thought, as we whizzed along the bike path and counted our friends the ducks.

Acknowledgments

Many people have helped me during the years of writing this book, and I am deeply thankful to all of them. For reading chapters, talking over ideas, and for sustaining support and friendship, I thank John Adler, Anne Becker, Daniel Becker, Meryl Botkin, Susan Coates, Rachel Conrad, Katrin Borland de Marneffe, Dianne Elise, Toni Vaughn Heineman, Stephen Hinshaw, Jeanne Burns Leary, and Mary Margaret McClure. Particular thanks to Gary Kamiya for his comments on the entire draft, and to Leslie Ann Fuchs, Laura Klein, and Kate Moses for their enthusiasm and crucial early feedback.

Friends, acquaintances, colleagues, and scholars I've admired from afar all came to my aid in myriad ways, offering the chance reference or anecdote, taking time to answer my e-mails, or consulting with me about some aspect of their expertise. I am grateful to them all for their assistance. I particularly wish to thank Karen Betzner, Karen Breslau, Ellen Burkhart, Lee Rubin Collins, Carolyn Pape Cowan, Diane Doucette, Richard Fabian, Renee Carroll Ghosh, Tracy Haughton, Alan Heineman, Susan Hill, Linda James, Nancy Kaplan, Lynne Layton, Alicia Lieberman, Vivian Steir Rabin, Maria Rivera, Rebecca Rogers, Alan Rubenstein,

Rebecca Saletan, Donald Schell, Stephen Seligman, and Judith Sternberg Turiel. An unexpected pleasure of working on this book has been reconnecting with old friends and trading perspectives on parenthood. For their insights and camaraderie, I thank Amy Givens, Patricia Howard Hudson, Hester Kaplan, Lizzie Leiman Kraiem, Liz Schein Krengel, Jessica Marshall, and Erika Peterson Munson. Though for reasons of discretion they remain unnamed, I am also hugely indebted to all the people I have encountered in the course of work and parenthood who have shared with me their struggles and their stories.

For their scholarly example, their encouragement, and their contribution to my intellectual development, I thank my teachers, particularly Nancy Chodorow, Philip Cowan, Carol Gilligan, and the late Enrico Jones. My gratitude also goes to my children's many excellent teachers and caregivers, at school, at preschool, and at home. Dara Blachman, Susanna Bonetti, and Lynne Foster helped me track down references, and I thank them for their diligence.

I can't say enough wonderful things about my agent, Tina Bennett, who is supremely gifted as both editor and advocate. Our work together has been a professional high point, and I thank her for her integrity, guidance, and good humor at every step of the way. I have also been blessed to work with my editor, Judy Clain, whose responsiveness, vision, and extraordinary fluidity between emotion and intellect have made for a highly satisfying collaboration. My sincere thanks also go to Judy's assistant, Claire Smith, and to all the superb professionals at Janklow & Nesbit and Little, Brown.

I am fortunate to have an extended family who lavish me with unwavering loyalty, interest, and pride. I offer my enduring appreciation to them all. I am especially thankful to my parents-in-law, Kathleen Jacobson Becker and John Becker, for their generous care; to my stepparents, Barbara Rowe de Marneffe and Anthony Ferranti, for the many gifts they have shared with me and our family; and most of all, to my devoted parents, Nancy Edmonds Ferranti and Francis de Marneffe, who gave me life and taught me to love it.

For their steadfast support and enfolding affection, I am grateful to my friends Debra Fine, Maureen Katz, Elizabeth Lloyd Mayer, Sheila Sammon Milosky, and Susan Morrison. Among these cherished companions I count my brother, Peter de Marneffe, on whom I can always rely for a great conversation, and my sister, Colette de Marneffe, my inspiration and best friend.

Finally, from my deepest heart, I thank my beloved children, for being who they are, and my husband, Terry Becker, for everything.

Acknowledgments for the Second Edition

It is a privilege to revisit my ideas in a second edition, and a great pleasure to do so in the intellectual company of my now-adult daughter, Sophia Colette Becker. I would like to thank Sophie and her friends Alexandra Glass-Katz and Lisa Martine Jenkins (beautiful writers both) for their careful reading of the first edition and for their comments and perspectives. I owe a particular debt of gratitude to Rumur Dowling, also part of my "millennial team," for his blazingly efficient and extraordinarily valuable research and editorial assistance. I expect great things from all of them! For their thoughtful input, I thank my colleagues David Blacker,

Claudia Califano, Erika Christakis, and Hillary Grill. I sincerely appreciate the ongoing support of my friends Deborah Fine, Maureen Katz, Susan Morrison, Arietta Slade, and Dawn Smith; my siblings, Peter and Colette de Marneffe; and my parents and extended family.

I thank my editor, Colin Harrison, for his exceptional insight, heart, and expertise. I always leave our conversations happier than when I began, which is no easy feat where writers are concerned, and for which I credit his impressive skill as a professional and as a person. I am extremely grateful to Scribner for publishing this second edition, and to Sarah Goldberg and the entire Scribner team for their contributions to its completion. As always, my profound thanks to my agent, Tina Bennett, who believed in *Maternal Desire* from its inception and has now been a guiding intellectual beacon and trusted advocate for almost two decades.

My deepest love and thanks as always to my husband, Terry, and our children, Sophie, Alex, and Nicholas. In addition to them, I would like to dedicate this edition to my late mother-in-law, Kathleen Jacobson Becker, in loving memory, and to my mother, Nancy Edmonds Ferranti, in enduring gratitude and love.

Notes on Sources

2 **honed my thinking on parenthood and intimate relationships:**
My later thinking on couples, including raising older children
and the empty nest, can be found in my book *The Rough Patch*
(2018).

3 **recognized as a hyped-up distraction:** See, for example, Peskowitz,
The Truth Behind the Mommy Wars (2005).

4 **the variable and complex ways they interact:** For a fuller treatment of this issue, see de Marneffe, "The (M)other We Fall in
Love With."

5 **Researchers in fields as diverse:** See, for example, Pascuzzi,
"Mothers at a Loss"; Shabot, "Name as Oppression and/or Lib-
eration"; Schultheiss, "To Mother or Matter"; Ropers-Huilman
and Enke, "Catholic Women's College Students' Construction";
Duane, "An Infant Nation"; Quesenberry, Trauth, and Morgan,
"Understanding the 'Mommy Tracks' "; Dagher, Hofferth, and
Lee, "Maternal Depression, Pregnancy Intention."

5 **"value and meaning of what they do":** Kawash, "New Directions
in Motherhood Studies," 989.

5 **"description of the world which will truly be ours":** Rich, *Of
Woman Born*, 15–16.

5 **claim more cultural terrain:** See Elkin, "Why All the Books About
Motherhood?" and Garbes, "Why Are We Only Talking About
'Mom Books' by White Women?"

5 **simplistic, if not tone-deaf:** For high-brow and low-brow versions, see Badinter, *The Conflict*, and Johnson, "How Stay-at-home Moms Hurt Gender Equality."

6 **modes of resilience:** Zraly, Rubin, and Mukamana, "Motherhood and Resilience," 416, 430.

6 **bear their ambivalence and self-judgment:** Baraitser and Noack, "Mother Courage," 184–86.

6 **"her own voice and subjectivity":** Bueskens, "Introduction," 27. See also Stone, *Feminism, Psychoanalysis, and Maternal Subjectivity*, and Baraitser, *Maternal Encounters: The Ethics of Interruption*.

6 **"without attempting, in a desperate way, to control them":** Wilson, "Maternal Reliance: Commentary on Kristeva," 107. See also Kristeva, "Reliance, or Maternal Eroticism."

6 **"lessens the threat of the difference":** Lorde, *Sister Outsider*, 56.

1. THE "PROBLEM" OF MATERNAL DESIRE

15 **childbearing as the root of women's oppression:** Firestone, *Dialect of Sex*.

15 **"because only meaner things are within her reach":** Eliot, *Felix Holt*, chap. 27.

18 *enabling the other to come into him- or herself:* See Chetrit-Vatine, *Ethical Seduction of the Analytic Situation*, chap. 2.

19 **a "luxury" many parents feel they can't afford:** See, for example, Cooke, "In the Middle Class, and Barely Getting By."

19 **American women are having fewer children than they would like:** Stone, "American Women Are Having Fewer Children."

20 **to the capacity for emotional intimacy:** For an overview, see Siegel, *Developing Mind*.

20 **reducing the emotional stress of parenthood in particular:** Carstensen, *Long Bright Future*, 68–69.

21 **In Victorian times, blooming young women contracted odd symptoms:** See Breuer and Freud, "Studies on Hysteria." In *The History of Sexuality*, the philosopher Michel Foucault brilliantly demonstrated how incessant, seemingly "free" social discussion of sex serves to regulate and define sexual expression. Similarly, though it may seem that people "can't stop talking about moth-

erhood," their very volubility may serve to obscure, and even discount, important aspects of maternal experience.

2. FEMINISM

23 **the most usual dedication of a feminist book:** Among many examples are Mitchell, *Psychoanalysis and Feminism*; Olsen, *Tell Me a Riddle*; Faludi, *Backlash*; Ludtke, *On Our Own*; and Hays, *Cultural Contradictions of Motherhood.*

24 **Third- and fourth-wave feminism:** For an accessible introduction to feminism's "waves," see Grady, "The waves of feminism."

25 **" 'Revolution' is too pallid a word":** Ehrenreich and English, *For Her Own Good*, 5.

25 **profound changes in family life and the lives of women:** Cott, *Bonds of Womanhood*, chap. 1. The studies I cite focus mostly on middle-class women in the northeastern United States.

26 **love, nurturance, and good works:** Ryan, *Cradle of the Middle Class*, 106; Lasch, *Women and the Common Life*, 93–120.

26 **continually acknowledged and amplified:** Sklar, *Catharine Beecher*, chap. 11.

26 **advocating for social betterment:** Cott, *Bonds of Womanhood*, 200–201; Smith-Rosenberg, "Beauty, the Beast," 126.

27 **tells a more one-sided tale:** See, for example, Warner, *Perfect Madness*; Wolf, *Beauty Myth*.

27 **absence of an ideal of tender affection in the family:** See, for example, Aries, *Centuries of Childhood*; and Stone, *Family, Sex, and Marriage.*

27 **"very much a social construction":** Schor, *Overworked American*, 92.

28 **"came to dominate child-rearing ideology":** Schor, 93.

28 **to oversee children's development was conceived as progress:** See, for example, Ryan, *Cradle of the Middle Class*, 231–32; and Cott, *Bonds of Womanhood*, 200.

29 **"Am I doing enough?":** Cott, *Bonds of Womanhood*, 88.

29 **little more than a "social fiction":** Wolf, *Beauty Myth*, 15.

30 **"the foe of waxed floors":** de Beauvoir, *Second Sex*, 587.

30 **whether "home production" (housework and caregiving) should**

be included: Coyle, "Way We Measure Economies Is Inherently Sexist."

31 the fundamentally different characters of the two endeavors: See, for example, Schor, *Overworked American*, 94–98.

31 to compare the work of mothers to that of domestic servants: See, for example, Mattis, "'Vulgar Strangers in the Home.'"

31 a professional ballplayer forgo pay because he enjoys his job: Crittenden, *Price of Motherhood*, 8, 79.

32 "finding nurses and housekeepers": Kolbert, "Mother Courage."

33 to care for those of more privileged families: See, for instance, Glenn, "Social Construction of Mothering," 7. Parrenas, *Servants of Globalization*; Ehrenreich and Hochschild, *Global Woman*; and Hondagneu-Sotelo, *Domestica*.

33 their own domestic spheres: For discussion of this point, see Collins, *Black Feminist Thought*, 54–55; and Williams, *Unbending Gender*, chap. 5.

33 to legitimize the notion of women's "difference": Faludi, *Backlash*, 312–31; Hewlett, *Lesser Life*; Friedan, *Second Stage*: Gilligan, *In a Different Voice*.

33 tendency "to conflate 'mothers' with 'women'": Pollitt, *Reasonable Creatures*, 43; see also Ireland, *Reconceiving Women*.

34 "more interested in family life than men": Kaminer, *True Love Waits*, 109–10.

34 particular requirements of mothering: See Kaminer, *Fearful Freedom*, 212–13 and chap. 10. For a nuanced discussion of feminist themes of equality and difference, see Scott, "Deconstructing Equality-versus-Difference."

35 "which challenges gender stereotypes and roles": Kaminer, 5–6. Kaminer's concern references a long-standing tension within feminism between treating women as individuals and treating them as a class with certain common characteristics. For a historical perspective on this tension, see Cott, *Grounding of Modern Feminism*.

36 "You work, you get paid": Harper's Forum, "Giving Women the Business," 50.

37 "somebody actually needed me to be that": Morrison, in Moyers and Tucher, *World of Ideas*, quoted in Bassin et al., *Representations of Motherhood*, 2.

37 **"like serious applicants for the space program":** Erdrich, *Blue Jay's Dance*, 11–12.

38 **"being a 'normal' girl and becoming a mother":** Mamo, *Queering Reproduction*, 58–61.

38 **"anything tied too closely to the female animal":** Nelson, *Argonauts*, 13–14.

39 **"deeply and primally" from their mothers:** Rich, *Of Woman Born*, 246–47.

40 **"children's psychological adjustment or gender development":** Golombok, *Modern Families*, 202.

40 **family's relationship to their larger social environs:** Golombok, 203.

40 **"the profound taste we have for children":** Leclerc, *Parole de femme*, 148 (my translation).

41 **people's desires with respect to love relationships and children:** Some sources include Mamo, *Queering Reproduction*; Gibson, *Queering Motherhood*; Park, *Mothering Queerly*; and Adams, *Mad Mothers*.

41 **"any gender, any sentient being":** Nelson, *Argonauts*, 72.

41 **"serving as a buoy, as a lifeline":** Chetrit-Vatine, *Ethical Seduction*, 39.

41 **"the stubborn reality of the flesh":** De Marneffe, *Rough Patch*, 11.

45 **"to risk letting the other teach me who I am":** Bauer, *Simone de Beauvoir*, 236.

3. PSYCHOANALYSIS

50 **male bias of psychoanalysis:** See for example, Chodorow, *Femininities*.

50 **experiences as mothers and ambitious women:** Sayers, *Mothers of Psychoanalysis*.

50 **"incompatibility between motherhood and career":** Langer, *Motherhood and Sexuality*, ix–x. Langer alludes to Lundberg and Farnham, *Modern Woman*.

51 **yet she herself felt drained by it:** Sayers, *Mothers of Psychoanalysis*, 33.

51 **hampered her own ability to care for her child:** Roazen, *Helene Deutsch*, 134, 136.

51 **fire caregivers to whom he had become attached:** Roazen, 135; and Sayers, *Mothers of Psychoanalysis*, 34, 40.

51 **"the tragedy of motherhood":** Deutsch, *Motherhood*, 302–17.

52 **"it is neither pure dutifulness nor love":** Deutsch, 291.

52 **"the interests of her own individuality":** Deutsch, 228.

52 **"they are missing something important":** Deutsch, 292–93.

52 **"my great childhood love":** Quinn, *Mind of Her Own*, 170.

52 **Horney's own experience in mothering her infant:** Quinn, 171.

53 **"to take an independent position":** Quinn, 172.

53 **"the whole period when the infant needs her care?":** Horney, "Flight from Womanhood," 60.

53 **for the sexual capacities they don't possess:** Kelman, "Introduction," 20.

53 **"part of their maternal instincts":** Langer, *Motherhood and Sexuality*, x.

55 **characterized by a sense of "merger" or oneness:** Chodorow, *Reproduction of Mothering*, for example see page 87.

56 **replenish and enrich our individuality:** Some classic sources include Loewald, *Papers in Psychoanalysis,* especially chaps. 5, 12, and 21; Stern, *Interpersonal World of the Infant*; Kaplan, *Oneness and Separateness*; Gergely and Watson, "Social Biofeedback Model of Parental Affect-Mirroring."

56 **melting into each other that mothers and likely babies experience:** For a discussion of the psychological processes underlying this experience, see Stern, *Interpersonal World of the Infant*, 104–11.

57 **"deny its mother's departure or separateness":** Chodorow, *The Reproduction of Mothering*, 59.

57 **a powerful motive to give care:** See, for example, George and Solomon, "Development of Caregiving" and "Representational Models of Relationships"; and Solomon and George, "Defining the Caregiving System."

58 **Margaret Mahler terms rapprochement:** Mahler, Pine, and Bergman, *Psychological Birth of the Human Infant*.

58 **illustrates maternal limit-setting with examples of the mother's leaving the child:** See, for example, Benjamin, *The Bonds of Love*, 212–13; "Omnipotent Mother," 134–36; and *Like Subjects, Love Objects*, 37–38.

59 **"sacrificed her own independence":** Benjamin, *Bonds of Love*, 79.

59 **"difficult for either one of them to accomplish separation":** Benjamin, 96.

60 **"transformative claims that motherhood would make upon our identities":** Chodorow, "Preface to the Second Edition," in *The Reproduction of Mothering*, xvii.

60 **"deep attunement but also difference":** Benjamin, "*The Bonds of Love*: Looking Backward," 6.

60 **perils of putting a child's needs before her own:** See, for example, Peters, *When Mothers Work*.

61 **"a repudiation of true agency and desire":** Gerhardt, Sweetnam, and Borton, "Intersubjective Turn in Psychoanalysis," 26.

61 **oversimplifies a complex and meaningful internal process:** For further discussion of this issue, see Baraitser, "Oi Mother, Keep Ye Hair On!," and de Marneffe, "What Exactly *Is* the Transformation of Motherhood?"

62 **mothers as full persons:** Benjamin, *The Bonds of Love*, 23.

62 **the meaning of that desire with respect to mothers' identities and goals:** Some writings that do approach these issues include Bassin, "Maternal Subjectivity"; Stern, *Motherhood Constellation*; Stern and Bruschweiler-Stern, *Birth of a Mother*; and Dimen, "Strange Hearts."

62 **"little miracle[s] of specificity":** Sander, "Thinking Differently," 20.

62 **patterns of pleasurable relating and intimacy throughout life:** Beebe and Lachmann, *Infant Research and Adult Treatment*, chap. 5.

63 **to achieve a gratifying rapport:** See Beebe and Lachmann, 103, for a fuller description of the meaning of these findings.

63 **"soothing of the infant at times of stress":** Lyons-Ruth, "Rapprochement or Approchement," 9.

63 **"maintaining warm relatedness":** Lyons-Ruth, 12.

64 **"the affective-intuitive and the intellectual":** Deutsch, *Motherhood*, 296–97.

64 *feels with* and *thinks about* **her child:** De Marneffe, *Rough Patch*, 49–58.

65 **"via the hearts, likes, etc., of social media platforms":** Van Cleaf, "Pleasure of Connectivity," 12.

65 **an estimated 4 million self-identified mom bloggers:** Hidalgo, "Open Letter."

66 **the miscommunications, the repairs, the repeated attempts to connect:** Tronick, "Emotions and Emotional Communication." See also Beebe and Lachmann, *Infant Research and Adult Treatment*, chaps. 7 and 8.

66 **"are mutual attention and delight":** Beebe and Lachmann, 85–86.

66 **too tightly matched nor too mismatched:** Jaffe et al., "Rhythms of Dialogue in Infancy." *Coordination* can be understood as the "degree of predictability of one person's behavior from that of the other" or "whether or not two parallel streams of behavior are correlated" (Beebe and Lachmann, *Infant Research and Adult Treatment*, 32, 99).

67 **"more 'space,' more room for uncertainty":** Beebe and Lachmann, *Infant Research and Adult Treatment*, 103.

67 **predicts her own child's security:** Main, Kaplan, and Cassidy, "Security in Infancy"; Hesse, "Adult Attachment Interview"; Pearson et al., "Earned- and Continuous-Security."

67 **"the infant's signals are accurately interpreted by the caregiver":** Fonagy and Target, "Mentalization," 95. See also Fonagy et al., *Affect Regulation, Mentalization*; and Slade, "Development and Organization of Attachment," 1154–55. For a foundational paper on the relationship between reflectivity, flexibility of attention, coherence of discourse, and caregiver responsiveness, see Main, "Metacognitive Knowledge."

72 **"people who are winning":** Bailey, "What Ever Happened to the Mommy Blog?"

4. PLEASURE

76 **we will reproduce the next generation:** For a thorough treatment of the mammalian bases of maternal feelings, see Hrdy, *Mother Nature*.

77 **"frozen yogurt desserts to my beloved mother":** Hays, *Cultural Contradictions of Motherhood*, xv.

79 **second only to those produced by death:** " '[Childbirth produces] more pronounced changes than at any time other than death,'

says Raphael Good, an ob-gyn and psychiatrist at the University of Miami" (*Newsweek*, July 2, 2001, 26).

79 **"tripped into the boundless":** These were Frost's words: "My poems—I should suppose everybody's poems—are all set to trip the reader head foremost into the boundless" (Bomford, *Symmetry of God*, 52).

80 **reading the Seuss story they knew:** DeCasper and Fifer, "Of Human Bonding," 1174–76. The interpretation of this research is drawn from Mitchell, *Relationality*, 8–9.

80 **"low legato murmurs for comforting":** Pinker, *Language Instinct*, 279.

80 **appears to be universal:** Fernald, "Human Maternal Vocalization," cited in Pinker, *Language Instinct*, 279.

81 **"the girl's fling of gesture and posture":** Stern, *Interpersonal World of the Infant*, 141.

82 **"by the mothers themselves":** Stern, 148.

83 **awareness of oneness is apprehended by the conscious mind:** Bomford, *Symmetry of God*, 58–59.

83 **"the chances of seeing it go down":** Scarry, *On Beauty and Being Just*, 18.

84 **"he has the experience of his own creativity":** Coates, "Having a Mind of One's Own," 22–23.

84 **sensitive responsiveness:** Allen, *Restoring Mentalizing*, 3.

84 **responds to them appropriately and promptly:** Allen, 7.

85 *understanding feelings* **is fundamental to rewarding relationships:** Holmes and Slade, *Attachment in Therapeutic Practice*, 61.

85 **lovable and worthy of care:** Allen, *Restoring Mentalizing*, 7.

85 **"a happy child is a safe child":** Holmes and Slade, *Attachment in Therapeutic Practice*, 55.

85 **memories of their own early attachment relationships:** Slade et al., "Mothers' Representations of Their Relationships," 613.

86 **are judged "insecure" when assessed at one year:** Holmes and Slade, *Attachment in Therapeutic Practice*, 10.

86 **attentive to *and* accepting of our experience:** Allen, *Restoring Mentalizing*, 27.

87 **"trying to avoid one's own mind—a futile endeavor":** Allen, 28.

87 **we need to also cultivate them toward ourselves:** Allen, 28; Neff, *Self-Compassion*.

87 **no matter how challenging our childhood was:** Mikulincer and

Shaver, *Attachment in Adulthood*, 142; Mehta, Cowan, and Cowan, "Working Models of Attachments."

88 **"about her own breakdown at the pediatrician's":** Elisa Camahort, BlogHer '06 session discussion on day two, May 20, 2006, "Mommy Blogging Is a Radical Act!," *Blogher*, www.blogher.com. Cited in Van Cleaf, "Blogging through Motherhood," 10.

88 **having children gives a woman confidence in her creativity:** In Nina Winter's *Interview with the Muse*, Faye Weldon said, "Another thing that seems quite helpful to the creative process is having babies. It does not distract at all from one's creativity. It reminds one that there is always more where that came from and there is never any shortage of ideas or of the ability to create. The process of being pregnant and then of having the baby and getting up in the night only puts one more in touch with this fecund part of oneself" (42).

89 **and "linear" time (history):** Kristeva, "Women's Time," 192. See also Moi, "Introduction."

92 **"in the body, as much as the mind":** Enright, "My Milk."

92 **a nondeclarative, nonverbal sensitivity to their interactions:** See Stern et al., "Non-interpretive Mechanisms."

94 **new, meaningful, or challenging:** Csikszentmihalyi, *Flow*, 65.

94 **"now enriched by new skills and fresh achievements":** Csikszentmihalyi, 66.

95 **the family-building phase of people's lives:** Carstensen, *Long Bright Future*, 68–69.

95 **foster stimulation and experimentation:** Csikszentmihalyi, *Creativity*, 128–44, and *Flow*, 71–90.

95 **"transporting a person into a new reality":** Csikszentmihalyi, *Flow*, 74.

97 **wound around to saying that motherhood is "hell":** Peri and Moses, *Mothers Who Think*.

97 **"from a place that you don't even know the register of":** Lambert, "Image and the Arc of Feeling."

98 **"he would be, quite simply, ill or not alive":** Graybeal, "Kristeva's Delphic Proposal," 35.

98 **"unskilled work done under compulsion":** Csikszentmihalyi, *Flow*, 143.

98 **"what would be wrong with me?":** Csikszentmihalyi, 148.

5. AMBIVALENCE

104 **"how vulnerable and disrespected you already feel"**: Lamott, "Mother Anger," 94–95.

105 **not that they are a rarity or a crisis**: For the classic paper on "normal" maternal hate, see Winnicott, "Hate in the Counter-transference."

107 **15 percent of new mothers suffer from diagnosable clinical depression**: Postpartum Support International, http://www.postpartum.net/learn-more/depression-during-pregnancy-postpartum/.

108 **"all the other side of the intensity of love"**: Chira, *Mother's Place*, 62.

109 **finding a way to manage the guilt and anxiety**: See Parker, *Mother Love/Mother Hate*, 6; Baraitser and Noack, "Mother Courage."

109 **caring for children is a recipe for marginalization**: See Crittenden, *Price of Motherhood*.

110 **"embarrassed by having to consider the issue"**: Folbre, *Invisible Heart*, 35.

110 **"steering clear of bathetic girly pathologies"**: Grigoriadis, "Baby Panic," 22.

111 **"'schlepping us around in the Navigator'"**: Gardner, "Mom vs. Mom," 25.

111 **"the kind of work that Barbara Bush did"**: Burggraf, *Feminine Economy and Economic Man*, 129.

112 **"I've got more eggs than she does!"**: Grigoriadis, 24.

112 **"Pinterest era of modern motherhood"**: Siemens, "Spoiler: Having It All Sucks."

113 **child-rearing as Mommy Olympics**: Wasserstein, "Competitive Moms," 259.

113 **"years after they have become adults"**: Angier, *Woman*, 255.

114 **"ancient, and also worth heeding"**: Angier, 257.

114 **"with their mothers and less with their fathers"**: Stern and Bruschweiler-Stern, *Birth of a Mother*, 132–33.

114 **"benign mother figures"**: Stern and Bruschweiler-Stern, 131.

114 **or at least incomplete**: See, for example, Orbach, *Fat Is a Feminist Issue*, 50; Wolf, *Beauty Myth*, 204–5; Debold, Wilson, and Malave, *Mother-Daughter Revolution*, chaps. 2 and 5; Brown and Gilligan, *Meeting at the Crossroads*, 219–21. For a critical discussion, see Hirsch, "Feminist Discourse/Maternal Discourse," 165.

116 **reiterated in countless fairy tales:** The theme of deprivation of a younger girl or woman by an older woman is common; beauty is the focus in *Snow White*, lovability in *Sleeping Beauty*, and food in *Hansel and Gretel*.

117 **how pregnancy would aesthetically alter her body:** For an excellent study of women's relationships to the (pregnant) body, see Balsam, *Women's Bodies in Psychoanalysis*.

117 **ways of "holding herself together":** For a relevant discussion of attitudes toward body perfection and emotional dependency, see Lemma, "Copies without Originals."

118 **"determination, cool, emotional discipline, mastery, and so on":** Bordo, *Unbearable Weight*, 171.

120 **"fascinating and relaxing as hell":** Havrilevsky, "Ask Polly: I'm Terrified of Having Kids!"; Van Cleaf, "Pleasure of Connectivity," 11.

120 **"the ambivalent state of mind for maternal development":** Parker, *Mother Love/Mother Hate*, 59.

121 **"the single most important aspect of mothering":** Parker, 6–7.

121 **and drain them of confidence:** See, for example, Parker, 24; Benjamin, *Bonds of Love*, chap. 5; Thurer, *Myths of Motherhood*; and Douglas and Michaels, *Mommy Myth*.

122 **"the good enough mother":** See, for example, Winnicott, "Transitional Objects" and "Use of an Object."

123 **"will feel real and be truly a personal experience":** Winnicott, "Capacity to Be Alone," 30, 34. See also Fonagy, *Attachment Theory and Psychoanalysis*, 98–99.

124 **"in which spiderlings live and grow, were impenetrable":** Byatt, *Still Life*, 187.

125 **"put down rational foot after rational foot, with difficulty":** Byatt, 161.

125 **"Time moved on":** Byatt, 163.

125 **"with some pain cleared this small space":** Byatt, 166.

6. CHILDCARE

129 **Disruption is the rule rather than the exception:** For childcare workers' perspectives on these same issues, see Ehrenreich and Hochschild, *Global Woman*.

130 **"I should have time to get a good nanny" (October 21, 1962):** From Payne, *Between Ourselves*, 181–84.

130 **the basic need for food and shelter:** Maslow, *Motivation and Personality*, chap. 4.

131 **turnover is too high:** Whitebook, Phillips, and Howes, *Worthy Work*, table 3.5, 40.

131 **is not good for children:** See Clarke-Stewart, *Daycare*, 100–102.

132 **"faux stay-at-home mom":** Pollitt, *Subject to Debate*, xv.

132 **artificial constructions irrelevant to their lives:** Gross, "Women and Their Work." For an insightful discussion of how polarized concepts of work and family fail to capture mothers' experiences, see Garey, *Weaving Work and Motherhood*.

133 **"taking care of their teachers":** Whitebook, Phillips, and Howes, *Worthy Work*, 17.

134 **at the expense of time spent caring for her children:** See, for example, Siemens, "Complicated Truth about Stay-at-Home Motherhood."

134 **to care for their own children at home:** See Williams, *Unbending Gender*, chap. 5.

134 **"much of the (under)-paid work they could find":** Crittenden, *Price of Motherhood*, 17.

135 **"treat the children like their closest kin":** Angier, "Primate Expert Explores."

135 **women were largely excluded:** Burggraf, *Feminine Economy and Economic Man*, 13.

136 **absorbing nature of both work and child-rearing:** Hrdy, *Mother Nature*, 50–52, 109–13.

137 **"children overwhelmingly prefer their parents to their caregivers":** Chira, *Mother's Place*, 123. For sources supporting this claim, see Chira, notes to chap. 6.

138 **negative effects on women's careers:** Scarr, "American Child Care Today," 100.

138 **"less motivated to maintain continuous, full-time employment":** Scarr, 99.

138 **"the underground market of unregulated care":** Scarr, 105.

138 **this shadowy, "gray-market" imagery:** For a discussion of the downside of for-profit day care centers, including cutting corners

on staff pay, training, and staff-to-child ratios, see Clarke-Stewart, *Daycare*, 54–55.

139 **"not do permanent damage to children?":** Scarr, "American Child Care Today," 106.

139 **as if the agendas could be so clearly separated:** Michel, *Children's Interests/Mothers' Rights*.

141 **"driven us back on this very crude monism":** Robinson, *Death of Adam*, 4.

141 **Joan Williams argues that in the American workplace:** The argument that follows is in Williams, *Unbending Gender*.

142 **"stiff headwinds from domesticity":** Williams, 38.

144 **in ten locations between 1991 and 2006:** NICHD website, https://www.nichd.nih.gov.

145 **related to less secure attachment scores for children:** NICHD Early Child Care Research Network, "Effects of Infant Child Care." "Minimal amounts of childcare" were defined in the statistical analysis as ten hours or fewer per week.

145 **strength of this connection was fairly weak:** NICHD Early Child Care Research Network, "Child Care and Mother-Child Interaction." For a review of the research linking attachment security to caregiver sensitivity, see Belsky, "Interactional and Contextual Determinants," 251–54.

145 **reflecting their personal caregiving approach:** See Jaeger and Weinraub, "Early Nonmaternal Care and Infant Attachment," for a fuller discussion of these alternatives.

146 **precisely because she was away so long:** See, for example, Ahnert and Lamb, "Shared Care," 1044–45.

148 **attunement to their emotions:** See, for example, Cozolino, *Neuroscience of Human Relationships*; Siegel, *Developing Mind*; Schore, *Affect Dysregulation*.

148 **a wage somewhere between that of animal caretakers and fast-food cooks:** Whitebook, Phillips, and Howes, *Worthy Work*, 26.

149 **"how life acquires the savour of longing":** Cusk, *Life's Work*, 206.

149 **the need to establish a nursing schedule:** Scarr, Phillips, and McCartney, "Working Mothers," 1405.

150 **"wants to be happy, to have fun":** Leach, *Your Baby and Child*, 8.

150 **"both my selves fit together with an audible click":** Chira, *Mother's Place*, xviii.

7. FERTILITY

151 **20 percent chance of success:** Silber, *How to Get Pregnant*, 57; and Nofziger, *Fertility Question*.

153 **having a baby after one round of IVF:** Rabin, "College Students Want Children."

154 **declined a whopping 52.4 percent:** Levine et al., "Temporal Trends in Sperm Count."

155 **during their prime childbearing years:** Luker, *Dubious Conceptions*, 172–73.

155 **provide economic and educational resources to their children:** Bui and Miller, "Age That Women Have Babies."

156 **"the occasion of public handwringing":** Luker, *Dubious Conceptions*, 17.

156 **"stand-in for status":** Wan, Letter to the Editor.

157 **"they'll regret it later if they don't":** Daum, "Opting Out of Motherhood."

158 **"face doubt from external sources need to hear your stories":** Comments on Miller, "Americans Are Having Fewer Babies."

158 **her feelings have changed:** See, for example, Chodorow, "'Too Late.'"

158 **"linked to the terror of loss":** Collins, "Mother at Last," 57.

160 **"I wanted a baby as badly as anybody did":** Rossi, "In Vitro," 63.

161 **"I'm going to burn this house down":** For memoirs that describe similar feelings, see Bartholet, *Family Bonds*; and Bialosky and Schulman, *Wanting a Child*.

161 **"she would come around eventually":** Lopate, "Lake of Suffering," 108–9.

162 **"this was not her final word on procreation":** Shacochis, "Missing Children," 41.

162 **"voluminous contents onto the tile floor":** Shacochis, 45.

163 **"frozen and put on the shelf":** Hodder, "New Fertility," 98–99.

163 **only 2 to 12 percent chance that a frozen egg will ultimately result in a birth:** La Ferla, "These Companies Really, Really."

164 **"women and their partners prefer to experience childbearing?":** Turiel, *Beyond Second Opinions*, 291.

164 **not yet found a partner or don't have a stable relationship:** Murphy, "Lots of Successful Women."

166 **"a pregnant Demi Moore doing acrobatics on TV":** Kitroeff and Silver-Greenberg, "Pregnancy Discrimination Is Rampant."

166 **Ruth Bader Ginsburg challenged the firm's lawyer:** Kitroeff and Silver-Greenberg.

167 **"when all pregnant women are able to assert their workplace rights":** Brown, Letter to the Editor.

167 **"living, breathing human being in the space between one's hip-bones":** Rossi, "In Vitro," 62.

167 **"while ripening my fruit":** Colette, *L'Étoile Vesper*, quoted by de Beauvoir in *Second Sex*, 560.

169 **"attentiveness, gentleness, forgetting oneself ":** Kristeva, "Women's Time," 206.

170 **"driven by 'baby hunger'":** Ludtke, *On Our Own*, 432–34.

170 **"resolving feelings about infertility":** Bartholet, *Family Bonds*, 31.

171 **"so clearly the children meant for me":** Bartholet, xiv–xv.

171 **"could not imagine loving a 'biological' child more":** Eisenberg, "Adoption Paradox," 82.

171 **similarly intense and involving journey into parenthood:** See, for example, Waterman, *Birth of an Adoptive*.

171 **"who have a financial interest in moving things along":** Boggs, *Art of Waiting*, 168.

172 **"ART requires a decision, a commitment":** Boggs, 158.

172 **Melanie Klein calls the *depressive position*:** Klein, *Envy and Gratitude*.

8. ABORTION

175 **nature didn't much care how sick I felt:** For a review article on the normal immunological suppression, and enhancements, of pregnancy, see Priddy, "Immunologic Adaptations during Pregnancy."

178 **the sober matter of fetal life:** Robert Bork wrote, "The vast majority of all abortions are for convenience." See Bork, "Inconvenient Lives," and Luker, *Abortion and the Politics of Motherhood*, 203.

178 **desire as a "thought-through feeling":** Gopnik, "Double Man," 91.

179 **"mired in metaphysics or theology about the beginning of life":** Roiphe, *Fruitful*, 50–51.

181 **"violent invasion of the personal space of the body"**: Bordo, "Are Mothers Persons?," 73–74.

182 **"easily ignored in the interests of fetal well-being"**: Bordo, 76.

182 **52 percent of the pregnant women were black**: "Feticide Playbook, Explained."

182 **"to 'indulge' Madyun's 'desires' at the expense of the safety of her fetus"**: Bordo, 78.

182 **to treat religious convictions as optional and expendable**: See Carter, *Culture of Disbelief.*

182 **what a given intervention means to *her***: Bordo, "Are Mothers Persons?," 79.

183 **"material incubator of fetal subjectivity"**: Bordo, 94.

184 **the relationship between herself and the developing fetus**: For a philosophical treatment of this issue, see Young, "Pregnant Embodiment."

185 **"carry a baby to delivery without an undue burden"**: Bordo, "Are Mothers Persons?," 93.

187 **resources for caring for others and herself are not limitless**: For the source of this argument, see Bolton, "Responsible Women."

189 **"'Honey, did you think it was so easy to be a woman?'"**: Gorney, *Articles of Faith,* 78.

189 **murderer to have loved her victim**: For a riveting treatment of the question of a mother murdering her child out of love, see Toni Morrison's novel *Beloved.*

189 **the belief that individual human life is sacred**: Dworkin, *Life's Dominion,* chaps. 1 and 2.

190 **"a complex, reasoning being from, as it were, nothing"**: Dworkin, 83.

190 **"a person will make and remake himself"**: Dworkin, 84.

190 **greater weight to the human creative contribution**: Kristin Luker catalogs many of the social characteristics that differentiate women who hold pro-choice and pro-life views. See *Abortion and the Politics of Motherhood,* chap. 8.

191 **"it is necessary to live them so that they live"**: Leclerc, *Parole de femme,* 108–9 (my translation).

193 **"a stance which in effect pits women against their children"**: Harper's Forum, "Is Abortion the Issue?," 36.

193 **the health and welfare of children a primary goal:** See, for example, Wolf, "Our Bodies Our Souls," 859–60; and MacKinnon, "Reflections on Sex Equality Under Law," discussed in Dworkin, *Life's Dominion*, 56–57.

194 **Good Samaritans with respect to their pregnancies:** This argument is made in Judith Jarvis Thomson's classic paper, "Defense of Abortion."

9. FATHERS

195 **" 'oh, it is awful, awful' and she burst into tears":** *Lawrence (MA) Telegram*, June 4, 1903.

201 **his role as "virtual father" to a generation of lost young men:** Chensvold, "YouTube's New Father Figure."

201 **qualitative differences exist between the two:** Peterson, "Proper Role of Parents" (at 0:21 and 0:58).

201 **"That is not a morally acceptable alternative":** Peterson, *12 Rules for Life*, 192.

202 **"when they come to need you":** Peterson, 225.

202 **"like it just about killed him":** Peterson, "Fathering and Manhood" (at 2:10).

203 **'No, what do *you* think?':** Brockes, "Single at 38?"

203 **a useful model of close relationships:** See, for example, Cummings and Davies, *Marital Conflict and Children*.

203 **to achieve a coparenting alliance:** See McHale, *Charting the Bumpy Road*.

204 **a family in which two adults have a relationship with each other:** See, for example, Heineman, "Boy and Two Mothers."

205 **both male and female children are predominantly cared for by women:** See, for example, Chodorow, "Oedipal Asymmetries"; and Dinnerstein, *Mermaid and the Minotaur*.

208 **men's unemployment or underemployment is one of the major risk factors for divorce:** Killewald, "Money, Work, and Marital Stability."

209 **"it is over the giving and receiving of gratitude":** Hochschild and Machung, *Second Shift*, 18.

210 **"wondered what I did all day":** For research on how a father's realistic appraisal of the challenges of caring for children con-

tributes to a mother's acceptance of her own ambivalence, see Boulton, *On Being a Mother*.

211 **share the world of parenting and she allows him in:** See, for example, Gottman and Silver, *Seven Principles*, 212; Shapiro, Gottman, and Carrere, "Baby and the Marriage"; and Cowan and Cowan, *When Partners Become Parents*, 101–2.

211 **hard to move from a twosome to a threesome:** See de Marneffe, *Rough Patch*, 34–38.

211 **though problems still abound:** See, for example, Williams, *Unbending Gender*, chap. 4; and Crittenden, *Price of Motherhood*, chaps. 7 and 8; Bianchi, Subaiya, and Kahn, "Gender Gap"; Wallerstein, Lewis, and Blakeslee, *Unexpected Legacy of Divorce*, chaps. 7 and 8.

213 **whereas fathers tended to take it much harder:** Rubin, *Women of a Certain Age*, 36.

213 **less than half feel they are doing "a very good job" raising them:** Parker and Livingston, "7 Facts about American Dads."

214 **fathers can become overly identified with their work:** See, for example, Hochschild and Machung, *Second Shift*.

216 **"their path is connected to their heart":** This phrase is from Kornfield, *Path with Heart*, quoted in hooks, *All about Love*, 80.

217 **"nurturing one's own or another's spiritual growth":** hooks, *All about Love*, 4, quoting Peck's *Road Less Traveled*.

217 **"points they are having difficulty getting across":** Wile, *After the Honeymoon*, 165.

218 **"feeling that it has gotten across":** Wile, 47.

10. TIME WITH CHILDREN

222 **"the grains of sand as they slid lightly away":** Tomasi di Lampedusa, *Leopard*, 277–78.

223 **"then shall I know even as also I am known":** "Nostalgia for the present" is a phrase recollected from a commentary on the Chinese philosopher Chuang-Tzu, the source of which I was unable to locate. The 1 Corinthians 13:12 quotation is from the King James Version of the Bible.

225 **"a person who is not expected to set her own agenda in the world":** de Beauvoir, *Second Sex*, 301; and Bauer, *Simone de Beauvoir*, 171.

226 **a primary source of parental dissatisfaction:** Galinsky, "1997 National Study."

227 **held steady for the last fifty years and, if anything, have decreased:** Sullivan and Gershuny, "Speed Up Society?"

227 **leisure time is up:** Robinson and Godbey, "Busyness as Usual"; "How Americans Spend Their Time."

227 **In a study of eleven Western countries:** Dotti Sani and Treas, "Educational Gradients."

227 **or doing more than one activity at once:** Robinson and Godbey, *Time for Life*, 38–42.

228 **a "serve-and-return" style of conversation:** Christakis, "Dangers of Distracted Parenting," 12. Christakis is citing the phrase of Jack P. Shonkoff, MD.

229 **age-old dichotomy of "having" as opposed to "being":** See, for example, Fromm, *To Have or to Be?*

231 **the dehumanizing aspects of the marketplace:** Hays, *Cultural Contradictions of Motherhood*, 18.

231 **high-intensity, child-focused chauffeuring:** For a classic study on class differences with respect to child-rearing approaches, see Lareau, *Unequal Childhoods*.

236 **less easily dispatched there:** Hochschild, *Time Bind*, chap. 4.

237 **the degradation of our capacity to appreciate:** Robinson and Godbey, *Time for Life*, 316.

237 **"one living reality which is a new *you*":** Merton, *Love and Living*, 28, quoted in hooks, *All about Love*, 187.

238 **"The liberation of the heart, which is love":** This phrase is the Buddha's, from Salzberg, *Lovingkindness*, 1, quoted in hooks, *All about Love*, 83.

Bibliography

Adams, Sarah L. *Mad Mothers, Bad Mothers, and What a "Good" Mother Would Do.* New York: Columbia University Press, 2014.

Ahlberg, Janet, and Allan Ahlberg. *Peek-A-Boo!* New York: Viking, 1990.

Ahnert, Lieselotte, and Michael E. Lamb. "Shared Care: Establishing a Balance between Home and Child Care Settings." *Child Development* 74, no. 4 (2003): 1044–49.

Allen, Jon G. *Restoring Mentalizing in Attachment Relationships: Treating Trauma with Plain Old Therapy.* Washington, DC: American Psychiatric Press, 2013.

Angier, Natalie. "Primate Expert Explores Motherhood's Brutal Side." *New York Times,* Science section, February 8, 2000.

————. *Woman: An Intimate Geography.* Boston: Houghton Mifflin, 1999.

Aries, Philippe. *Centuries of Childhood: A Social History of Family Life.* Translated by Robert Baldick. New York: Alfred A. Knopf, 1962.

Badinter, Elisabeth. *The Conflict: How Modern Motherhood Undermines the Status of Women.* New York: Metropolitan Books, 2011.

Bailey, Sarah P. "What Ever Happened to the Mommy Blog?" *Chicago Tribune,* January 29, 2018. https://www.chicagotribune.com/life styles/parenting/ct-mommy-blog-disappear-20180129-story.html.

Balsam, Rosemary M. *Women's Bodies in Psychoanalysis.* New York: Routledge, 2012.

Baraitser, Lisa. *Maternal Encounters: The Ethics of Interruption.* London: Routledge, 2008.

————. "Oi Mother, Keep Ye' Hair On! Impossible Transformations of Maternal Subjectivity." *Studies in Gender and Sexuality* 7, no. 3 (2006): 217–38.

Baraitser, Lisa, and Amelie Noack. "Mother Courage: Reflections on Maternal Resilience," *British Journal of Psychotherapy* 23, no. 2 (2007): 171–88.

Bartholet, Elizabeth. *Family Bonds: Adoption and the Politics of Parenting.* Boston: Houghton Mifflin, 1993.

Bassin, Donna. "Maternal Subjectivity in the Culture of Nostalgia: Mourning and Memory." In *Representations of Motherhood,* edited by Donna Bassin, Margaret Honey, and Meryle Mahrer Kaplan, 162–73. New Haven, CT: Yale University Press, 1994.

Bauer, Nancy. *Simone de Beauvoir, Philosophy, and Feminism.* New York: Columbia University Press, 2001.

Beebe, Beatrice, and Frank M. Lachmann. *Infant Research and Adult Treatment: Co-constructing Interactions.* Hillsdale, NJ: Analytic Press, 2002.

Belsky, Jay. "Interactional and Contextual Determinants of Attachment Security." In *Handbook of Attachment: Theory, Research, and Clinical Applications,* edited by Jude Cassidy and Phillip R. Shaver, 249–64. New York: Guilford, 1999.

Benjamin, Jessica. "Beyond Doer and Done to: An Intersubjective View of Thirdness." *Psychoanalytic Quarterly* 73, no. 1 (2004): 5–46.

———. "*The Bonds of Love*: Looking Backward." *Studies in Gender and Sexuality* 14, no. 1 (2013): 1–15.

———. *The Bonds of Love: Psychoanalysis, Feminism, and the Problem of Domination.* New York: Pantheon, 1988.

———. *Like Subjects, Love Objects: Essays on Recognition and Sexual Difference.* New Haven, CT: Yale University Press, 1995.

———. "The Omnipotent Mother: A Psychoanalytic Study of Fantasy and Reality." In *Representations of Motherhood,* edited by Donna Bassin, Margaret Honey, and Meryle Mahrer Kaplan, 129–46. New Haven, CT: Yale University Press, 1994.

Bialosky, Jill, and Helen Schulman, eds. *Wanting a Child.* New York: Farrar, Straus and Giroux, 1998.

Bianchi, Suzanne M., Lekha Subaiya, and Joan R. Kahn. "The Gender Gap in the Economic Well-Being of Nonresident Fathers and Custodial Mothers." *Demography* 36, no. 2 (May 1999): 195–203.

Boggs, Belle. *The Art of Waiting: On Fertility, Medicine, and Motherhood.* Minneapolis: Graywolf Press, 2016.

Bolton, Martha Brandt. "Responsible Women and Abortion Decisions." In *Having Children: Philosophical and Legal Reflections on Parenthood,* edited by Onora O'Neill and William Ruddick, 40–51. New York: Oxford University Press, 1979.

Bomford, Rodney. *The Symmetry of God.* London: Free Association Books, 1999.

Bordo, Susan. "Are Mothers Persons?: Reproductive Rights and the Politics of Subjectivity." In *Unbearable Weight: Feminism, Western Culture, and the Body,* 71–97. Berkeley: University of California Press, 1993.

———. *Unbearable Weight: Feminism, Western Culture, and the Body.* Berkeley: University of California Press, 1993.

Bork, Robert. "Inconvenient Lives." *First Things* 68 (December 1996): 9–13.

Boulton, Mary Georgina. *On Being a Mother: A Study of Women with Pre-school Children.* New York: Tavistock Publications, 1983.

Breuer, Josef, and Sigmund Freud. "Studies on Hysteria." In *The Standard Edition of the Complete Psychological Works of Sigmund Freud,* edited by James Strachey, 2: 3–181. London: Hogarth Press, 1955.

Brockes, Emma. "Single at 38? Have That Baby." *New York Times,* June 23, 2018. https://www.nytimes.com/2018/06/23/opinion/sunday/single-at-38-have-that-baby.html.

Brooks, Gwendolyn. "the mother" (1945). In *The Norton Anthology of African American Literature,* edited by Henry Louis Gates Jr. and Nellie Y. McKay, 1579–80. New York: Norton, 1997.

Brown, Laura. Letter to the Editor. *New York Times,* June 25, 2018.

Brown, Lyn Mikel, and Carol Gilligan. *Meeting at the Crossroads: Women's Psychology and Girls' Development.* Cambridge, MA: Harvard University Press, 1992.

Bueskens, Petra. "Introduction." In *Mothering and Psychoanalysis: Clinical, Sociological and Feminist Perspectives,* edited by Petra Bueskens. Bradford, ON: Demeter Press, 2014, 50.

Bui, Quoctrung, and Claire C. Miller. "The Age That Women Have Babies: How a Gap Divides America." *New York Times,* August 4, 2018. https://www.nytimes.com/interactive/2018/08/04/upshot/up-birth-age-gap.html.

Burggraf, Shirley P. *The Feminine Economy and Economic Man: Reviving the Role of Family in the Post-industrial Age.* Reading, MA: Addison-Wesley, 1997.

Byatt, A. S. *Still Life.* New York: Scribner, 1985.

Carstensen, Laura L. *A Long Bright Future*. New York: Public Affairs, 2011.

Carter, Stephen L. *The Culture of Disbelief: How American Law and Politics Trivialize Religious Devotion*. New York: Basic Books, 1993.

Chensvold, Christian. "YouTube's New Father Figure." *NationalReview .com*, June 17, 2017. https://www.nationalreview.com/2017/06 /jordan-p-peterson-self-help-guru-father-figure/.

Chetrit-Vatine, V. *The Ethical Seduction of the Analytic Situation*. London: Karnac, 2014.

Chira, Susan. *A Mother's Place: Taking the Debate about Working Mothers beyond Guilt and Blame*. New York: HarperCollins, 1998.

Chodorow, Nancy J. *Femininities, Masculinities, Sexualities: Freud and Beyond*. Lexington: University Press of Kentucky, 1994.

———. "Oedipal Asymmetries and Heterosexual Knots." In *Feminism and Psychoanalytic Theory*, 66–78. New Haven, CT: Yale University Press, 1989.

———. *The Reproduction of Mothering: Psychoanalysis and the Sociology of Gender*. 2nd ed. Berkeley: University of California Press, 1999.

———. " 'Too Late': Ambivalence about Motherhood, Choice, and Time." *Journal of the American Psychoanalytic Association* 51, no. 4 (2003): 1181–98.

Christakis, Erika. "The Dangers of Distracted Parenting." *Atlantic*, July/August 2018. https://www.theatlantic.com/magazine /archive/2018/07/the-dangers-of-distracted-parenting/561752/.

Clarke-Stewart, Alison. *Daycare*. Rev. ed. Cambridge, MA: Harvard University Press, 1993.

Clarke-Stewart, Alison, and Greta Fein. "Early Childhood Programs." In *Handbook of Child Psychology*. Vol. 2, *Infancy and Developmental Psychobiology*, edited by Paul Mussen, 917–1000. New York: Wiley, 1983.

Coates, Susan W. "Having a Mind of One's Own and Holding the Other in Mind: Commentary on Paper by Peter Fonagy and Mary Target." *Psychoanalytic Dialogues* 8, no. 1 (1998): 115–48.

Collins, Karen. "A Mother at Last." *Harper's Bazaar*, January 2003, 57.

Collins, Patricia Hill. *Black Feminist Thought: Knowledge, Consciousness, and the Politics of Empowerment*. New York: Routledge, 1990.

Cooke, Emily. "In the Middle Class, and Barely Getting By." *New York Times*, July 9, 2018. https://www.nytimes.com/2018/07/09/books /review/alissa-quart-squeezed.html.

Cott, Nancy F. *The Bonds of Womanhood: "Woman's Sphere" in New England, 1780–1835*. New Haven, CT: Yale University Press, 1977.

————. *The Grounding of Modern Feminism*. New Haven, CT: Yale University Press, 1987.

Cowan, Carolyn Pape, and Philip A. Cowan. *When Partners Become Parents: The Big Life Change for Couples*. New York: Basic Books, 1992.

Coyle, Diane. "The Way We Measure Economies Is Inherently Sexist." *World Economic Forum*, April 13, 2016. https://www.weforum.org/agenda/2016/04/why-economic-policy-overlooks-women/.

Cozolino, Louis. *The Neuroscience of Human Relationships*. 2nd ed. New York: Norton, 2014.

Crittenden, Ann. *The Price of Motherhood: Why the Most Important Job in the World Is Still the Least Valued*. New York: Metropolitan Books, 2001.

Csikszentmihalyi, Mihaly. *Creativity: Flow and the Psychology of Discovery and Invention*. New York: HarperCollins, 1996.

————. *Flow: The Psychology of Optimal Experience*. New York: Harper Perennial, 1991.

Cummings, E. Mark, and Patrick T. Davies. *Marital Conflict and Children: An Emotional Security Perspective*. New York: Guilford, 2010.

Cusk, Rachel. *A Life's Work: On Becoming a Mother*. New York: Picador, 2001.

Dagher, Rada K., Sandra L. Hofferth, and Yoonjoo Lee. "Maternal Depression, Pregnancy Intention, and Return to Paid Work After Childbirth." *Women's Health Issues* 24, no. 3 (2014): e297–e303.

Daum, Meghan. "Opting Out of Motherhood." HarpersBazaar.com, February 20, 2015. https://www.harpersbazaar.com/culture/features/a10040/opting-out-of-motherhood-0315/.

de Beauvoir, Simone. *The Second Sex*. Translated by H. M. Parshley. New York: Vintage Books, 1974.

Debold, Elizabeth, Marie Wilson, and Idelisse Malave. *Mother-Daughter Revolution: From Betrayal to Power*. Reading, MA: Addison-Wesley, 1993.

Decasper, A., and W. Fifer. "Of Human Bonding: Newborns Prefer Their Mothers' Voices." *Science* 208 (1980): 1174–76.

de Marneffe, Daphne. "'The (M)other We Fall in Love With Wants to be There': Reply to Commentaries." *Studies in Gender and Sexuality* 10, no.1 (2009): 27–32.

————. *The Rough Patch: Marriage and the Art of Living Together*. New York: Scribner, 2018.

———. "What Exactly *Is* the Transformation of Motherhood?: Commentary on Lisa Baraitser's Paper." *Studies in Gender and Sexuality* 7, no. 3 (2006): 239–48.

Deutsch, Helene. *Motherhood.* Vol. 2, *The Psychology of Women.* New York: Grune and Stratton, 1945.

Dimen, Muriel. "Strange Hearts: On the Paradoxical Liaison between Psychoanalysis and Feminism." In *Freud: Conflict and Culture*, edited by Michael Roth, 207–20. New York: Alfred A. Knopf, 1998.

Dinnerstein, Dorothy. *The Mermaid and the Minotaur: Sexual Arrangements and Human Malaise.* New York: Harper Colophon Books, 1976.

Dotti Sani, Guilia M., and Judith Treas. "Educational Gradients in Parents' Child-Care Time across Countries, 1965–2012." *Journal of Marriage and Family* 78 (2016): 1083–96. https://doi.org/10.1111/jomf.12305.

Douglas, Susan, and Meredith Michaels. *The Mommy Myth: The Idealization of Motherhood and How It Has Undermined Women.* New York: Free Press, 2004.

Duane, Anna Mae. "An Infant Nation: Childhood Studies and Early America." *Literature Compass* 2 (2005): 1–9.

Dworkin, Ronald. *Life's Dominion: An Argument about Abortion, Euthanasia, and Individual Freedom.* New York: Alfred A. Knopf, 1993.

Ehrenreich, Barbara, and Deirdre English. *For Her Own Good: 150 Years of the Experts' Advice to Women.* New York: Anchor Press/Doubleday, 1978.

Ehrenreich, Barbara, and Arlie Russell Hochschild, eds. *Global Woman: Nannies, Maids, and Sex Workers in the New Economy.* New York: Metropolitan Books, 2003.

Eisenberg, Evan. "The Adoption Paradox." *Discover*, January 2001, 80–89.

Eliot, George [Mary Ann Evans]. *Felix Holt, the Radical.* 1866. Reprint, New York: Penguin, 1995.

Elkin, Lauren. "Why All the Books About Motherhood?" theparisreview.org, July 17, 2018. https://www.theparisreview.org/blog/2018/07/17/why-all-the-books-about-motherhood/.

Enright, Anne. "My Milk." *London Review of Books* 22, no. 19 (October 5, 2000).

Erdrich, Louise. *The Blue Jay's Dance: A Birth Year.* New York: Harper Perennial, 1995.

Faludi, Susan. *Backlash: The Undeclared War against American Women.* New York: Anchor Books/Doubleday, 1991.

Fernald, Anne. "Human Maternal Vocalization to Infants as Biologically Relevant Signals: An Evolutionary Perspective." In *The Adapted Mind: Evolutionary Psychology and the Generation of Culture,* edited by J. H. Barrow, L. Cosmides, and J. Tooby, 391–428. New York: Oxford University Press, 1992.

Firestone, Shulamith. *The Dialectic of Sex: The Case for Feminist Revolution.* New York: Bantam Books, 1972.

Folbre, Nancy. *The Invisible Heart: Economics and Family Values.* New York: Free Press, 2001.

Fonagy, Peter. *Attachment Theory and Psychoanalysis.* New York: Other Press, 2001.

Fonagy, Peter, Gyorgy Gergely, Elliot L. Jurist, and Mary Target. *Affect Regulation, Mentalization, and the Development of the Self.* New York: Other Press, 2002.

Fonagy, Peter, and Mary Target. "Mentalization and the Changing Aims of Psychoanalysis." *Psychoanalytic Dialogues* 8 (1998): 87–114.

Friedan, Betty. *The Feminine Mystique.* New York: Dell, 1970.

———. *The Second Stage.* New York: Summit Books, 1981.

Fromm, Erich. *To Have or to Be?* New York: Harper and Row, 1976.

Foucault, Michel. *The History of Sexuality.* New York: Vintage, 1980.

Galinsky, Ellen. "The 1997 National Study of the Changing Workforce. Families and Work Institute, 1997." www.familiesandwork.org/nationalstudy.html.

Garbes, Angela. "Why Are We Only Talking About 'Mom Books' by White Women?" thecut.com, November 1, 2018. https://www.thecut.com/2018/11/why-are-we-only-talking-about-mom-books-by-white-women.html.

Gardner, Ralph, Jr. "Mom vs. Mom." *New York,* October 21, 2002, 21–25.

Garey, Anita I. *Weaving Work and Motherhood.* Philadelphia: Temple University Press, 1999.

George, Carol, and Judith Solomon. "The Development of Caregiving: A Comparison of Attachment Theory and Psychoanalytic Approaches to Mothering." *Psychoanalytic Inquiry* 19 (1999): 618–46.

———. "Representational Models of Relationships: Links between Caregiving and Attachment." *Infant Mental Health Journal* 17 (1996): 198–216.

Gergely, Gyorgy, and John Watson. "The Social Biofeedback Model of Parental Affect-Mirroring." *International Journal of Psychoanalysis* 77 (1996): 1197–1228.

Gerhardt, Julie, Annie Sweetnam, and Leann Borton. "The Intersubjective Turn in Psychoanalysis: A Comparison of Contemporary Theorists: Part 1: Benjamin." *Psychoanalytic Dialogues* 10, no. 1(2000): 5–42.

Gibson, Margaret F., ed. *Queering Motherhood: Narrative and Theoretical Perspectives.* Bradford, ON: Demeter Press, 2014.

Gilligan, Carol. *In a Different Voice: Psychological Theory and Women's Development.* Cambridge, MA: Harvard University Press, 1982.

Glenn, Evelyn Nakano. "Social Constructions of Mothering: A Thematic Overview." In *Mothering: Ideology, Experience, and Agency,* edited by Evelyn Nakano Glenn, Grace Chang, and Linda Rennie Forcey, 1–29. New York: Routledge, 1994.

Golombok, Susan. *Modern Families: Parents and Children in New Family Forms.* Cambridge, UK: Cambridge University Press, 2015.

Gopnik, Adam. "The Double Man: Why Auden Is an Indispensable Poet of Our Time." *New Yorker,* September 23, 2002.

Gorney, Cynthia. *Articles of Faith: A Frontline History of the Abortion Wars.* New York: Simon & Schuster, 1998.

Gottman, John M., and Nan Silver. *The Seven Principles for Making Marriage Work.* New York: Crown, 1999.

Grady, Constance. "The Waves of Feminism, and Why People Keep Fighting over Them, Explained." vox.com, July 20, 2018. https://www.vox.com/2018/3/20/16955588/feminism-waves-explained-first-second-third-fourth.

Graybeal, Jean. "Kristeva's Delphic Proposal: 'Practice Encompasses the Ethical.' " In *Ethics, Politics, and Difference in Julia Kristeva's Writing,* edited by Kelly Oliver, 32–40. New York: Routledge, 1993.

Grigoriadis, Vanessa. "Baby Panic." *New York,* May 20, 2002, 20–25.

Gross, Jane. "Women and Their Work: How Life Inundates Art." *New York Times,* Money and Business section, August 23, 1998.

Harper's Forum. "Giving Women the Business: On Winning, Losing, and Leaving the Corporate Game." *Harper's,* December 1997, 47–58.

———. "Is Abortion the Issue?: Strong Sentiments in Search of a Discussion." *Harper's,* July 1986.

Havrilevsky, Heather. "Ask Polly: I'm Terrified of Having Kids!" thecut.com, July 12, 2017, https://www.thecut.com/2017/07/ask-polly-im-terrified-of-having-kids.html.

Hays, Sharon. *The Cultural Contradictions of Motherhood.* New Haven, CT: Yale University Press, 1996.

Heineman, Toni Vaughn. "A Boy and Two Mothers: New Variations on an Old Theme or a New Story of Triangulation? Beginning Thoughts on the Psychosexual Development of Children in Non-traditional Famiies." *Psychoanalytic Psychology* 21, no. 1 (2004).

Hesse, Erik. "The Adult Attachment Interview: Protocol, Method of Analysis, and Selected Empirical Studies, 1985–2015." In *Handbook of Attachment: Theory, Research, and Clinical Applications*, 3rd ed., edited by J. Cassidy and P. Shaver, 553–97. New York: Guilford, 2016.

Hewlett, Sylvia Ann. *A Lesser Life: The Myth of Women's Liberation in America.* New York: William Morrow, 1986.

Hidalgo, Candis Lynn. "Open Letter to New Mom Bloggers: The 9 Reasons Why You're Failing." *Huffington Post*, February 23, 2016. https://www.huffpost.com/entry/open-letter-to-new-mom-bl_b_9288760.

Hirsch, Marianne. "Feminist Discourse/Maternal Discourse: Speaking with Two Voices." In *The Mother/Daughter Plot: Narrative, Psychoanalysis, Feminism.* Bloomington: Indiana University Press, 1989.

Hochschild, Arlie Russell. *The Time Bind: When Work Becomes Home and Home Becomes Work.* New York: Metropolitan Books, 1997.

Hochschild, Arlie Russell, with Anne Machung. *The Second Shift: Working Parents and the Revolution at Home.* New York: Viking, 1989.

Hodder, Harbour Fraser. "The New Fertility." *Harvard Magazine*, November/December 1997.

Holmes, Jeremy, and Arietta Slade. *Attachment in Therapeutic Practice.* London: Sage, 2018.

Hondagneu-Sotelo, Pierrette. *Domestica: Immigrant Workers Cleaning and Caring in the Shadows of Affluence.* Berkeley: University of California Press, 2001.

hooks, bell. *All about Love: New Visions.* New York: William Morrow, 2000.

Horney, Karen. "The Flight from Womanhood: The Masculinity-Complex in Women as Viewed by Men and Women" (1926). In *Feminine Psychology*, edited by Harold Kelman, 54–70. New York: Norton, 1973.

"How Americans Spend Their Time: Working Less despite Job Growth." *Wall Street Journal*, June 28, 2018. https://www.wsj.com/graphics /time-use-2018/.

Hrdy, Sarah Blaffer. *Mother Nature: A History of Mothers, Infants, and Natural Selection.* New York: Pantheon, 2000.

Ireland, Mardy. *Reconceiving Women: Separating Motherhood and Female Identity.* New York: Guilford, 1993.

Jaeger, Elizabeth, and Marsha Weinraub. "Early Nonmaternal Care and Infant Attachment: In Search of Process." *New Directions for Child Development* 49 (1990): 71–90.

Jaffe, Joseph, Beatrice Beebe, Stanley Feldstein, Cynthia Crown, and Michael D. Jasnow. "Rhythms of Dialogue in Infancy." *Monographs of the Society for Research in Child Development* 66, no. 2, serial no. 265 (2001): 1–132.

Johnson, Emma. "How Stay-at-home Moms Hurt Gender Equality." wealthysinglemommy.com, February 20, 2018. https://www .wealthysinglemommy.com/how-stay-at-home-moms-hurt-gen der-equality/

Kaminer, Wendy. *A Fearful Freedom: Women's Flight from Equality.* Reading, MA: Addison-Wesley, 1990.

———. *True Love Waits: Essays and Criticism.* Reading, MA: Addison-Wesley, 1996.

Kaplan, Louise. *Oneness and Separateness: From Infant to Individual.* New York: Simon & Schuster, 1978.

Kawash, Samira. "New Directions in Motherhood Studies." *Signs* 36, no. 4 (2011): 969–1003.

Kelman, Harold. "Introduction." In Karen Horney, *Feminine Psychology*, edited by Harold Kelman, 7–31. New York: Norton, 1973.

Killewald, Alexandra. "Money, Work, and Marital Stability: Assessing Change in Gendered Determinants of Divorce." *American Sociological Review* 81, no. 4 (2016): 696–719. https://doi.org/10 .1177/0003122416655340.

Kitroeff, Natalie, and Jessica Silver-Greenberg. "Pregnancy Discrimination Is Rampant inside America's Biggest Companies." *New York Times*, June 15, 2018. https://www.nytimes.com/interac tive/2018/06/15/business/pregnancy-discrimination.html.

Kitzinger, Sheila. *Ourselves as Mothers: The Universal Experience of Motherhood.* Reading, MA: Addison-Wesley, 1995.

Klein, Melanie. *Envy and Gratitude and Other Works, 1946–1963*. New York: Free Press, 1975.

Kolbert, Elizabeth. "Mother Courage." *The New Yorker*, March 8, 2004. https://www.newyorker.com/magazine/2004/03/08/mother-courage.

Kornfield, Jack. *A Path with Heart: A Guide through the Perils and Promises of Spiritual Life*. New York: Bantam Books, 1993.

Kristeva, Julia. "Reliance, or Maternal Eroticism." *Journal of the American Psychoanalytic Association* 62, no. 1 (2014): 69–85.

———. "Women's Time." In *The Kristeva Reader*, edited by Toril Moi, 187–213. New York: Columbia University Press, 1986.

La Ferla, Ruth. "These Companies Really, Really, Really Want to Freeze Your Eggs." *New York Times*, August 29, 2018. https://www.nytimes.com/2018/08/29/style/egg-freezing-fertility-millennials.html.

Lambert, Craig. "Image and the Arc of Feeling." *Harvard Magazine*, January/February 2001, 39–43.

Lamott, Anne. "Mother Anger: Theory and Practice." In *Mothers Who Think: Tales of Real-Life Parenthood*, edited by Camille Peri and Kate Moses. New York: Villard, 1999.

Langer, Marie. *Motherhood and Sexuality*. Translated by Nancy Caro Hollander. New York: Guilford, 1992.

Lareau, Annette. *Unequal Childhoods: Class, Race, and Family Life*. Berkeley: University of California Press, 2003.

Lasch, Christopher. *Women and the Common Life: Love, Marriage, and Feminism*. New York: Norton, 1997.

Lasch-Quinn, Elisabeth. "Mothers and Markets." *New Republic*, March 6, 2000, 34–37.

Leach, Penelope. *Your Baby and Child: From Birth to Age Five*. New York: Alfred A. Knopf, 1992.

Leclerc, Annie. *Parole de femme*. Paris: Grasser, 1974.

Lemma, Alessandra. "Copies without Originals: The Psychodynamics of Cosmetic Surgery." *Psychoanalytic Quarterly* 79 (2010): 129–57.

Levine, Hagai, Niels Jørgensen, Anderson Martino-Andrade, Jaime Mendiola, Dan Weksler-Derri, Irina Mindlis, Rachel Pinotti, and Shanna H. Swan. "Temporal Trends in Sperm Count: A Systematic Review and Meta-regression Analysis." *Human Reproduction Update* 23, no. 6 (2017): 646–59. https://doi.org/10.1093/humupd/dmx022.

Loewald, Hans. *Papers in Psychoanalysis*. New Haven, CT: Yale University Press, 1980.

Lopate, Phillip. "The Lake of Suffering." In *Wanting a Child*, edited by Jill Bialosky and Helen Schulman, 106–19. New York: Farrar, Straus and Giroux, 1998.

Ludtke, Melissa. *On Our Own: Unmarried Motherhood in America*. New York: Random House, 1997.

Luker, Kristin. *Abortion and the Politics of Motherhood*. Berkeley: University of California Press, 1984.

———. *Dubious Conceptions: The Politics of Teenage Pregnancy*. Cambridge, MA: Harvard University Press, 1996.

Lundberg, Ferdinand, and Marynia Farnham. *Modern Woman: The Lost Sex*. New York: Harper Brothers, 1947.

Lvons-Ruth, Karlen. "Rapprochement or Approchement: Mahler's Theory Reconsidered from the Vantage Point of Recent Research in Early Attachment Relationships." *Psychoanalytic Psychology* 8 (1991): 1–23.

MacKinnon, Catharine A. "Reflections on Sex Equality under Law." *Yale Law Journal* 100 (1991): 1281–1328.

Mahler, Margaret, Fred Pine, and Anni Bergman. *The Psychological Birth of the Human Infant*. New York: Basic Books, 1975.

Main, Mary. "Metacognitive Knowledge, Metacognitive Monitoring, and Singular (Coherent) vs. Multiple (Incoherent) Models of Attachment: Findings and Directions for Future Research." In *Attachment across the Life Cycle*, edited by C. M. Parkes, J. Stevenson-Hinde, and P. Marris, 127–59. London: Routledge, 1991.

Main, Mary, Nancy Kaplan, and Jude Cassidy. "Security in Infancy, Childhood, and Adulthood: A Move to the Level of Representation." In *Growing Points of Attachment Theory and Research*, edited by Inge Bretherton and Everett Waters. Monographs of the Society for Research in Child Development 50 (1–2), serial no. 209 (1985): 66–104.

Mamo, Laura. *Queering Reproduction: Achieving Pregnancy in the Age of Techno-science*. Durham, NC: Duke University Press, 2007.

Maslow, Abraham H. *Motivation and Personality*. 2nd ed. New York: Harper and Row, 1970.

Mattis, Ann. "Vulgar Strangers in the Home: Charlotte Perkins Gilman and Modern Servitude." *Women's Studies* 39 (2010): 283–303.

McBride, James. *The Color of Water: A Black Man's Tribute to His White Mother*. New York: Riverhead Books, 1996.

McHale, James P. *Charting the Bumpy Road of Coparenthood: Understanding the Challenges of Family Life.* Washington, DC: Zero to Three, 2007.

Mehta, Neera, Philip A. Cowan, and Carolyn P. Cowan. "Working Models of Attachments to Parents and Partners: Implications for Emotional Behavior between Partners." *Journal of Family Psychology* 23 (2009): 895–99.

Merton, Thomas. *Love and Living.* Edited by Naomi Burton Stone and Patrick Hart. New York: Farrar, Straus and Giroux, 1979.

Michel, Sonya. *Children's Interests/Mothers' Rights: The Shaping of America's Child Care Policy.* New Haven, CT: Yale University Press, 2000.

Mikulincer, Mario, and Phillip R. Shaver. *Attachment in Adulthood: Structure, Dynamics, and Change.* 2nd ed. New York: Guilford, 2016.

Miller, Claire C. "Americans Are Having Fewer Babies. They Told Us Why." *New York Times,* Comment section, July 5, 2018. https://www.nytimes.com/2018/07/05/upshot/americans-are-having-fewer-babies-they-told-us-why.html#commentsContainer.

Mitchell, Juliet. *Psychoanalysis and Feminism: Freud, Reich, Laing, and Women.* New York: Pantheon, 1974.

Mitchell, Stephen A. *Relationality: From Attachment to Intersubjectivity.* Hillsdale, NJ: Analytic Press, 2000.

Moi, Toril. "Introduction" to "Women's Time." In *The Kristeva Reader,* edited by Toril Moi, 187–88. New York: Columbia University Press, 1986.

Morrison, Toni. *Beloved.* New York: Plume, 1988.

Moyers, Bill, and Andie Tucher. *A World of Ideas: Public Opinions from Private Citizens.* New York: Public Affairs Television, 1990.

Murphy, Heather. "Lots of Successful Women Are Freezing Their Eggs. But It May Not Be About Their Careers." *New York Times,* July 3, 2018. https://www.nytimes.com/2018/07/03/health/freezing-eggs-women.html?action=click&module=RelatedLinks&pgtype=Article.

Neff, Kristin D. *Self-Compassion.* New York: HarperCollins, 2011.

Nelson, Maggie. *The Argonauts.* Minneapolis: Graywolf Press, 2015.

New York Times Editorial Board. "Fetal Playbook, Explained." *New York Times,* December 28, 2018. https://www.nytimes.com/interactive/2018/12/28/opinion/abortion-murder-charge.html.

NICHD Early Child Care Research Network. "Child Care and Mother-

Child Interaction in the First Three Years of Life." *Developmental Psychology* 35, no. 6 (1999): 1399–1413.

———. "The Effects of Infant Child Care on Infant-Mother Attachment Security: Results of the NICHD Study of Early Child Care." *Child Development* 68, no. 5 (1997): 860–79.

Nofziger, Margaret. *The Fertility Question.* Summertown, TN: Book Publishing Company, 1982.

Olsen, Tillie. *Tell Me a Riddle.* New York: Delta/Seymour Lawrence, 1994.

Orbach, Susie. *Fat Is a Feminist Issue.* New York: Galahad Books, 1982.

Park, Shelley M. *Mothering Queerly, Queering Motherhood.* Albany, NY: SUNY Press, 2013.

Parker, Kim, and Gretchen Livingston. "7 Facts about American Dads." Pew Research Center, June 13, 2018. http://www.pewresearch.org/fact-tank/2018/06/13/fathers-day-facts/.

Parker, Rozsika. *Mother Love/Mother Hate: The Power of Maternal Ambivalence.* New York: Basic Books, 1995.

Parrenas, Rhacel Salazar, ed. *Servants of Globalization: Women, Migration, and Domestic Work.* Stanford, CA: Stanford University Press, 2001.

Pascuzzi, Francesco. "Mothers at a Loss: Identity and Mourning in *La Sconosciuta* and *Milyang.*" In *Italian Motherhood on Screen*, edited by Faleschini Lerner and Maria Elena D'Amelio, 117–35. London: Palgrave Macmillan, 2017.

Payne, Karen, ed. *Between Ourselves: Letters between Mothers and Daughters.* Boston: Houghton Mifflin, 1983.

Pearson, Jane, Deborah Cohn, Philip Cowan, and Carolyn Pape Cowan. "Earned- and Continuous-Security in Adult Attachment: Relation to Depressive Symptomatology and Parenting Style." *Development and Psychopathology* 6, no. 2 (1994): 359–73.

Peck, M. Scott. *The Road Less Traveled.* New York: Simon & Schuster, 1978.

Peri, Camille, and Kate Moses, eds. *Mothers Who Think: Tales of Real-Life Parenthood.* New York: Villard, 1999.

Peskowitz, Miriam. *The Truth Behind the Mommy Wars* (2005).

Peters, Joan K. *When Mothers Work: Loving Our Children without Sacrificing Ourselves.* Reading, MA: Addison-Wesley, 1997.

Peterson, Jordan. "Fathering and Manhood | Jordan Peterson." https://www.youtube.com/watch?v=IdezhDdI_Zs.

————. "The Proper Role of Parents (Particularly Fathers)." https://www.youtube.com/watch?v=-JQHcHoUk3c.

————. *12 Rules for Life: An Antidote to Chaos.* New York: Penguin Random House Canada, 2018.

Pinker, Steven. *The Language Instinct: How the Mind Creates Language.* New York: William Morrow, 1994.

Pollitt, Katha. *Reasonable Creatures: Essays on Women and Feminism.* New York: Alfred A. Knopf, 1994.

————. *Subject to Debate: Sense and Dissents on Women, Politics, and Culture.* New York: Modern Library, 2001.

Priddy, Kristen D. "Immunologic Adaptations during Pregnancy." *Journal of Obstetric, Gynecologic, and Neonatal Nursing* 26, no. 4 (1997): 388–94.

Quesenberry, Jeria L., Eileen M. Trauth, and Allison J. Morgan. "Understanding the 'Mommy Tracks': A Framework for Analyzing Work-Family Balance in the IT Workforce." *Information Resources Management Journal* 19, no. 2 (2006): 37–53.

Quinn, Susan. *A Mind of Her Own: The Life of Karen Horney.* New York: Summit Books, 1987.

Rabin, Roni C. "College Students Want Children, but Don't Know When Fertility Declines." *New York Times,* August 1, 2018. https://www.nytimes.com/2018/08/01/well/college-students-want-children-but-dont-know-when-fertility-declines.html.

Rich, Adrienne. *Of Woman Born: Motherhood as Experience and Institution.* New York: Norton, 1995.

Roazen, Paul. *Helene Deutsch: A Psychoanalyst's Life.* Garden City, NY: Anchor Press/Doubleday, 1985.

Robinson, John P., and Geoffrey Godbey. "Busyness as Usual." *Social Research* 72, no. 2 (2005): 407–26.

————. *Time for Life: The Surprising Ways Americans Use Their Time.* University Park: Pennsylvania State University Press, 1997.

Robinson, Marilynne. *The Death of Adam: Essays on Modern Thought.* Boston: Houghton Mifflin, 1998.

Roiphe, Anne. *Fruitful: A Real Mother in the Modern World.* Boston: Houghton Mifflin, 1996.

Ropers-Huilman, Rebecca, and Kathryn A.E. Enke. "Catholic Women's College Students' Constructions of Identity: Influence of Faculty and Staff on Students' Personal and Professional Self-

Understanding." *NASPA Journal About Women in Higher Education* 3, no. 1 (2010): 88–116.

Rossi, Agnes. "In Vitro." In *Wanting a Child*, edited by Jill Bialosky and Helen Schulman, 60–68. New York: Farrar, Straus and Giroux, 1998.

Rubin, Lillian. *Women of a Certain Age: The Midlife Search for Self.* New York: Harper and Row, 1979.

Ryan, Mary P. *The Cradle of the Middle Class: The Family in Oneida County, New York, 1790–1865.* Cambridge, UK: Cambridge University Press, 1981.

Salzberg, Sharon. *Lovingkindness.* Boulder, CO: Shambala, 2002.

Sander, Louis W. "Thinking Differently: Principles of Process in Living Systems and the Specificity of Being Known." *Psychoanalytic Dialogues* 12, no. 1 (2002): 11–42.

Sayers, Janet. *Mothers of Psychoanalysis: Helene Deutsch, Karen Horney, Anna Freud, Melanie Klein.* New York: Norton, 1991.

Scarr, Sandra. "American Child Care Today." *American Psychologist* 53, no. 2 (1998): 95–108.

Scarr, Sandra, Deborah Phillips, and Kathleen McCartney. "Working Mothers and Their Families." *American Psychologist* 44, no. 11 (1989): 1402–9.

Scarry, Elaine. *On Beauty and Being Just.* Princeton, NJ: Princeton University Press, 1999.

Schor, Juliet B. *The Overworked American: The Unexpected Decline of Leisure.* New York: Basic Books, 1991.

Schore, Allan N. *Affect Dysregulation and Disorders of the Self.* New York: Norton, 2003.

Schultheiss, Donna E. Palladino. "To Mother or Matter: Can Women Do Both?" *Journal of Career Development* 36, no. 1 (2009): 25–48.

Scott, Joan W. "Deconstructing Equality-versus-Difference: Or the Uses of Poststructuralist Theory for Feminism." In *Feminist Social Thought: A Reader*, edited by Diana Tietjens Meyers, 758–70. New York: Routledge, 1997.

Seuss, Dr. [Theodor Seuss Geisel]. *Horton Hatches the Egg.* New York: Random House, 1940.

Shabot, Sara Cohen. "Name as Oppression and/or Liberation: A Feminist Reading of Triple Cronica De Nombre." *Journal of Iberian and Latin American Research* 22 (2016): 173–86.

Shacochis, Bob. "Missing Children." In *Wanting a Child*, edited by Jill Bialosky and Helen Schulman, 40–59. New York: Farrar, Straus and Giroux, 1998.

Shapiro, Alyson Fearnley, John M. Gottman, and Sybil Carrere. "The Baby and the Marriage: Identifying Factors That Buffer against Decline in Marital Satisfaction after the First Baby Arrives." *Journal of Family Psychology* 14, no. 1 (2000): 59–70.

Siegel, Daniel J. *The Developing Mind.* 2nd ed. New York: Guilford, 2012.

Siemens, Rachel. "The Complicated Truth about Stay-at-Home Motherhood." manrepeller.com, September 13, 2018. https://www.manrepeller.com/2018/09/the-complicated-truth-about-stay-at-home-moms.html.

———. "Spoiler: Having It All Sucks." manrepeller.com, February 17, 2017, https://www.manrepeller.com/2017/02/women-having-it-all.html.

Silber, Sherman J. *How to Get Pregnant.* New York: Scribner, 1980.

Sklar, Kathryn Kish. *Catharine Beecher: A Study in American Domesticity.* New Haven, CT: Yale University Press, 1973.

Slade, Arietta. "The Development and Organization of Attachment: Implications for Psychoanalysis." *Journal of the American Psychoanalytic Association* 48, no. 4 (2000): 1145–74.

Slade, Arietta, Jay Belsky, J. Lawrence Aber, and June L. Phelps. "Mothers' Representations of Their Relationships with Their Toddlers: Links to Adult Attachment and Observed Mothering." *Developmental Psychology* 35, no. 3 (1999): 611–19.

Smith-Rosenberg, Carroll. "Beauty, the Beast, and the Militant Woman." In *Disorderly Conduct: Visions of Gender in Victorian America.* New York: Oxford University Press, 1986.

Solomon, Judith, and Carol George. "Defining the Caregiving System: Toward a Theory of Caregiving." *Infant Mental Health Journal* 17 (1996): 183–98.

Stern, Daniel N. *The Interpersonal World of the Infant: A View from Psychoanalysis and Developmental Psychology.* New York: Basic Books, 1985.

———. *The Motherhood Constellation: A Unified View of Parent-Infant Psychotherapy.* New York: Basic Books, 1995.

Stern, Daniel N., and Nadia Bruschweiler-Stern. *The Birth of a Mother: How the Motherhood Experience Changes You Forever.* New York: Basic Books, 1998.

Stern, Daniel N., Louis W. Sander, Jeremy P. Nahum, Alexandra M. Harrison, Karlen Lyons-Ruth, Alec C. Morgan, Nadia Bruschweiler-Stern, and Edward Z. Tronick. "Non-interpretive Mechanisms in Psychoanalytic Psychotherapy: The 'Something More' Than Interpretation." *International Journal of Psychoanalysis* 79 (1998): 903–21.

Stone, Alison. *Feminism, Psychoanalysis, and Maternal Subjectivity.* London: Routledge, 2014.

Stone, Lawrence F. *The Family, Sex, and Marriage in England, 1500–1800.* New York: Harper and Row, 1977.

Stone, Lyman. "American Women Are Having Fewer Children Than They'd Like." *New York Times*, February 13, 2018. https://www .nytimes.com/2018/02/13/upshot/american-fertility-is-falling -short-of-what-women-want.html.

Sullivan, Oriel, and Jonathan Gershuny. "Speed Up Society? Evidence from the UK 2000 and 2015 Time Use Diary Surveys." *Sociology* 52, no. 1 (2018): 20–38.

Thomson, Judith Jarvis. "A Defense of Abortion." *Philosophy and Public Affairs* 1, no. 1 (Fall 1971): 47–66.

Thurer, Shari L. *The Myths of Motherhood: How Culture Reinvents the Good Mother.* Boston: Houghton Mifflin, 1994.

Tomasi di Lampedusa, Giuseppe. *The Leopard.* 1958. Reprint, New York: Pantheon, 1991.

Tronick, Edward Z. "Emotions and Emotional Communication in Infants." *American Psychologist* 44, no. 2 (1989): 112–19.

Turiel, Judith Steinberg. *Beyond Second Opinions: Making Choices about Fertility Treatment.* Berkeley: University of California Press, 1998.

Van Cleaf, Kara M. "Blogging through Motherhood: Free Labor, Femininity, and the (Re)Production of Maternity." Unpublished dissertation, 2014.

———. "The Pleasure of Connectivity: Media, Motherhood, and the Digital Maternal Gaze." Unpublished manuscript.

Wallerstein, Judith, Julia Lewis, and Sandy Blakeslee. *The Unexpected Legacy of Divorce: A 25-Year Landmark Study.* New York: Hyperion, 2000.

Wan, Helen. Letter to the Editor. *New York Times*, August 9, 2018.

Warner, Judith. *Perfect Madness: Motherhood in the Age of Anxiety.* New York: Riverhead, 2005.

Wasserstein, Wendy. "Competitive Moms." *Harper's Bazaar*, September 2002, 259–60.

Waterman, Barbara. *The Birth of an Adoptive, Foster, or Stepmother: Beyond Biological Mothering Attachments.* London: Jessica Kingsley, 2003.

Whitebook, Marcy, Deborah Phillips, and Carollee Howes. *Worthy Work, Still Unlivable Wages: The Early Childhood Workforce 25 Years after the National Child Care Staffing Study.* Berkeley: Center for the Study of Child Care Employment, University of California, Berkeley, 2014.

Wile, Daniel B. *After the Honeymoon: How Conflict Can Improve Your Relationship.* New York: Wiley, 1988.

Williams, Joan. *Unbending Gender: Why Family and Work Conflict and What to Do about It.* New York: Oxford University Press, 2000.

Wilson, Mitchell. "Maternal Reliance: Commentary on Kristeva." *Journal of the American Psychoanalytic Association* 62, no. 1 (2014): 101–11.

Winnicott, D. W. "The Capacity to Be Alone" (1958). In *The Maturational Processes and the Facilitating Environment,* 29–36. New York: International Universities Press, 1965.

———. "Hate in the Counter-transference." *International Journal of Psychoanalysis* 30 (1949): 69–74.

———. "Transitional Objects and Transitional Phenomena" (1953). In *Playing and Reality,* 1–25. New York: Tavistock Publications, 1971.

———. "The Use of an Object and Relating through Identifications" (1969). In *Playing and Reality,* 86–94. New York: Tavistock Publications, 1971.

Winter, Nina. *Interview with the Muse: Remarkable Women Speak on Creativity and Power.* Berkeley, CA: Moon Books, 1978.

Wolf, Naomi. *The Beauty Myth: How Images of Beauty Are Used against Women.* New York: Anchor Press/Doubleday, 1991.

———. "Our Bodies Our Souls." In *Vice and Virtue in Everyday Life.* 4th ed., edited by Christina Sommers and Fred Sommers, 843–60. New York: Harcourt Brace, 1997.

Young, Iris Marion. "Pregnant Embodiment: Subjectivity and Alienation." *Journal of Medicine and Philosophy* 9 (1984): 45–62.

Zraly, Maggie, Sarah E. Rubin, and Donatilla Mukamana. "Motherhood and Resilience among Genocide-Rape Survivors," *Ethos* 41, no. 4 (2013): 411–39.

Index

abortion, 21, 24, 176–77; desire and selfhood in relation to, 177–83; as legal matter, 180–82; maternal desire and, 225–26; opponents of, 178, 185, 189; pregnancy as relationship and, 183–88; pro-life feminism and, 192–94; question of sacredness and, 188–92
adolescence, 64, 82, 91, 228
adoption, 106, 170–71, 184, 187
Adult Attachment Interview (AAI), 85, 86
agency, 25, 44, 61, 62, 198
Ahlberg, Janet and Allan, 229
Alcott, Abigail, 28–29
Alcott, Louisa May, 29
Allen, Jon, 87
ambivalence, maternal, 6, 14, 97, 103–9; about roles, 109–13; eating and body-image issues, 116–20; mothers' relationships with their own mothers, 113–16;

as universal phenomenon, 108; upside of, 120–24
Angier, Natalie, 113–14
anthropology, 5, 6
Apgar scores, 112
"Are Mothers Persons?" (Bordo), 180
Art of Waiting, The (Boggs), 171
assisted reproduction technology (ART), 156, 164–65, 172
attachment, 4, 57; pleasure and, 84–88; secure, 66, 67, 85–87, 144
autonomy, 4, 56; agency and, 10; autonomous self in capitalist society, 46; balance of needs and, 69–70; mother's assertion of, 59; sexual, 16

babysitters, 100, 119, 127, 147. See also caregivers; day care
Backlash (Faludi, 1991), 33
Bartholet, Elizabeth, 170, 171

About the Author

Daphne de Marneffe, PhD, is a psychologist and the author of *The Rough Patch: Marriage and the Art of Living Together*. In her clinical practice, she offers psychotherapy to couples and individuals. She teaches and lectures widely on marriage, couple therapy, adult development, and parenthood. She is a contributing editor at *Parents* magazine, and her work has been featured in the *New York Times*; *O: The Oprah Magazine*; and on NPR and *Talks at Google*. She and her husband have three children and live in the San Francisco Bay Area.

Turn the page to read the first chapter of

THE ROUGH
PATCH

Marriage and the Art of Living Together

---

by Daphne de Marneffe

"Anyone in any relationship at any stage of life could stand
to learn from the wisdom in these pages."

—Andrew Solomon, National Book Award–winning
author of *Far from the Tree* and *The Noonday Demon*

1

The Rough Patch: An Introduction

You are forty-three. You have been married twelve years. You didn't marry too young. You had your adventures and your choices. You now have two little girls (ten and seven), or two little boys, or one of each. You were in love when you married. That's what you've always believed, at least, although now sometimes you wonder. You knew you were different from each other, but at the beginning that was fine—it helped you feel stable, or it helped you grow, and it was even exciting, as you noticed how much you wanted to reach out and understand and even indulge each other's differences. Yet now you feel *too* different. Sometimes you drive each other crazy. Or leave each other feeling deeply hurt. Or kind of neutral. Or each of these, at different times.

A lot of advice is out there to help you deal with the problem. Social scientists tell you that people are happier at sixty-five than forty-five, so if you wait it out another twenty years, you might feel better. The couple specialists, the work-family balance people, the sex and intimacy experts, all have something to say that almost fits. But somehow they don't get at the crux of the problem. The crux is that you feel lost, or lonely, or at times almost blindingly miserable.

297

Sometimes you feel you can't breathe. It's true that you're exhausted at work, or your mother's ill, or your hormones are out of whack. But it's hard to believe that that's the whole story. You didn't always feel this stuck in your relationship. There was a time when the marriage made sense.

What changed? And why? Perhaps you felt fine about your marriage, until you surprised yourself by becoming infatuated with someone else. Or maybe you were absorbed by the care of your kids when they were small and didn't give much thought to your personal satisfaction. But now your older daughter/son spends time texting her/his friends (how did that happen so quickly?) and doesn't seem interested in being around you on the weekends. Even if the child-centered marriage didn't foster much passion, at least it provided a meaningful framework. Now things are shifting. What felt tolerable before doesn't anymore. You are left wondering, where am I in all this? Who have I become?

It's not quite fair, but you can't help blaming your partner for how dissatisfied you sometimes feel. It's hard to imagine putting up with her/his workaholism/drama/withdrawal/insensitivity for another few decades. Yet you know feeling this way is wrong somehow. Marriage takes work. Immature people think relationships should be easy or fun; selfish people leave when the going gets rough. You've always been a good worker; you're great at work. But it's not clear what you are working for. Deep down, you aren't sure things can change. And the truth (shameful and hard to utter) is that sometimes you feel you're not sure you *want* things to change anymore. You don't want to have to work so hard for whatever incremental satisfactions you might gain. Occasionally you feel a whiff of freedom, and it is shockingly exhilarating.

You feel guilty about it, but on the other hand, you are still youngish. You deserve to have some intimacy and passion and real connection in your life. You won't have your energy or looks forever. How long is it reasonable to go on like this?

But you don't want to make any destructive decisions. That's the path your sister/uncle/best friend took, and look where it left them. The kids, let's face it, suffered. Shuttling back and forth between houses, forced to witness their parents' heartaches at way too close a range, and no money saved for college. And the adults imported their same old problems into the next relationship. Lately, though, you find yourself calling to mind the success stories: the kids who seem to have emerged unscathed, and the parents who seem so much happier, like new people. Still, you don't want to divorce. It would be easier, better, if you could find a way not to be so unhappy in your marriage. Or maybe not to be so unhappy, period.

THE ROUGH PATCH. "Lonely." "Confused." "Stuck." "Stirred up." "Going through the motions." "Falling apart." I see a hitting-the-wall unhappiness in the middle slice of life, when people struggle, alone or in pairs, to figure out why their marriages don't feel right. In my work as a therapist, I am reminded every day of people's conundrums:

- Is my problem that I need to find a way to resuscitate some loving feeling toward my partner? Or is it my own harsh insistence that I shouldn't give up?
- I know I should *think* about my predicament, but I'm so sick of thinking. I just want to *feel* for a change.

- I know my infatuation with my coworker is a "fantasy," but why does it feel like the most real thing in my life?
- Reminding myself how grateful I should be for what I have just makes me feel worse.
- Can I, or should I, spend the rest of my life with minimal affection or sex?
- Can I, or should I, keep living with my partner's substance use/spending habit/mental illness?
- My partner is withdrawing from me but I don't know if I can, or want to, change in the ways (s)he wants me to.
- If my greatest goal is to give my children a happy childhood, how can I do that if I am unhappy in my marriage? Yet what if trying to find more happiness for myself comes at the expense of theirs?

People who seek my help often feel they are caught between what they *should do* and what they *feel*. When I spoke with Lisa, a professional, she had just turned forty-seven, and she struggled with the sound of it. "I never felt middle-aged. Then I turned forty-seven. It's a number that sticks in my mind. Forty-seven is a big deal. Fifty is a big deal." Why? "I feel like I should have figured it out by fifty." She hadn't figured it out; she felt more confused than ever. Feeling exhausted from work, parenthood, and family life, and alienated from her husband of fifteen years, she found herself acting entirely against her values, embarking on an affair with a younger man. "I was shocked to be with someone I was excited about—texting and calling someone I can communicate with, without the burden of all the family stuff. My physical relationship with my husband is dismal, and I sort of chalked it up to the inevitable effect of aging.

What's funny is this guy reminds me of my husband—smart, professional—but ten years younger. Now I've really become a middle-aged cliché: almost fifty, in a rut in my marriage, finding someone young and exciting . . ."

I am struck by how often people try to dismiss their marital distress as "cliché," embarrassed to have fallen prey to the "midlife crisis," a construct toward which they felt, until recently, comfortably disparaging. We're voyeuristically critical toward middle-age flameouts—"She's divorcing him and marrying their tenant!" "He ran off with a lap dancer and now he's bringing her to the kids' soccer games!"—partly to protect ourselves. We feel vulnerable to life's surprises and attempt to fortify ourselves through the communal conviction that people should be more grown-up. Finding ourselves susceptible to feelings that we so recently judged as selfish or immature in others is a rude awakening, especially destabilizing when we felt, not so long ago, pretty confident and successful about our choices.

But humbled as we are by our lack of originality, we may privately feel something momentous is happening. We feel we are waking out of a stupor, and that we can't bear to go back and re-anesthetize ourselves. Perhaps we had a strange sort of relief in plunging into the child-rearing years, when our own desires were back-burnered. Serving our children's needs allowed us to take a break from wanting things for ourselves, and all the complicated dilemmas it engendered. But somewhere inside we knew this wasn't a tenable long-term solution. Kids grow up. Statistically, we may be looking at another forty years of life. Unlike in the 1950s, it's no longer realistic to wait for our two-pack-a-day habit to kill us at sixty-two. It's obvious we can't keep swallowing the vague adage that "marriage is compromise," if compromise means suppressing whole swaths of our personalities. Life is too long, and too short. We have to find some way to stay vital, engaged, desiring, and *ourselves* while being married, if married is what we want to be.

When we trivialize the rough patch as a "middle-aged cliché," we are actually trying to find a way to disarm the intensity of the forces we are grappling with. We hope that if we can distance ourselves from others' crises or minimize our own, we might escape their disruptiveness. But something important and meaningful is occurring in the rough patch—even if we don't yet know exactly *what* that meaningful or important thing *is*. We don't call it a cliché when a two-year-old starts saying no, or when a teenager starts experimenting with sex; we consider these to be common expressions of what it *means* to be a two-year-old or a teenager. Both the toddler and the teenager are trying to grow, to become more complex and whole—the toddler's task is striving for autonomy, the teenager's is figuring out how to be a sexual person. Though the tasks are different, the challenges of the rough patch are in some sense the same. Like the toddler and the teenager, we are looking to discover and fully express who we are, while staying connected to others. We want to take risks and feel secure. We want autonomy and connectedness in optimal balance. These are *completely valid goals* at any age. We have every right, and even a responsibility, to pursue them. So what makes the rough patch so *rough*?

THE MIDPOINT OF LIFE represents the moment of *maximal conflict* between our drive to seek external solutions to our emotional dilemmas and our recognition that, ultimately, they don't work. In the rough patch we are forced to realize, often against our will, that the life-building activities of youth—job, relationship, children, house—have not taken care of what's unresolved within. We still yearn—for what we're not sure— and what we've achieved doesn't entirely fill us.

But it's not only that external achievements have not taken care of internal problems. It's that we've begun to take a more complicated view of ourselves. By virtue of experience, we *know* more, and this unsettles us from three directions.

First, we know more now about time and loss. Our own eventual mortality is becoming less of an abstraction and more of a fact. We've almost inevitably suffered some disappointments and setbacks along the way. The spiritual wisdom of the ages is starting to make visceral sense. No person, job, or acquisition, no matter how wonderful, can ever entirely fill our sense of incompleteness. We even begin to sense that those who "have everything" are in exactly the same boat.

Second, the passage of time gives a new urgency and poignancy to the state of our intimate relationships. This is our *life*. Can this relationship last for the next four decades? Is now the time to reckon with that question? We may begin to feel tendrils of doubt, the upwelling of inconvenient longings and needs, an uneasy sense that suppression or chronic discord will not be sustainable. We may encounter dread, fear, and a desire to escape through work, or screens, or drink. We're dimly aware we may have to lose in order to gain, that painful upheavals may be the cost of emotional growth or inner peace. Oscillating between what is and what could be, between reality and possibility, between embracing and relinquishing, we feel disoriented and confused.

When things feel bad, two options may loom up in our minds: *endure* (for the children, the shared history, the finances, the stability, the vow) or *strive* (for something more, another chance, a better relationship). Surrender or escape. Give in or start over. Depressive resignation or manic flight. These occur to us largely because it's not at all clear where else to go. But the thought that soon follows is that we want to be honest, and we ask ourselves, what is the line between seizing vitality and manically defending against decline? What's the difference between "settling" and acceptance? How might the effort to have more in our lives unwittingly result in less? When does accepting limits help us to make the most of what we have, and when does it signal premature resignation? Our dawning awareness of life's limits means we know that we've reached the point where dismantling what we have and starting something new does not come cheap. We know there's really no such thing as "starting over," only starting something different and trailing the inevitable complications in our wake. The acting out we see around us, which till now we've casually dismissed, begins to looks like one way that people try to combat the stasis of depression with the action of escape, attempting to transcend (at least temporarily) the "hitting a wall" feeling that this life stage can induce.

Finally, as time presses in, we inevitably confront questions of value. What are our values about marriage? What might it mean to stay or to go? "An open secret in our world is that we do not know what legitimizes either divorce or marriage," wrote the philosopher Stanley Cavell. Deep down, many of us don't know where we stand on marriage. Sociologists find that people absorb highly contradictory cultural messages and hold stunningly inconsistent romantic narratives within themselves. We believe, for example, *both* that couples should stay together for the children *and* be free to pursue their own happiness. We maintain that relationships that begin with exciting strong attraction are simultaneously highly desirable and likely to be "unrealistic." We espouse the romantic worldview that marriage derives meaning from the unique specialness of our mates, their status as "one and only." Yet we endorse the more functionalist ethos that life is long and people "grow apart," and that different people may be better partners at different stages of life. We're constantly trying to strike a psychic balance between the ideals of freedom and domestic life. If we are even moderately self-aware, we know enough to be suspicious of the ways our longed-for romantic and sexual experiences conform so predictably to scripts handed to us by Hollywood and advertising. But unless we can nest a sexually or romantically compelling element within our long-term relationship, we fear we won't make it through the decades that yawn before us.

Trying to ground our marital values in universal principles seems next to impossible. Not many rules are left. The rules that remain are all pretty much self-assigned, and this seems true even among those who strain to obey a higher law. Studies indicate that people on the religious right divorce *more* often than other people, not less. Orthodox communities that insist on the sanctity of marriage vows often have benighted views of women's rights and purvey an oppressive model of marriage. Instead of shared social values or universal principles, the most robust determinants of whether people get married and stay married are money and education. Demographic research over the past two decades demonstrates that people who command more economic resources and education marry and stay married at higher rates than do people with fewer resources. Greater resources not only correlate with fewer divorces; they allow for more choices in living arrangements. But regardless of their position on the economic spectrum, increasing numbers of people view the goal of long-term monogamy as separate from the goal of being a good parent.

Still, for many of us, our qualms about divorce relate directly to our children—their feelings and their growth into loved and loving adults. Couples often feel that children are the most compelling reason to revitalize a marital bond. The psychoanalyst Wilfred Bion wrote, "There is absolutely no substitute for parents who have a loving relation with each other. No amount of talk or theory is going to take the place of parents who love each other." Where children are concerned, parents sharing a loving bond comes close to an absolute good. But parents sometimes feel they don't have a loving bond. People want to stay married for the children, but *also* because they have a loving relationship.

On the values questions about marriage and divorce, the culture at large doesn't offer much guidance. For one thing, it keeps throwing us back on youthful preoccupations and sows panic about "giving up" on "our potential." The market's desire-stoking engines promote the mirage that there's nothing about our dispiriting situation that we can't buy, or trade in, or surgically alter our way out of. For another, the culture continues to play the seductive refrain that romantic passion is the preeminent conduit to personal renewal. Even if you entertain the idea that long-term monogamy *could* be an enduring vessel for romantic love, you will face countless reminders that new love is essential to life, and its monomaniacal focus is a state to be prolonged and nurtured. Its attenuation signals not the bittersweet end of an era, but a sign that a relationship is static, dead, and in need of correction. At minimum, it demands the purchase of candles, massages, and getaway hotel packages.

I am an enthusiastic proponent of psychotherapy, but aspects of therapy culture can encourage the tendency to scrutinize our love relationships and find they come up short. To get through the rough patch you may have to enlarge your perspective and expand your focus beyond your marriage's minute emotional ebb and flow, but such outward focus arouses therapeutic suspicion that you are "not taking care of your marriage" or "not being emotionally present." Consumerism urges us to look at the small details and slice them as thin as possible (how else are we going to be convinced we need the next iPhone?), and this mentality can seep into our view of relationships, encouraging us to focus on tiny details and amplify pockets of discontent. Where does an admirable attention to personal growth end and a "more-different-better" mind-set begin? It's a fine line we can't always detect, and the cultural surround encourages us to blur it.

Glowing youth. Passionate sex. Romantic love. All great things. I'd say they are among some of the very best things. But that's different from saying that the only way through the rough patch, to a sense of renewed vitality or purpose, is to somehow double down on our preoccupation with them. With that kind of striving, people too often end up in misdirected solutions, relational or otherwise, that can only temporarily relieve their desolation. The reality that life is lived in one direction means that things we might have had in concrete form at earlier points in life—youthful beauty, our high school sweetheart, Herculean sexual stamina—become increasingly costly and delusional to pursue. As time passes, the stakes of not squarely facing the reality of loss, of relinquishing what you can't actually have, *get higher*. We have to develop and refine other capacities, *inner* capacities, if we want the second half of life to go well.

Of course, living in America at this cultural moment means not always knowing what constitutes a realistic acceptance of limits. Our cultural heroes are guys who hang out in their dorm rooms fooling around on their computers, until, at twenty-six, they become internet billionaires. Teenagers inhale the daily doings of suddenly world-renowned YouTube personalities, aspiring to their instantaneous and magical reach, while their parents look on with mystified boredom. We all now live with prosthetic minds called smartphones that extend our communication and knowledge exponentially, while colonizing our consciousness in as-yet incomprehensible ways. Seventy-year-olds can look fifty, through good health or body modification, and the "longevity dividend"—the twenty to thirty more years than our grandparents had—means that a whole life phase is only now being truly charted.

Yet even as we extend the boundaries of the possible to previously unimaginable limits, we live in bodies that die, and most of us believe we have only one life on this earth. If this leads some of us toward a "seize the day" impulse to escape marital malaise, it leads many others back toward their marriages in hopes of making them more fulfilling. If these people turn to self-help, they may encounter the secular religion of health, where research findings suggest that it's worth staying married as protection against heart-attack risk. When in doubt, these writings seem to imply, we should think of marriage as part of a fitness routine, even if couching it as a good workout rather than the marriage of true minds lacks for a bit of inspirational grandeur. More psychologically oriented are the studies of happiness, which document that changing some key habits—setting goals, practicing gratitude, cultivating optimism—can improve our relationships to a surprising degree. Working in the spiritual genre is the raft of latter-day sages who counsel that the ego is a delusion, and detachment holds the key to personal transformation. When we're unhappy in our personal relationships, they suggest, it derives from our limited view of love, namely our attachment to form (i.e., the personal) over formlessness (i.e., infinity and transcendence).

Certainly it's a relief to breathe in the practical, empowering spirit of positive psychology, which pinpoints the aspects of happiness we can attain through effort and healthy routines. Ironically, though, the well-intentioned messages about the health benefits of long-term relationships, as well as the New Age–inflected spiritual formulas, carry with them an astonishingly simplistic view of the one thing that lies at the beating heart of marriage: our *emotions.*

Our emotions form the core of our sense of meaning. They define and create our central love relationships. It's fine to intone about detaching from the ego, until you admit that the ego is part of the self, and self is grounded in emotions, and emotions happen within a body. Marriage, like parenthood, inevitably and necessarily involves the stubborn reality of the flesh. That's one reason why marriage and parenthood are so hard. When we move from airy abstraction to actual human relationships, we quickly realize that the only route toward wisdom, love, and a sense of aliveness is *through* the sensitive and skillful management of emotion. As the philosopher Immanuel Kant put it, the dove may wish that the air had no resistance so that it could fly higher, yet resistance is the very thing that allows the dove to fly. Likewise, we can't escape our bodies or emotions; we can only discover who we are and how to love from *within* our fleshly human medium.

What most people want from marriage is affection, trust, safety, fun, soothing, encouragement, excitement, and comfort. They want to have companionship and be left alone in all the right ways, neither intruded upon nor abandoned. They want to be seen, accepted, valued, and understood for who they are. *All* of this stands or falls on the quality of emotional sharing and communication. That's why the rough patch inescapably calls us to struggle with our emotions on a whole new level of awareness, and to figure out what they mean for our relationships. This is a profound personal and relational journey. There aren't any shortcuts. Relationships are messy and complicated. No wonder the deceptive simplicity of all the checklists and tweets and seemingly endless reminders that our happiness is under our own control can come to intimidate rather than reassure us.

From the last three decades of psychological research, we know that our minds are formed in relationships. This means not simply that our minds are *concerned* with relationships (which they are), but that relationships shape the ways we process and experience reality. Psychology has made huge strides in mapping the connections between early attachment, emotional development, and adult intimate relationships. Throughout life, our emotions signal what's important, and what's important—at any age—is satisfying relationships. In a real sense, then, marriage picks up where childhood left off. As a close relationship that engages body, heart, and mind, marriage offers a powerful lifelong vehicle for knowing another, being known, and developing our deep emotional life.

Overall, research finds that the most important factors in whether our relationships are satisfying all have to do with emotions: how we tune into our emotions, experience them, manage them, communicate about them, calm them enough to respond to others, and align them with our behavior and goals. Throughout this book, I will sum up the key capacities of healthy emotional relating as *curiosity, compassion,* and *control.* When we're curious, we are open to trying to understand our own and the other's truth. When we're compassionate, we feel empathy for our own and the other's struggles. When we exert self-control, we contain and communicate our emotional responses to others in ways that are accurate, sensitive, and likely to get heard. The triad of curiosity, compassion, and (self-)control takes us toward a sense of personal agency, and away from holding our partner responsible for our own feelings. It helps us build the inner capacities we need to reckon well with the rough patch.

Finding a way to be happy in marriage depends on our ability to exercise emotional skill, flexibility, and resilience. But it also depends on something else: our ability to value both the needs of the individual partners and the needs of the marriage. Rough-patch breakdown often occurs when people lose track of one side or the other. Sometimes, they've conceptualized marriage as demanding a suppression of individuality, and they reach a point when that solution is no longer sustainable. Or, they find themselves only able to advocate for their own needs, in a sort of zero-sum survival strategy, without being able to hold on to a vision of the marriage as a resource for comfort and excitement, stability and growth. Throughout life, we continually learn about ourselves through pressing up against the personalities of others. Ideally, we don't simply react, but use our interactions with others to increase our self-awareness. The result is greater self-definition, which leads to the possibility of more authentic connection. This recurrent back-and-forth of relating to self and other is the engine of adult development, as well as the engine of growth in marriage. If the emotional interactions are basically healthy, we gradually become more self-realized as individuals and more deeply relational as partners.

But marriage itself, not to mention the romantic ideology that surrounds it, so easily tends to produce misunderstanding about who's responsible for whose emotions. It's almost as if the ideal of passionate fusion that we welcomed so blissfully at the outset returns, like a swamp monster, in the form of chronic confusion about who's doing what to whom. As time goes on, if people don't step up to the challenge of communicating in an emotionally healthy way, they fall into the trap of thinking that individual and couple needs are doomed to conflict. They now imagine there's no way around the unshakable reality of competing agendas. In both cases, people overlook that their way of handling their *own* emotions powerfully influences the very ways they conceive of, and participate in, marriage. Throughout these pages, we will be looking closely at the individual—not only because it receives short shrift in writings on couples, but because, paradoxically, individual development represents one of the most potent paths to marital happiness.

Since marriage presents one challenge after another, we need to bring our best resources, as individuals and as a couple, to solve them. Three of the biggest challenges—children, sex, and work—pervade the emotional climate of marriage, and accordingly, they thread through every chapter of this book. More specific challenges, such as money or aging, are addressed in individual chapters. I hope that couples will read this book together, or at least sequentially. I also hope that each reader will embrace the opportunity to focus on three questions: Who do I want to be as an individual? Who do I want to be as a partner? And how do the two fit together?

My goal is to create more breathing room around these questions. In a broad sense, I believe that the vast and troubling energies of the rough patch will have been harnessed for good if they contribute to personal progress on the following fronts:

- Becoming a more loving person. Really. By this I don't mean going on loving-kindness retreats that are stealth missions to indulge a crush on your meditation teacher, but rather engaging full-heartedly in becoming more kind and compassionate, toward others *and* yourself.
- Seeing your partner's perspectives and experience as equal in importance to your own. This means recognizing narcissism for what it is (it's not just you, we *all* have it). Relating to others as genuine people, rather than need satisfiers or projections of your own psyche, is a lifelong effort, never complete.

- Expressing emotion skillfully rather than simply emoting. Marriage offers a ready-made dumping ground for our bad moods and tendency to blame and judge. Taking responsibility for how you express yourself, and repairing after negative interactions, pave the way for closeness.
- Developing a nuanced relationship to your fantasy life. That means cultivating awareness that actions and thoughts aren't the same thing, building confidence in the difference between them, and using your imagination and fantasy life as a source of creativity rather than for numbing out and escapism.
- Discovering the need for committed living, where a value higher than your own emotional weather prevails. In adulthood, a sense of purpose and meaning derives from the dual psychological movement toward *deepening inward* and *expanding outward*. We in the rough patch need to use the fuel of waning youth and the whisper of mortality to vitalize and intensify our self-awareness, love for others, and our engagement with the world.

ONE OF MY guiding assumptions as a therapist is that you shouldn't stay in a marriage if there's no hope for it to become a secure, loving relationship. Another guiding assumption is that staying in a marriage, even if it is difficult, can be one of the most effective ways of developing a secure, loving relationship. Anyone can decide that being married to one's partner is not the way one wants to pursue an intimate life. But people can undertake that decision under pressures that they don't understand. They feel pushed, pulled, and not free to flexibly choose. For many of the people who seek my help, I believe that working through the problems in their marriage is a more direct and ultimately satisfying route to a secure, loving bond than leaving.

In all my talk of the responsibility of the individual in marriage, I might be mistaken for endorsing two common ideas. The first is that the duty of a mature adult (especially one with children) is to *suck it up*. So what if you are unhappy? Distract yourself. The second is that *marriage takes work*, a position that consigns me, in some people's minds, to the camp of puritanical libido-killers who advocate a work ethic for everything from sex to fine dining ("Are you still *working* on your prime rib?").

As to the first, I believe that the things we feel are lacking in the rough patch are all good things to want and to strive for: a sense of aliveness, the flexibility to change, the desire to feel, to love and be loved. We should not give up on the goal of having them in our intimate relationship. But we should also think about those goals more broadly—not only in terms of our marriage, but also in terms of the opportunity the rough patch presents for taking responsibility for, and recommitting to, who one is. The challenge of the rough patch is not only to discover whether it is possible to find a way to be happy with one's partner, but to reckon—yet again—with our relationship to ourselves and to the world.

As to the second, the idea that marriage takes work: if you ask older married people, they'll sometimes say one of their proudest accomplishments is their marriage. They say this because it wasn't always easy, God knows, and because they recognize the marriage for the creative project that it is. But people generally abhor the idea of marriage as work, not only because it reinforces the message that somehow marriage is the death knell for spontaneity, excitement, and fun, but also because it depressingly pits our current experience of marriage against the very hopes and pleasures that gave rise to it in the first place.

But this interpretation entirely misnames the activity at the center of the enterprise. The "work" involved is not the drudgery of cleaning the bathroom or the mind-numbing repetition of the assembly line. The work is in facing authentic emotion and vulnerability. The work is in the challenge of *opening up*—to being present, to listening, to learning about feelings, to having hard conversations, to facing reality. The work is in having the courage to take risks, and to speak one's truth and listen to the other, in the effort to create an intimate relationship.

When people don't take those risks, they shut down and disengage, and then marriage can't possibly feel like anything but boring and static. They start telling themselves, "I shouldn't have to work this hard." But if it's too depressing to think about working on your relationship, think about working on yourself. Not only is it true that the less you work on yourself, the more effort other people put in to deal with you (have you ever noticed how often people stepping forth to renew themselves leave wreckage for others?). It is also true that making the effort to look within, and to struggle with your own demons, repays you in more fulfilling relationships.

The rough patch offers the possibility to become a more integrated person. I don't think there's any way around the fact that wrestling with the conflicts that arise is a psychological journey of self-understanding that can take every ounce of your fortitude. It entails holding in tension both the intense reality of what you are going through, and the ability to take some distance from it. The challenge is to arrive at an understanding of your life that is self-compassionate but not self-serving, satisfying but also true.

People are so often caught feeling that their situation is both impossibly complicated and insufferably trite. Simply *knowing more* about the titanic forces with which we all grapple, in midlife and marriage, can help us apply more compassion and less judgment toward ourselves and others, and to exercise more patience and wisdom in discerning our individual path. As will be obvious, I am not in the business of keeping fatally flawed marriages together. Certain marriages should end. Rather, I am interested in the states of mind that beset people in the rough patch, and what they can teach us about living the rest of our lives with verve, creativity, and commitment. The rough patch, for all its pain and bewilderment, presents an opportunity—to know ourselves, to expand our scope, to grow, and to grow up.